Acclaim for Bree .... book,
Crush Your Divorce & Keep Your Faith

Yahoo! Finance: "Sullivan-Howell uses scripture to encourage, not shame, women going through the trauma of divorce. She guides them to build spiritual, emotional and financial stability throughout the process. Her legal expertise helps demystify navigating complex divorce proceedings as a woman of faith."

"With a mission to reconnect with the promises of God's Word to give hope and comfort, *Crush Your Divorce® & Keep Your Faith* author and attorney Bree Sullivan-Howell shares experiences and lessons learned from over two decades as a leading divorce attorney, along with insights from her own divorce journey."

Fox: "*Crush Your Divorce®* offers practical solutions centered on biblical truth and grace for women navigating marital dissolution." "Women need compassion and empowerment during chaotic marital dissolution. Sullivan-Howell is helping fill this gap through her unique work supporting Christian women navigating divorce. She offers faith-based services for those facing divorce all the way through rebuilding life after the divorce is finalized. Her book and online resources remove the veil of silence and stigma."

"*Crush Your Divorce®* aims to teach why it's not unladylike or unChristian to stand up for yourself, as well as help people gain valuable, practical insight into the nuts and bolts of a divorce case—including strategies on how to help your lawyer prepare your case to win."

ABC: *"Crush Your Divorce®* helps Christian women find their voice during a divorce, especially those experiencing abandonment or abuse."

NBC: "Sullivan-Howell's message offers a path forward, bringing God's light into the darkness of divorce and empowering women to crush its hold over their lives. There is hope, healing and wholeness after divorce ends a Christian marriage. Sullivan-Howell is helping lead the way."

CRUSH YOUR YOUR DIVORCE

& keep your faith

CRUSH YOUR DIVORCE

& keep your faith

BREE SULLIVAN-HOWELL, J.D.

Luke 1:45

Bree Sullivan-Howell

PALMETTO
PUBLISHING
Charleston, SC
www.PalmettoPublishing.com

Copyright © 2023 by Crush Your Divorce, LLC

Cover art: Sharon Heard
Headshot: Ursula Page Photography

Hardcover ISBN: 979-8-8229-2958-6
Paperback ISBN: 979-8-8229-2959-3
eBook ISBN: 979-8-8229-2960-9

Dedication

For JH and my redheads, the reasons my heart beats.

Table of Contents

*Author's Note

The stories in this book and people named herein are <u>PURELY HYPOTHETICAL</u> composite characters based on general themes drawn from the multidimensional experiences of those close to me, random case studies I've researched, fact patterns from publicly available case law, and online divorce survivor blogs I've studied over the years. These stories are here to let you know you are not alone, to show you the importance of perseverance and to demonstrate that joy is possible on the other side of this challenging time. They are not any particular person's story, and all names are <u>purely fictitious</u>. Don't even try to guess who I might be talking about in each hypothetical, as they are <u>not real people</u>.

<u>BIG Disclaimer</u>: Nothing in the book should be construed as legal advice for your particular situation. Laws differ from state to state. You MUST seek your own attorney in your jurisdiction for in-dividualized guidance tailored to address the particular issues of your unique story. While I hope my words give you food for thought and help you frame questions for your lawyer, and I'm thankful you're interested in my insight, ***I cannot advise you, and I do not represent you in your case just because you picked up my book***.

There is a Resource section at the end of each chapter to give you other helpful things to read and listen to as you walk your divorce journey. There is so much wisdom out there, and we should nev-er stop learning and growing! Questions for Reflection are likewise included at the end of each chapter for you to consider during your quiet time and in group study with your friends and supporters.

I've also included a soundtrack of tunes pertinent to the struggles explored in each chapter, as music can be such a great source of comfort. I pray it will be a balm on your sweet, shattered heart, empower you and lighten your mood as you wrestle with your situation and begin to heal. Check out my "Crush Your Divorce | Keep Your Faith" playlist on Spotify.

I'm praying for you, Dear Reader, to be strengthened and encouraged to look forward to the new day to come after your divorce is over. I pray boldly for God to work mightily in your life, draw you close, and be glorified in your story. Divorce or no divorce, your relationship with Him is the most important thing you have. May you praise Him in your storm and also in the victories to come.

xo xo, BSH

Where I'm Coming From

I wrote this book because, not too long ago, I was you. When I filed for divorce after nearly two decades of marriage, I was a bundle of nerves and riddled with fear even though I'd guided hundreds of clients through their divorces. I'd seen firsthand the emotional highs and lows, the bewilderment clients felt as they started the process with no idea what to expect, the empowerment that came when the case was finalized and hope was restored. But until I went through the process myself, I didn't fully grasp my clients' plight.

The lessons of this book come from twenty-plus years of law practice and from seven months of my own personal Divorce Hell. I know firsthand the agonizing lead-up to the end of a marriage. I know the pain of being unfairly criticized, gossiped about, disparaged, and made to feel altogether "less than" for choosing to walk away.

And, best of all, I know the unforeseen, unbridled euphoria that followed almost as soon as the judge signed the papers. For me, divorce was a turning point, a joyous fresh start, a world-is-your-oyster moment. Transformational.

My prayer is that you will be blessed, encouraged and comforted by my words as you try to make sense of this time of your life. I pray that your divorce will be the redemptive experience it was for me.

When *I* was the divorce client, I was scared to death and totally dependent on others for guidance and reinforcement. Counselors and friends kept me going. My attorney's paralegal let me literally cry on her shoulder. God bless the paralegals!

I cried too many tears to count. Dropped ten pounds. Grieved for my children. Lost friendships I didn't expect to lose. Battled insomnia. Sought counsel. Felt the anger. Struggled with how best to settle the case to buy my peace. Learned self-care. Prayed often. Learned to adapt and compartmentalize. Made new friends. Gained fresh perspective. Started a new life. Crafted my comeback and found exuberant happiness.

I've been in your shoes and survived. I'm here to tell you—you will, too.

As a child of divorced parents, I also know the child's life following a divorce. I learned early what works and what doesn't by being coparented in two homes and being part of a blended family. Parenting my own children through divorce and its aftermath continues to humble me and teach me new and valuable life lessons.

Why "Crush Your Divorce"?

Crush Your Divorce may seem an odd title for a book written to women, especially Christian women, for we aren't exactly known for going around crushing things. But I chose this title because it captures the attitude of empowerment I want you to have. I encourage my clients to take control of their lives and play OFFENSE, not DEFENSE. Like in football, defense is important, but it's offense that scores touchdowns, and touchdowns are necessary for victory. I want you to look back years later and be proud of how you confronted, conquered, and, well, *crushed* this difficult time in your life. Proud that you got through a very hard thing.

Your divorce isn't something that's happening *to you.* It's something you have to attack with tenacity, grit, and wisdom if you're going to succeed.

You've heard of "putting on your game face." Divorce is just like that. You have to put your emotions to the side so you can take care of business. I'll show you how you can get smart, Crush Your Divorce, and mend your heart—all so that you can start over with a new purpose and a fresh perspective.

Sister, this is *your* life, and you have a say in your future, even if your husband has tried to strip you of your voice. This divorce is likely the most daunting obstacle you've ever faced. But it's your opportunity to dig deep and find out what you're made of. To face your fears. To take control of your future. To create a foundation for a wonderful new life you never imagined. How strong you will be for having gone through it!

This book offers emotional support and empathy while also equipping you with information and smart strategies for success in your divorce case. Your divorce feels like a mountain you must climb. *Crush Your Divorce* will make that mountain a little less frightening and give you confidence to know you can positively CRUSH your goal of getting to the other side.

How to Use This Book

This book is divided into three parts.

Part One will help you unpack the chaotic emotional upheaval you're feeling. How did you get here? What can you do to ease the pain? How should you behave and communicate while your divorce case is underway? We'll help you process these questions and put yourself in the best position to win your case.

Post-separation abuse is a sad reality for many women. Part Two will arm you with strategies to beat your abuser at his own game, without losing your composure or stooping to his level.

In Part Three, we'll give you a step-by-step guide of what to expect. No one, unless they've been divorced before, knows what to expect in their case. We'll get into the nuts and bolts and outline the practical things you can do to help your lawyer. By the end of this section, you'll be ready to tackle your case head-on, with your head fully in the game to optimize your chances for success. You will understand that you and your lawyer are a team.

Your divorce is an opportunity to start fresh and create a glorious "new normal" for yourself and your kids. Ending my marriage was the most life-affirming decision of my life. It can be the same for you!

I'm working on a second book, soon to follow this one, in which I'll lay out the financial, relational and other considerations to keep in mind as you start over as a single woman. It's going to be epic! Get excited!

Hear me, Dear One. You are *valuable*. You are *loved*. You don't have to live in fear. Stop enduring mistreatment. It's okay to stand up for yourself and say, "no more." Be the heroine in your own life story. Show your kids a better way to live. You can do it! You will survive. And in time, you will laugh again.

Your husband may have broken you, but God never will. You can trust Him with your heart. You can trust Him with your life. You can trust Him with your family. There is a plan for you, and it is *good*. Trust that plan, rip that Band-Aid off the wounds of your heart, and let the healing begin.

Questions for Reflection

1. Why did you pick up this book? What are you hoping to glean from its pages?

2. Are you ready to go through divorce? Have you known it was coming for some time, or is it an overwhelming surprise to you?

3. Do you have faith that you will get through it?

4. Do you trust God with your heart and his plan for your life?

5. Are you ready to sort through your thoughts and feelings, get smart, prepare a strong case, and get it behind you? Have you prayed that God will be with you through it all?

Chapter Soundtrack

"Not for a Moment (After All)"—Meredith Andrews

"Exhale"—Plumb

"I Will Rest in You"—Jaci Velasquez

"You Learn"—Alanis Morissette

Part I

Pregame: Get Your Head on Straight

1

Is This Really My Life?

"Everything that looks too perfect is too perfect to be perfect."
—Dejan Stojanovic

It was a blazing hot August day in South Georgia. The majestic, red-brick Dawson United Methodist Church of my childhood, with its mahogany pews and exquisite stained-glass windows, was bursting with 350 loved ones, standing room only. Bouquets of fragrant white roses and freesia were everywhere. In my satin A-line dress with pleated waistline, low-V back, and gathered bustle, I felt like a princess. My shoes were pearl-embellished, beige heels purchased the previous week from Dillard's. My late grandmother's sparkling diamond watch, pulled from the safe deposit box the day before, adorned my bronze wrist—thank you, self-tanner! The bridesmaids' dresses were the prettiest candle-glow yellow with bedazzlements along the neckline. My Aunt Lisa had done my nails in a French manicure, just as she had for high school proms and homecoming dances.

All the pieces had fallen perfectly into place. I had just graduated from college and would start law school right after the honeymoon—with a full scholarship to boot. "Mark," with his impressive resume and brilliant business mind, had already finished his first year of post-graduate coursework. Our future looked so bright! We had only known each other seven months, but I was sure he was The One.

Crowned with Touch-of-Sun-lightened hair styled in a stately French twist, I stood in the narthex, arm-in-arm with my sweet dad who had taken a third job that summer to pay for all of this. The organist began to play Pachelbel's "Canon in D" and groomsmen seated the mothers. My eyes puddled over as Daddy, looking so dapper in his tuxedo and ecru-colored rose boutonniere, cupped my hand and joked (probably to make me laugh because my tears have always unnerved him), "You know it's not too late to run. I'll get you out of here if you want."

I giggled, but I wasn't going anywhere.

The lead-up to the wedding had been a whirlwind. Mark and I had gotten engaged on Easter Sunday, and I was hardly able to keep the secret until my candlelight ceremony at the Kappa Delta chapter meeting the following Monday night, where I got to blow out the candle on its third go-round in our circle. Excitement was in the air. I dove into wedding planning, as the engagement period was to be just four months long.

The engagement announcement was in all the local newspapers. The china and silver patterns had been selected and—thanks to the generosity of so many southern ladies—purchased for us. I'd already written hundreds of thank-you notes, with more still to go. The wedding showers had been like something from a storybook, with our families and close friends in attendance to give congratulations and best wishes.

I felt like the luckiest girl in the world to have found love before I finished college, as everyone at the KD house knew it got harder to find someone after that. I loved Mark's parents and having been an only child, couldn't wait to have his sisters as my own. As my in-laws said to me, Mark had dated some "very fine young ladies at Wake Forest," and I felt I had won.

Oh, bless my foolish heart. If only I could go back and have a word with my twenty-two-year-old self! I now know I should have gone through at least one football season with him before getting married. Where I live, who a man really is comes out during football season.

While all the wedding hoopla was South Georgia Society perfection, the marriage itself—but for the three beautiful children it produced—was a total freaking disaster. All the trappings—the college degrees, the pretty house, the Easter photos, the preschool programs, the cute kids, the soccer weekends—looked so solid to the world, but the relationship underneath had little substance. And I knew that deep in my soul as early as my honeymoon.

Never in my wildest dreams could I have imagined all the heartbreak to come. But then, no one ever thinks on their wedding day that their marriage will end in divorce.

How Did You Get Here?

Like me, you probably never predicted that you would be facing divorce. Maybe you're on the verge of losing hope that you will ever be happy again. Maybe you aren't sure where you fit in the world anymore.

Maybe your husband just left you out of the blue without explanation or forewarning. You're reeling because it doesn't make sense, maybe because you never gave him a reason to leave or because you thought you were a happy couple. You're asking yourself: *Was it all a lie? If my marriage was fake, is anything real? Is nothing sacred? Is nothing trustworthy? Does my mother even love me? Are my friends really my friends?*

Perhaps your divorce isn't coming upon you suddenly. Maybe you've been hurting and suffering in silence for years, enduring the pain and praying for a breakthrough that never came. Maybe you've stayed for the kids or to keep up the Instagram-perfect appearance your family projects to the world. Maybe you've stayed to protect your husband from the humiliation he will suffer if others hear about the things he's done. Maybe you've been surviving your marriage for years, and you're just exhausted.

Maybe you've stayed because you're too scared to make a change. You've endured your husband's meanness or indifference because you don't see another viable alternative. You've built your life around him, and you're afraid of trying life alone. In your bravest moments, you've dared to wonder if God has a better life waiting for you apart from your husband, but you're afraid to step out in faith. The "known set of problems" in your marriage feels safer than the unknown that awaits you apart from him.

You've picked up this book because you're hurting, yearning for peace and healing, and seeking practical guidance on what to do next. You're wondering if all the happy times of your marriage were a lie. Maybe you're grappling to discern the truth of your life story, and you want to proceed with class and grace. Above all, you want to honor God in how you deal with this painful situation, and you're not sure what that looks like.

How ever you arrived at this place, your world is rocking, spinning out of control, and feels like utter chaos. You're overwhelmed and can't make sense of your feelings. You don't know what you will tell your family or your kids. Perhaps you've even been served divorce papers and have no clue what to do next, or you need to file for divorce but cannot find the courage to do it. You can barely function, but now you're going to have to pull it together to build a legal case against this guy you once thought was your soul mate?! You have no idea how you're going to get through this. You are crying out to the Lord in desperation, praying for this hell to end, but there is no end in sight. You're standing at the bottom of a proverbial mountain you must climb, but you neither want to climb it nor do you have the energy to do so.

Sometimes God's Answer is "No"

I thought for nearly two decades that my marriage could be great if only I could do more, pray harder, or love my husband bigger. I spent countless, raw hours pouring out my heart to the Lord—in my closet, in my car, during worship—begging Him to change our hearts, to make us an epic Christian couple with a powerful "success story" testimony, which I repeatedly promised to use to advance His Kingdom and glorify His name, if only He would redeem us. And, in all fairness, I feel sure my husband did some praying of his own. Neither of us wanted the marriage to end if it could be good.

It eventually became more and more clear to me that God's answer was simply "no." The marriage was dead and not coming back to life. Game Over. All that was left to do was to acknowledge the death for what it was, grieve it, and find the courage to do something about it.

You cannot, in your own strength, ever pray hard enough to fix a broken marriage and make it good. You are not that powerful, so stop putting that pressure on yourself as if you are.

Have you prayed for God to deliver your marriage? Is His answer "no" for you, as it was for me? If it is, I'm here to tell you this is not the end of your story. You can—and will—find the strength to get your head together and persevere. For yourself. For your children. For other women who are watching on the sidelines and who you can inspire through your story.

So, What Now?

I meet women just like you every week, and the common theme is fear of an unknown, post-divorce future. I want you to know that you are not alone. It's become my life's work to help women bring order to the chaos, clarify the uncertain, and come up with a plan tailored to their needs to make them more likely to succeed, as single—and secure—women.

If you're reading this book, I bet you're a lot like I was toward the end of my marriage. I knew early on that things weren't right but stayed because I didn't want to be seen as a failure or disappoint my family. I absolutely didn't want to give up on Jesus' ability to heal and restore. I wanted Christ to be glorified in my struggle. By the end of my marriage, I was living each day literally looking forward to death, not in the suicidal sense but because I just couldn't wait to be in Heaven, where there would be no more tears, just joy. I thought my struggle would earn me some kind of crown in the afterlife. I yearned so deeply to run into His arms and hear those sweet words, "Well done, my good and faithful servant" (Matt. 25:21). Praise God my story didn't end there. Yours won't either, friend.

Sis, the Lord had something better for me. He was preparing me to face my fears and break free of my toxic marriage. It took a really long time, but I finally got there when the circumstances were right. It was God's timing, not mine.

The Church teaches us Christian women not to be anxious, but in every situation, "by prayer and petition, present our requests to God" (Phil. 4:6). We are taught that love covers over a multitude of sins (1 Pet. 4:8) and that we are to forgive our husbands' transgressions "seventy times seven times" (Matt. 18:21), just as Jesus has forgiven us. We read in Romans 5 that struggling produces good character, and that we have hope if only we can persevere through sufferings. And we are told all the time how much "God hates divorce" (Mal. 2:16). Good Christian girls stick it out and stay married no matter what, right?

But there's only so much your heart can take.

Dear One, I know the exhaustion and hopelessness you're feeling. *Know one thing above all else*: you are God's dearly loved child (Eph. 5:1), and He sent his only Son to die in order prove it to you. How awesome is that?! It grieves Him for your heart to be hurting, just like it grieves us mothers when our own children hurt. He has not called you to be anyone's doormat, my friend. He has not called you to live a life with a man who is unfaithful or hateful to you. There is a time when you must draw a line and say enough is enough.

Only you know in your spirit when the right time has arrived to change your life. God made our bodies to give physical reactions to our circumstances. If you are uneasy or feel unsafe in the presence of your husband, it's a tangible reaction from your very bones. If you are always on edge at home, waiting for the next explosion or argument, your body manifests that anxiety in a palpable way. You can't live this way for very long without significant impacts on your mental and physical health.

Your heart is broken, but Scripture tells us the Lord is near and will save you when your spirit is crushed (Ps. 34:18). He heals the brokenhearted and binds up their wounds (Ps. 147:3). He surely did it for me, and He will do the same for you.

Think of the crucifixion and how hopeless the disciples were when Jesus was killed that Friday. They thought all hope was lost, that their movement was dead. It's Friday right now for you, but Sunday's coming, my friend. And it's going to be a gLoRiOuS day! Having been through it myself, I can tell you that while it may not be easy, you will get through this pain and find your joy again, on a morning real soon. I'm praying over you as you read this, and I'm going to help you get there.

Questions for Reflection

1. Think back to your wedding day. What were you thinking and feeling?

2. How has your perspective changed since then?

3. What were your motivations for marrying in the first place? Was there pressure from others? Did you fear being alone or never finding someone if you didn't marry him?

4. Did you overlook warning signs that emerged during your engagement period, choosing to marry him anyway or hoping to change him after the wedding?

5. Did you have "cold feet" as you prepared for the wedding? What was your gut telling you then? Why did you marry him anyway?

6. How soon after your wedding did your relationship change to something that made you feel insecure or unsafe? What was it? Did you tell him? How did you cope with it? Why did you stay?

Chapter Soundtrack

"Ready to Run"—the Chicks

"American Honey"—Lady A

"Butterfly Kisses"—Bob Carlisle

"Suds In the Bucket"—Sara Evans

"Walkaway Joe"—Trisha Yearwood

"Going to the Chapel"—the Dixie Cups

"Sample in a Jar"—Phish

2

God Hates Divorce

"I'm pro marriage. Nearly 40 years of ups and downs to back that up. But when we as a church culture demonize divorce as the worst possible outcome—the sin of all sins—we truly have no clue on this everloving earth what some people are enduring. We do not submit to abuse. NO."

—Beth Moore, April 28, 2018, @BethMooreLPM on Twitter / X

I sat next to my Daddy in the back row (we always were back-row people) wearing the Gunne Sax lace dress I'd gotten for my eleventh birthday, resting my head on his blazer shoulder as I doodled on the church bulletin. My parents had been happily divorced for about a year by then, and it was my dad's weekend to spend with me.

The sermon topic that day was marriage, and the preacher was on a roll! Bits and pieces of that sermon stuck with me for the rest of my life.

Turn with me, dear friends, to the book of Malachi, where God tells us all how much He hates divorce.

❖ *The fabric of our society is being ripped apart by divorce.*

❖ *God's heart is GRIEVED by divorces and the breakup of marriages! The Lord doesn't want to see families in pain, doesn't want children's lives disrupted, doesn't want women raising children without fathers in the home . . .*

- *Studies show that children raised in single-parent or divorce homes are much more likely to commit crimes . . .*
- *Marriage is a SACRED VOW, and vows are to be taken SERIOUSLY. . . People of good character stay married to the spouse of their youth . . .*
- *You are to forgive your spouse when they hurt you—not just seven times, but "seventy times seven times!"*

For GOD HATES DIVORCE. He really, really does.

My parents' divorce had brought us all so much peace, and both of my parents were so much happier apart. And my dad was happily remarried to my stepmother, a lady who had brought such blessings to my life. My parents were coparenting beautifully. It was hard for me to process how God could hate anything about our situation.

Now I don't know about you, but I've been a rule follower since I was a very small child. I was never one to push boundaries or challenge authority. I wanted my parents, teachers, coaches, friends to like me, accept me, approve of me. The approval of others felt so good to me, so that if I heard something was in the Bible that I shouldn't do, I did my best not to do that thing. I thought it a good formula for a successful life: behave well, follow the rules, and things will go well. I was a good Christian girl or tried my best to be.

So, when I heard "God hates divorce" and "divorce grieves the heart of God" at such a young age and kept hearing it over the years from those I looked up to in the church, the message became etched into my conscience: "You must *never* get divorced or else you'll risk God hating *you*." I certainly want no part of anything God hates.

Before We Go Any Further

Let's address the elephant in the room: Does God really hate divorce?

In my years of Bible Belt law practice, I've heard countless "good Christian girls" like me echo the same concern again and again: "Will God hate me if I end my marriage?" Hurting women everywhere have wrestled with this question. No woman who loves the Lord wants to do anything to harm her relationship with Him. The fear of being hated by God keeps Christians—both women and men, I would argue—in unhealthy marriages, avoiding divorce at all costs, opting instead to endure abuse, which sets a terrible example for children and keeps these faithful people stuck, unable to pursue God's true best for their lives.

Matthew 19:5-6 tells us that we humans should not "put asunder" what God has joined together, and that men should leave their parents and "cleave to [their] wives." But what if a man is over there cleaving to *other* men's wives, or, instead of cleaving to his wife, he's running the other way or harming her? What then?

Unpacking the "God Hates Divorce" Passage

The widespread, oversimplified takeaway from Malachi 2:2-17 is "God hates divorce." So, you shouldn't get divorced. And if you *do* get divorced, you better watch out, because God hates divorce so much that He will also hate *you*, too, and you could be punished.

But the Malachi 2 Passage is not about married couples. It's a warning to Jewish priests who hadn't honored Him.

Have you ever taken the time to really analyze this passage for yourself, in context? A careful reading of the text reveals that it's more about man's unfaithfulness to God than about marriage (or legal divorce) between spouses. Malachi, a prophet, is calling out man's infidelity toward God and Man's rejection of Him. Nowhere in the text is Malachi telling women to stay with cheating men. Indeed, to the extent Malachi does touch on marriage, he's admonishing *men* to be true and faithful to their wives, to treat them well so that divorce never enters the discussion.

Somewhere along the way, well-meaning evangelical leaders (not God) distorted the meaning of this passage and began using it as a tool to keep marriages together, to convince married folks to stay married, on the valid idea that society functions better when families remain intact. But in their well-meaning efforts, church leaders have kept countless folks trapped in abusive marriages and caused society to lose trust in the Church as an institution. People don't trust institutions whose grand agendas take priority over loving people well.

Here's something you might not know: The current NIV version of Malachi 2:16 does not even contain the words "God hates divorce." That language was replaced when NIV Bible scholars completed their 2011 revision.

The 1984 NIV translation many of us grew up reading said, "'*I hate divorce,*" says the LORD, *the God of Israel, "and I hate a man's covering himself with violence as well as his garment,' says the Lord Almighty.* Between 1984 and 2011, Bible publishers went back and analyzed the words of the passage and felt that the 2011 translation was a more authentic interpretation of the original Hebrew text. No version of the original Bible contained the "God hates divorce" language. It wasn't until the 1611 A.D. King James Version (AV)—nearly two thousand years after the Bible came into existence—that those words appeared in any version of the book of Malachi.[1]

---

1   Gretchen Baskerville, *The Life-Saving Divorce: Hope for People Living in Destructive Relationships* (2020). See also https://lifesavingdivorce.com/malachitimeline/.

It's the Institution, Not the Person

Even if you accept the 1984 version as an accurate translation, it should be noted that the discussion was of God hating "divorce" and unfaithfulness. Nowhere in there does it reference God hating a person. Even if you want to argue that He hates marital divorce in general, the only logical conclusion to be drawn is that while He might hate the institution, He doesn't hate the poor soul enduring it. God is love,[2] and you are his dearly loved child.[3]

God Hates Other Things More Than He Hates Divorce

It's easy to see why God might hate divorce, for the heartbreak it brings can be nearly unbearable at times. Anyone who's been through it will tell you that. We're told again and again that God doesn't want any of His children to suffer, so it's logical to conclude that God would hate anything that causes suffering and hardship. But, friend, I believe Scripture supports the idea that He probably hates other things just as much, if not more.

He Hates for His Daughters to be Abused

Scripture is replete with examples of Jesus protecting women, respecting and revering women, empowering women, honoring and recognizing women as his friends, giving women a place in his ministry, receiving financial support from women, calling women by name and recognizing their humanity. Jesus called the little children to his side, telling his disciples not to hinder them from

---

2   1 John 4:16.

3   Ephesians 5:1.

approaching.[4] Never anywhere in Scripture do you see Jesus condoning the abuse of women or children. Never in Scripture do you see Jesus giving men license to treat women however they want. Men are, again and again, called to love their wives just as Jesus loves his bride, the Church. Bottom Line: God does not want any of His daughters to be abused, cheated on, or mistreated in any way. They're to be revered, cherished and protected. And He doesn't want defenseless children exposed to abuse, either.

Research over the past thirty years consistently shows that in high conflict marriages, children are better off if their parents divorce.[5] And when divorce became more accessible in the legal reforms of the 1970s and 1980s, lives were saved. One study found that suicide rates for wives diminished by eight to sixteen percent, while reports of domestic violence went down by thirty percent and homicides where women were killed in domestic disputes went down by ten percent.[6]

I humbly submit to you that God hates abuse of His children much more than He could ever hate divorce as an institution, for it is that institution which provides an avenue for setting the abused, demoralized, broken, hopeless woman free. Divorce breaks the chains that keep the abused woman bound to her abuser. Divorce in such a scenario is, indeed, a blessing straight from Heaven. After two decades in my front-row seat to these matters, you'll never convince me

———————————

4   Matthew 19:14.

5   http://lifesavingdivorce.com/abuse-and-kids, where you can read all about the various studies and resulting data on this important subject. "Staying for the children" is not a justification to remain in an abusive home.

6   Stevenson and Wolfers study, see more at http://www.lifesavingdivorce. com/divorcesaveslives.

otherwise. I've seen firsthand how God has used it to transform and improve lives and families, bringing women and children to safety.

Proverbs 6:16-19: Other Big Things God Hates (Newsflash: Divorce Isn't Listed)

How noteworthy that when God took the time to make lists of things he hates, divorce didn't make the list!

Proverbs 6:16-19 lists "six things the Lord hates, seven that are detestable to him." They are: "haughty eyes, a lying tongue, hands that shed innocent blood, a heart that devises wicked schemes, feet that are quick to rush into evil, a false witness who pours out lies, and a person who stirs up conflict in the community."

Arrogance is one that just really irks me. These are all those folks over there thinking they're better than you because they've stayed married and you didn't, or for some other reason. It's poppycock. Listen to who God says you are, not what they say about you. God hates dishonesty and pot-stirring (the creation of discord in the community), too. Think of the haters and gossips in your life. The seemingly perfect ones spouting off their judgments of you. God doesn't like it one bit, Friend.

The Church Often Fails the Divorcing Woman

After these decades of walking alongside the divorcing, I've come to understand that *no one* gets divorced until they see no other option. Divorce is not a best-case scenario or a piece of cake for anyone; it's a last-chance alternative, a life raft, a gateway to peace.

When I went through my divorce, my eyes were opened to all the ways humans can hurt one another. I did my best to mind my own business, taking it day-by-day and staying as quiet as I could about it, keeping my head down, not talking about it too much. But I should have known it wouldn't take long for my divorce to be the talk of the town. I guess they thought their comments wouldn't get back to me, but they always did. Oh, how I praise my God for the ones who stood in the gap, defended me, and let me know who my friends were not.

Managing a divorce is an emotional siege even in the most amicable of circumstances. But mine was a tough one, and judgment from others thoroughly kicked me while I was down. I'll never be able to erase their words from my memory.

I can still hear them now:

"You know she didn't even try when they went to counseling." (Wait... were you there?)

"You know he wants to reconcile but she just won't give him another chance." (Did they know how many attempted reconciliations there had already been? Did they know my marriage story? Uh, no.)

"She shouldn't be serving in the church now that she's filed for divorce." (I needed my church then more than ever before, and working alongside other believers in church service got me through it! Did they really think the Church should excommunicate me because I had ended my marriage? Where was the Christian love? I needed the hands and feet of Jesus, and these folks were giving off nothing but condemnation from afar. No one would say it to my face.)

"She must have a boyfriend. There's no other reason a woman like her would leave a stable financial situation like that." (What a bold assumption! I didn't even talk to another guy until after my divorce

was totally final, not that anyone took the time to ask me about it before spreading false narratives.)

"Mark is so handsome and has so much going for him. She's crazy to leave him and break up her family. Those poor children!" (None of them knew our story. And—this just in—a man's appearance doesn't make a hill of beans when you feel like your soul is dying.)

I never anticipated just how big some people's opinions would be. Most of them were people who didn't even know me, let alone know my marriage story. It was almost as if some of them—folks I had always considered friends—were enjoying my pain from afar, reveling in the gossip surrounding our breakup, freely opining about what I should or shouldn't be doing, as if it was any of their business. I pray they never have to walk in shoes like the ones I wore during my divorce. If only those people had just called me to offer a prayer or a kind word instead of judgment behind my back!

For some reason, it's sometimes human nature to want others to struggle rather than trying to help them. Unfortunately, there are those who feel better about themselves when others aren't doing so well. They're okay with your being happy, so long as you're not happier than *they* are. Can I get an Amen?

Hurt people hurt people. Pain is recycled, paid forward from person to person. It turns out that the very ones who judged me for getting divorced were the very ones struggling with issues of their own, bless them. And you know what? It would be wrong for me to judge them for those things. But what a blessing to know who your real friends are! All you can do is move on, knowing not to trust those folks who don't want your best.

We must be ever mindful to remove the planks from our own eyes—to clean up around our own back doorsteps—before casting stones at others.[7] Everyone has enough gunk to clean up in her own life before analyzing the gunk of another.

The Decision to Divorce Should Not Be Taken Lightly

Divorce should never be a flippant choice. I'm a believer in the possibility of marital reconciliation after infidelity and other sins between spouses. I've rejoiced with my clients and friends as their marriages were restored, healed, and transformed after intense counseling and the hard work was done to depart from bad behaviors. Everyone loves a happy ending, and I'm always rooting for my clients to stay married if it's healthy and safe for them to do so.

Repentance, reconciliation, and restoration are beautiful, inspiring things to behold. There's truly nothing better than a story of good overcoming evil, of triumph against all odds.

But when it *isn't* possible for Christians to reconcile, it's almost never because someone didn't try hard enough or was just harshly unforgiving. It's almost always because the patterns of deception, mistreatment, abuse or infidelity continue without true repentance, and it becomes clear that nothing will ever change. The forgiving, victimized spouse finally gives up hope, starts realizing her value as a child of God, and starts loving herself enough to make a change.

You'll never convince me God hates any part of that woman finally realizing her worth, saying "no more," getting away from her abusive husband, and starting to heal.

---

7   Matthew 7:3-5 and John 8:7.

A Word on Unequal Yokage

2 Corinthians 6:14 admonishes us not to hitch ourselves to unbelievers. In Bible times, two oxen were joined—or "yoked" together—by a wooden bar in order to complete agricultural work. To be effective as a team, those oxen must be of commensurate strength. If a weak ox is paired with a strong one, progress will be slow, frustrating and ineffective. Applied to marriage, this passage is warning us not to marry men who don't encourage us in our faith, or men whose faith isn't as strong as our own. When a believer marries an unbeliever, it's a recipe for conflict and strife, and sure not to be a productive, cooperative relationship.

Sometimes we make choices that were just wrong from the start. We convince ourselves something's a good decision because we *so* want it to be. We *so* want that happy ending, and we think we can force it, giving no thought to what the Lord might think about it!

As one client told me, "I made the decision to marry him when I was NOT listening to God. My divorce was necessary to undo something I never should have done in the first place. I knew in my heart it was the wrong decision when I did it." Ouch. What a tough realization to recognize you've ignored God's will for your life and gone your own way. In this woman's situation, divorce was the only way to rectify her defiance against her Lord.

I don't know who needs to hear this, but if a man is a stumbling block or hindering your intimacy with your Creator, you need to drop that man like a hot potato. Keeping that fool around, no matter his good qualities, is a mistake if he pulls you away from your God.

Marriage is Hard, But it Shouldn't Be That Hard

In addition to "God hates divorce," you've probably heard that "marriage is hard," that "marriage is work," or that "it's a choice to love someone." In other words, if you want a divorce, then you're just copping out when you should be willing to put in more work. The message is that you're lazy. And you are judged for that laziness by those who consider themselves "harder marriage workers" than you. And you're judged for your perceived lack of faith for "not trusting God enough" to save your marriage.

Look up social media posts under the hashtag #churchtrauma. So many women have been shamed into staying with abusive men because church leaders preached Malachi 2 at them, telling them they had to stay. That it was "the Christian thing to do."

To the Woman Trying to Change Her Man

I regularly meet women who are clinging to hope that their men will change, that their lives can be the storybook fairy tale they've always wanted. If you're a woman like this, I see you. I've *been* you.

Maybe you've heard how one spouse can sanctify the other by sticking by them and praying, loving them in spite of unkindness and bad treatment. Maybe you've made sanctifying your husband your life's work. And you're so very tired. You just can't keep it up any longer because it's killing your soul. But you're feeling shame over your lack of energy to try anymore. So many of my clients wrestle with that very same thing.

Let me tell you something. You can't be the Holy Spirit for your abusive husband or for anyone else. Stop wearing yourself out trying to be superhuman. You're not that powerful. You're wasting your good years on someone who doesn't appreciate it. The brokenness within your husband that made him cheat on you or abuse you will always be there until *he* does something about it.

I have a feeling you've lost that girl you once were as you've tried to please your man all this time. Do you even recognize yourself these days, as you labor to keep that crazy, mean, heartless man happy? God made you to be authentically you! You are special and unlike any other person.

Stop the martyrdom and start living as your authentic self. Let him figure out his own issues, Friend. Stop being who your husband wants you to be and start living in truth. Stop excusing abusive behaviors. Stop accepting his meanness as a fact of life. This is America (praise Jesus!), and you don't have to live that way.

I believed for many years that I could just love my first husband enough for the both of us. I told myself that God was pleased with my effort to stay in a terrible marriage, that He would call me a "good and faithful servant" upon my arrival at the Pearly Gates someday. I was literally living for the day of my death, thinking that my temporary suffering on earth would be rewarded in the next life. Looking back on it now, I know I spent years in an unnecessary Limbo Land of Misery. God didn't have me there. I had myself there. Divorce saved my life.

You Can Always Come Back Home

Nothing hurts quite like the sting of being rejected or hurt by someone you love. You can't make your husband love you if he doesn't. You must make peace with it and find a way to move on.

Righteous indignation certainly has a place if you've been wronged, and I believe God is big enough for our questions about how you got here. No matter the struggle, don't ever forget you are God's dearly loved child, and that you have not been forsaken, even when it might feel like it. He will bring you through this storm just like He's brought you through every other challenge since your birth. If you love Him, Scripture tells us you can trust Him to work all things together for your good. Your God will never reject you.

Sometimes it's easy to drift away from your faith foundations. Perhaps your husband didn't like church, so you stopped going. Or maybe you and your husband didn't entirely agree on spiritual matters, so you just stopped worshipping or practicing your faith altogether. Like the prodigal son's father, God is waiting for your return, Dear Sister, and He will welcome you back anytime you're ready. Don't let the judgment or condemnation you've received from other churchgoers keep you from the Father. Christians are all the time messing up what God's trying to do in the world. Your divorce can be a spiritual fresh start for you. He's been with you the whole time, working out the details of your life, even when you didn't know it. You can always come home.

Sweet Sister, I hope you will rest in God's love, knowing that while He hates the sins that broke down your marriage, He loves you, and He also loves your husband. Rest in that grace, knowing God is doing a powerful work in you, molding you into the woman He is calling you to be. Pour out your heart's deepest longings to Him. He's got you, girl.

Questions for Reflection

1. Have you ever heard the "God Hates Divorce" passage? What was your understanding of it until you read this chapter?
2. Has anyone ever used the "God Hates Divorce" passage to convince you to stay in an abusive marriage? What did they say, and how did it make you feel?

3. Have you ever heard gossip about a divorcing friend in which that woman was being judged for her decision, with "God hates divorce" being the primary argument? How did you respond?

4. Ponder the following scriptures and reflect on each one, applying them all to your present circumstances.

Romans 8:28   *1 Chronicles 16:11*   *Psalm 18:6*   *James 4:8*

1 Peter 5:7   *1 Thessalonians 5:17*   *Hebrews 13:5*   *Luke 15:11-32*

5. Have you strayed from your faith? What is your heart telling you to do to get back in tune with God's will for your life, back into intimate connection with Him? Do you know He'll take you back? Have you talked with Him about it?

Resources

www.flyingfree.com

The Life-Saving Divorce: Hope for People Leaving Destructive Relationships—Gretchen Baskerville

Is It Me? Making Sense of Your Confusing Marriage—Natalie Hoffman

www.amysjournal.com

Divorced and Delivered (podcast)— @divorcedanddelivered on Instagram

Lisa TerKeurst, Proverbs 31 Ministries Founder— @lysaterkeurst on Instagram.

Chapter Soundtrack

"You Are So Good to Me"—Third Day

"No Fear In Love"—Steffany Gretzinger

"Take You Back"—Jeremy Camp

"Softly and Tenderly"—classic hymn as performed by
Carrie Underwood

"Who Am I"—Casting Crowns

"Praise You In This Storm"—Casting Crowns

"Blessed Be Your Name"—Tree63

"Spoken For"—MercyMe

"Thy Will"—Hillary Scott & The Scott Family

"Lord I'm Ready Now"—Plumb

"All This Time"—Britt Nicole

"Steady Heart"—Steffany Gretzinger

"I Am Not Alone"—Kari Jobe

3

The Breaking Point

"Make your breaking point your turning point."
—Dennis Kimbro

Every woman has a point at which she can take no more of the thing that's crushing her spirit, a point where something must totally break so healing can start. That breaking point is different for each of us, but you know it in your bones when you've gotten there.

Pearl's Story

The morning I decided my marriage had to end started like any other. I was in the kitchen in my bathrobe, no makeup, hair not yet done and coffee not yet drunk. The kids were having breakfast, and I was standing at the kitchen island putting together their lunchboxes.

My kitchen had been updated with new cabinets just a few months before, and it was just beautiful. It's my favorite room in our house, and I worked hard to make it reflect my style. It still brings me joy just to walk in there. There were contractors in my kitchen for eight long months, and every detail was carefully selected.

While standing there making the sandwiches that morning, I asked my husband a simple question about his plans for the day, and he took offense. Not sure why.

He's suddenly raging, repeatedly opening and slamming, opening and slamming, opening and slamming my carefully organized silverware drawer. As I'm trying to find the right words to calm him down (story of my life, times 14.5 years), I hear the silverware flying around inside the cabinetry. The children freak out and run to the car, buckle themselves in. I bring their lunches outside and kiss their little heads while he is still inside raising cane.

After I return to the kitchen, he stops slamming the cabinet drawer, calls me a name, and leaves to take the kids to school. Rattled and hands shaking, I tearfully survey the damage and try to clean up the utensil upheaval. I tell myself, "He's just upset. It's just silverware. Everything is fine." Forks, spoons, cheese knives, and bottle stoppers had been flung to the drawer below, and I see with a flashlight that some items have landed deep inside the base cabinet, never to be recovered again. As I'm cleaning up this mess, my pep-talk-to-myself continues: "It could be worse. At least he didn't hit me or hurt the children. I can clean this up. Surely he loves me. He doesn't mean to act like that. He'll be over it by the time I see him later today."

In this moment of reorganizing and self-deception, I was still good with excusing the incident like I had done with every incident before. I was all set to move on to the next part of the abuse cycle, the love-bombing part.

And then suddenly I was no longer okay. No longer making any excuses. Just resolved that something had to give.

It's the smallest thing, really, and it doesn't make sense that this would be the final straw, but it was. You see, one of my favorite things about this new kitchen was that the drawers were soft shutting; they have these closure mechanisms that allow you to push the drawer gently to close it, and then the drawer sort of pulls itself the rest of the way shut, very quietly and smoothly. It was one of those tiny, everyday pleasures that gave me joy.

So, I go to close the silverware drawer after cleanup is complete, and wouldn't you know that the drawer bangs loudly against the cabinet base and refuses to close itself gently as usual.

That bang is my wakeup call. I collapse on the kitchen floor and weep.

In that moment, I know that I can no longer live with this man, someone who will have a tantrum at the drop of a hat, break nice things in our home, and call me horrible names, all just to demonstrate his position as the Alpha Male/Apex Predator in the household. I realize in that moment he has no respect for himself, let alone any respect for me. And I don't respect him, either.

He'd been acting this way for years, and I'd always forgiven him. But that day, I hit my limit. This isn't a love story, I suddenly realized. He doesn't value the things I value. He couldn't care less about my thoughts on any matter. He keeps me feeling uneasy. This is not rational, considerate adult communication. It doesn't feel normal. I don't feel safe. I'm certainly not loved. I'm taking care of everyone in this house, and no one is taking care of me.

He broke a five-dollar piece of hardware, and I decided that was it. Such a strange thing to be the final straw, but indeed it was. When a man lacks self-control and is driven by volatile emotions, it rarely ever gets better. I rode that roller coaster for years, hoping for change and seeing none. I was the walking embodiment of Einstein's definition of insanity—doing the same things over and over and foolishly expecting a different result. Something had to give.

About two weeks later, I found proof of his secret offer to buy a one-bedroom apartment downtown. Cash offer: no financing needed. As-Is. Furnished. Deeded in his name only.

Nothing says "it's over" like discovering your husband is using your savings to buy himself a bachelor pad. Bright. Neon. Flashing. Red. Flag. A sign straight from the Lord that I was free at last.

My heart skipped a beat. No more indecision. No more doubt. My next move was clear. I would finally file for divorce and damn the torpedoes. What happened next had to be better than this nightmare. I was more resolved than I'd ever been in my life about anything.

Every woman has a breaking point, and it's different for each one of us. Pearl's story is unique to her, but there are parts of it that ring true in most separation stories. Love covers over a multitude of sins, but sometimes there is such an accumulation of sins that you can take no more.

After decades of ups and downs, after forgiving her husband for the same mistreatment again and again, one friend says her "Mercy and Grace Switch" finally broke. She was done, with no more mercy or grace to give. Today, after a tumultuous divorce, she is happily remarried to the right man. She praises God that divorce was an option. May we all show abundant mercy and grace, but also have the good sense to know when it's time to flip the switch!

Rose Ann's Story

Rose Ann had been dealing with Dan's threats, emotional volatility, meanness and fits of rage—often in front of the children—for nearly two decades.

The silliest things would set him off, and I never knew when it was coming. It happened every week and always followed the same predictable pattern:

1. *He would blow up, yell, sometimes break something or throw something. Threats and cursing. More threats and cursing.*
2. *I would try to insulate the children. I did my best to keep peace by not talking back. I would withdraw and lie low.*

3. *He would eventually calm down after a day or two.*

4. *He would pretend nothing had happened, try to make me laugh, and proceed to behave fairly well for a few days. No apology, just humor, disarming charm and distraction—until the next time.*

5. *Another blowup would occur over some stupid thing.*

6. *Repeat Steps 2 through 4.*

From years of family law practice, I now know that this pattern is Standard Operating Procedure in many households. It can be very confusing, especially because his ability to string together enough good days to make you convince yourself that the well-behaved, charming version of your husband is "the real him," rather than the combative, rude, hurtful personality you see on his bad days. It's when the soul-crushing bad days outnumber the good ones that most women finally find the courage to leave.

For many of my clients, physical abuse is the final breaking point. I don't normally speak in absolutes, but if your husband is physically violent with you and/or your children, or violent with you in front of the children, you *must* leave. *Physical safety is not optional.* You must protect your children and yourself before irreversible damage is done.

A husband's unhealed addiction to pornography, alcohol, or drugs can also be a breaking point. I just don't believe God calls you to live with a man who regularly looks at other naked women or gets drunk or high every day. In such a case, you're not even living with a man as much as you are living with the addiction that's controlling him. There's a better life.

Adultery is, of course, another common deal-breaker. While many women will decide it's over the first time a husband cheats, you'd be amazed how many women stay and try to forgive him, at least the first time. Cheating is a choice, not a mistake, and it rarely ends with the first indiscretion. Dear One, as much as I'd like to tell you different, twenty years of experience in family law practice have taught me that if you forgive your cheating husband, chances are he'll cheat on you again. God doesn't want you to waste your life waiting to see how many more times.

Unrelenting verbal abuse can also break your marriage. Your husband's duty is to build you up, encourage you, be your soft place to land each day. Your home should be peaceful. Everyone has arguments from time to time, but if your husband's words undermine your confidence and self-esteem or make you feel "less than" or unworthy of love, something is seriously wrong. Sadly, many women continue to live this way because they lack the courage and self-assurance to stand up for themselves and break free. If this is your situation, sister, I'm praying right now that God will embolden you and give you the resolve you need to do something about it.

For me, there were a couple of final straws, but I need not mention the details here. Suffice it to say that I wanted my children to know there was a different way of living—and loving—than what they had experienced in our home up to that point. We all needed peace.

Once it Breaks, It's Irretrievably Broken

When you're done, you're just done. There's no going back when you reach that point. Dead things don't come back to life.

You are still that wonderful woman you were before this marriage broke your spirit and stole your hope. You aren't crazy. You are loved. You are good. You are smarter than you think. You're going to get through this and THRIVE on the other side. Keep the faith!

Questions for Reflection

1. Are you at your breaking point? How long did it take you to get here? Was it a slow process or a sudden fracture?

2. What were the things that happened to bring you to this place in your marriage?

3. What was the proverbial "final straw" for you?

4. What have you done to overcome this broken feeling? Has it helped? If not, why do you think not? If it did, how did it help?

5. Do you wish you could have a word with your younger self in the days leading up to your wedding? Is there anything that could have prepared you for what's happened during your marriage?

Chapter Soundtrack

"You Don't Even Know Who I Am"—Patty Loveless

"Whatever You Say"—Martina McBride

"Heartbreak Warfare"—John Mayer

"Forget About It"—Alison Krauss

"Who Will You Run To"—Heart

4

Know Your Worth

Life is too short to think you're unlovable because
someone didn't know how to love you.
—Dr. Caroline Leaf

S omewhere along the way, did someone make you feel you weren't "enough?" Not pretty enough? Smart enough? Talented enough? Good enough? So many women stay in abusive, toxic marriages because they do not believe they are worth loving.

Friend, if you're going to get through this divorce in good health and flourish on the other side, you must know you're worth fighting for.

Insecurities Keep Us Trapped in Bad Marriages

I often marvel at how the women I meet in my office are so miserable in their marriages but reluctant to do anything about it. Indeed, why did I live in misery as long as I did? I'm convinced it comes down to insecurity. We simply don't think we have what it takes to do life on our own.

We can retrain our brains to help us realize we are worthy and that we should expect to be treated well. This chapter will show you how.

Your Husband Does Not Define Your Worth

You are not defined by how your husband views you. Read that again.

Janie's Story

My husband, James, was encouraging and wonderful the whole time we were dating and engaged. Almost as soon as we were married, his treatment of me changed, and it was like I became his possession, his trophy, rather than his equal.

I had always enjoyed singing since my childhood, and I had been part of choral activities at church and in high school and college. Friends had even asked me to sing at their weddings, so I had always assumed I sounded okay, at least. It brought me joy!

One evening I was singing in the kitchen of our small apartment while cleaning the dinner dishes, and he walked in there, clasping his hands together against his sternum in opera-singer fashion. He began to mimic me, singing through his nose in the most unpleasant, twangy way, sounding almost like a kazoo. "Janie, I could hear you singing from the bedroom," James said. "You should never sing around other people ever again. I'm telling you this because I care about you and don't want you to embarrass yourself."

So, I stopped singing for the rest of my ten-year marriage. Unless I was totally alone in the car or just with my kids, I would never let anyone hear my voice. If James happened to walk into the room when I was singing lullabies to the children, I would immediately stop. The kids and I could be singing in the kitchen to some song they liked, giggling and dancing, and I would turn it down and shut off my voice the second James came home, almost like a scene from a John Hughes movie where teenagers are having a party and the parents come home early.

I realize now how sad that was. He stole my joy, and I was so insecure that I let him.

After I finally left James, I began singing with the praise team at my church. I sang with bands at weddings and with friends at karaoke.

My return to public singing is a small thing, but it has become a metaphor for reclaiming my life and pursuing happiness my own way, unrestricted by how James views me.

I'm not a professional, but I'm a pretty good singer. I'm convinced now that James just didn't want anyone to compliment or encourage me. He wanted to keep me under his control and making me insecure about this part of myself was a way he could keep me from having confidence. He knew he could treat me however he wanted and that I would never have the courage to leave him if I didn't feel good about myself. He did this in other ways, too. Told me I was ugly, my nose was too big, no one would ever love me, that I had fat ankles, that I couldn't make it without him.

His words do not define me, but it took me years to figure that out. I now live my best life each day, embracing the things that bring me joy. And proving him wrong.

Why They Tear Us Down

He wants you to think less of yourself so he can treat you however he wants. But why? I mean, he loved you enough to ask you to marry him, is proud of you at least to the extent he wanted to call you his wife, and takes you places as his forever date, right? It doesn't make sense.

The reason is that he knows, in his heart, how truly amazing you are. And, in his insecurity, he doesn't want some other, better guy to notice and turn your head. He doesn't want you to have the confidence to find financial independence, either, but that's another chapter.

His poor treatment of you, his assassination of your character, his snide remarks about your talents and interests, is really more a reflection of his view of himself than his real view of you. Realizing this truth is the key to unlocking your confidence and becoming unaffected by what he says about you. He is to be pitied for his insecurity, not hated for it. My goal for you is that his words slowly lose their power over you; that's when you know you've healed.

How the World Shapes Our View of Self

I spent my formative years allowing others to define me.

Flat-chested, nerdy, and sheltered, with limbs that didn't become proportional until college (for years, I could scratch my knees without bending down—no lie), mediocre skin and wavy brown hair that resisted straightening and became a poofy bouffant in the South Georgia humidity, I was awkward to say the least.

I was positively pining for a boy to notice me and ask me to go on a date, and I tied my sense of worth to appearance. I thought, if only I could fill out a little, have prettier hair or skin, be somehow cooler, a boy will notice me, and then I'll be accepted. And if a boy *didn't* notice me, that meant I must not be lovable.

After years of counseling clients, I now realize this is a worldview many women share. All too often, we tie our worth to what kind of man we can catch, to what kind of man we can *keep*. Rather than regarding ourselves as unique, gifted individuals with special insights, ideas and potential, we base all our value on how *one man* sees us, and in doing so tie all our happiness and contentment to whether that *one man* is happy with us at a given time. I don't know how things became that way, but this kind of marital patriarchy is still very much alive and well among many women I meet.

This patriarchal worldview stuck with me into adulthood. When I got married, I found sufficient value in the simple fact that I was married, and I reckoned I was one of the lucky ones to have found a husband who would love me.

Trying to please my husband, I slowly let my individuality diminish until my former self no longer existed. A friend recently remarked about how I had totally changed when I met Mark all those years ago. She was right! I had started dressing more matronly overnight, opting for drab clothing over the more fashion-forward, colorful selections of my college days. I let Mark talk me into chopping my long hair into a short bob that made my nose look like a beak. I didn't care that the haircut made me less confident. I was married, and I didn't want any extra attention, anyway.

I stopped being openly affectionate and warm. Always a hugger before, I somehow convinced myself it was unladylike or unrefined for a married woman to go around hugging people and saying "I love you" in public settings. Trying to be what I thought Mark wanted me to be, I lost my warmth. The fun parts of me died for a long time, only to emerge on girls' trips and the occasional social event if I had enough wine in me not to be self-conscious.

Determined to be Betty Crocker in the early days of marriage, I traded in the Stouffer's frozen entrees of my college years for original home-cooked recipes and tried a few new ones each week. I focused on keeping the house clean. We ate what he wanted to eat, and I cooked the way he wanted things cooked. I learned how to garden and arrange flowers. I subscribed to *Southern Living* and read all the articles on housekeeping and entertaining. I did what he wanted to do and stopped having opinions about where we spent free time. I did not make waves.

The truth is that the best parts, the fun parts, the interesting parts, of me disappeared in that marriage.

What I had previously cared about no longer mattered to me. What mattered was that someone had wanted to marry me, and I was what every other girl my age wanted to be—a married woman. My new identity was to be his "Missus," not an individual. I had no right to complain, even when daily life wasn't happy, because at least I was married and he wasn't going anywhere, or at least I didn't think he was.

What a load of bull.

I wish someone had taken me by the shoulders and shaken me into reality, and that's why I'm writing this book for you now. Consider me your shoulder shaker.

Maybe you've done some of the same things I did. Lost a bit (or maybe a big ol' chunk) of who you were before. Forfeited your beautiful individuality to meet whatever worldly standards you perceived in his family or in his peer group, hoping to be accepted. Set aside your passions and goals, losing your sense of life purpose, opting instead to help him pursue *his* dreams and attain *his* goals. And now you feel utterly broken that divorce is looming, thinking you aren't good enough, or that you're not being "[insert whatever adjective] enough" is what caused the marriage to fail.

If so, Dear Sister, you need to know you are not alone. Your worth is bigger than that silly man. It really has nothing at all to do with him, and everything to do with you.

Where Our Worth Comes From

To be happy in relationships with other people, first you must be single and secure as an individual.[8]

---

8 Wilkerson, Rich. "Single and Secure—Know Your Worth." VOUS Church. March 6, 2022, Miami, Florida. Sermon. *See also Single and Secure: Break Up With the Lies and Fall In Love With the Truth*, published in 2022

Humans have value because we are created beings, beloved children of the Most High God. Scripture tells us that we were "fearfully and wonderfully" made (Psalm 139:14) in God's own image (Genesis 1:26-28), that we are more precious to God, the Creator of the entire universe, than any other part of creation, as we are "just a little lower than the angels" (Psalm 8:4-8). He knows how many hairs are on each of our heads. He cares about the daily workings of our lives. He cares for the sparrows and meets their needs (Matthew 10:31), but meets our needs even more abundantly (Luke 12:7). He's almighty but also loves us the way we love our own children.

Our value comes from our very personhood, not from what other persons say or think about us.

And of all humankind, women are special in their own way! We bring lives into the world and then feed them from our bodies. We build up our children and teach them the way they should live, changing the world through their impact. We are master organizers, running our households and managing our children's schedules, and meeting the needs of everyone around us. We love big. We kiss the boo-boos and nurse the sick back to health. We serve our husbands with all our hearts. We show hospitality and kindness to others, feeding bellies, cleaning dirty baseball pants, and nurturing souls. We nurture our babies and let them know they're loved and protected. Women are amazing. God crafted us in a very special way.

Most amazing of all, God thought so much of us, wanted us in Heaven with Him so badly despite our tendency to sin against Him, that He sent His own son to die to buy our salvation. I'll never understand why He did that for little bitty me. But He did, and I'm ever so thankful.

Our identity is tied to Christ's sacrifice. It is not found in the praise of man.

Rich Wilkerson, pastor of VOUS Church in Miami, has given us powerful sermons that speak directly to this idea of knowing our worth.[9] Based on a passage from Numbers 27, Wilkerson preaches about four "single and secure" women who'd been denied their inheritance simply because they were women. They had no brothers, and the law of the land at the time was that a woman was unable to inherit her father's assets. Instead of taking the news of "no land for you" lying down, they fought like hell for what was theirs. And you know what? The rulers heard them loud and clear, and their efforts even resulted in a change in the law for other women like them! Talk about bold! They knew who they were as daughters of a wealthy father, and they weren't going to settle for less than their full entitlement of assets.

They changed the landscape for women everywhere from then on. Boss ladies! I can't wait to get to Heaven and get to know them.

Sometimes I think Christian women forget they are daughters of a King. We should know, like the women in Numbers, that we are entitled to certain basic treatment by virtue of the fact that we belong to the Lord, that we are human, that we are women, and that men are not any better than we are. Start embracing your worth, sister!

Stop Giving Discounts, And Don't Forget to Add Tax

When we downplay our worth, we "give discounts"[10] and expect less in our relationships. We don't stand up for ourselves. We don't speak our minds. We abandon our convictions and allow our morals to slip.

---

9   Id.

10   Id.

We allow our individual selves to be absorbed into the cultures of our husbands' families. We forget our foundations. We abandon our beautiful, premarital selves and become the faux women we think our husbands want us to be.

And, worst of all, we accept and allow poor treatment. We allow ourselves to be ignored. We allow ourselves to be used. We allow ourselves to be objectified. Diminished.

When you know your worth, your standards and expectations rise. You no longer discount your worth, and you start expecting more from those around you, i.e., you start "adding tax"[11] and expecting only the best treatment in your friendships and romantic relationships.

You are exactly what someone is searching for right now. God says you are amazing and wonderful, just as you are, even if your husband—and his mama—are able to see it. You are God's daughter! You do not have to settle!

Higher expectations result in better treatment from others in relationships. Better treatment from others yields more meaningful and fulfilling relationships. Fulfilling and encouraging human relationships are what life is all about. We are built for relationships, built to love each other, designed with a need for encouragement. When you feel encouraged and loved by others, your overall life experience improves, as you feel free to give that same encouragement back to them without fear of rejection.

Realize Your Value

Realizing your value as a human being is foundational to finding happiness in the future. When you are secure in your singleness, in

---

11 Id.

your humanity apart from any tie to another person, you have confidence that you're okay no matter what life throws at you. And this, my friend, is what makes other people want to be with you. It's an attitude that makes you magnetically attractive.

Have you ever had a friend who was so original, so full of joy and effervescence, so encouraging to others, so comfortable in her own skin that she had no concern whatsoever about what others thought of her? A woman you could sit with for hours just being entertained and enjoying the flow of communication as she uplifts you and makes you laugh with her view of the world and genuine kindness?

My mother is a woman like that.

She was part of a ministry of people who dressed up as clowns and witnessed to prison inmates in the name of Jesus; dressed as Katie the Clown in a red tinsel wig, there's no telling how many people she told of God's love for them.

She makes a cake from scratch for each family birthday. She is the first to comfort the bereaved after a death. She dances to Motown in the kitchen. She shoots a gun like Annie Oakley and knows how to use a chainsaw. She knows who she is in the Lord, and she couldn't care less if you like it or not.

This utter self-assurance is what has always made her so captivating. She loves the Lord and worships Him with no-holds-barred intensity, unafraid to lift her arms in praise or talk about Him with strangers. She has loved people with such reckless abandon all my life. People have always loved her because she first let them know how much *they* were loved.

She is the epitome of "single and secure," of confidence and strength, of the kind of person I want to be—fearless and bold, game-changing, difference-making, Jesus-loving, service-minded and fiercely protective of the oppressed. Untethered by societal expectations.

Friend, your divorce could be God's way of setting you free to be the woman you really want to be, unhindered by your husband's rules, unrestricted by his family's view of what is proper. Get excited that God has given you such great potential. Your life story is still yours to write! Make it your own!

One Last Thing: You Are Not a Failure

Your marriage may be failing, but this does not mean *you* have failed.

I meet with at least one woman each week who is distraught over her marriage ending. She's wrestling with feelings of inadequacy, thoughts of what she could have done differently to keep him from leaving, to make him love her and want her the way she wants and loves him.

Marriages fail because something just isn't right. It's never totally one spouse's fault, though many of us feel it's probably at least 90/10 in one direction. 😉 The truth is that marriages fall apart because humans are imperfect, and they can't—or won't—control how their imperfections inflict wounds on one another. I've seen it hundreds of times in my law practice: a woman can do everything in her power to save her marriage, by correcting her own behaviors in line with her husband's complaints, and nothing is ever enough for him.

Divorce doesn't mean you have failed or that you are lacking somehow. It just means the relationship was meant to end.

Relationships are two-way streets. You can focus on being your best self all day long, but if your husband isn't also working to be his best self, paying attention to your needs and endeavoring to be the best married man he can be, the marriage cannot thrive.

I vividly remember a conversation I had with my friend Katie sophomore year at Georgia when I was nursing some serious heartbreak after a boy had dumped me for another girl. Sitting in Apartment 3 in the KD house, I was saying how I must not be good/pretty/smart/accomplished enough for him, questioning what I could have done to avoid the breakup. Katie, wise beyond her years, said—and I'll never forget it— "It's not anything you did. Relationships are not about one person being good enough for the other. It's about what's *between you* that makes it work."

She helped me see that the experience was just not meant to last, not because either of us wasn't good enough for the other, but just because it wasn't a good fit. After all, we were just twenty and very few are mature enough for a serious relationship at that age anyway! It just wasn't meant to be. Some relationships are just so unhealthy that they need to die for the good of all parties, and that's okay. Sometimes even better than okay.

Questions for Reflection

1. Were you raised to believe you were worthy of love? What experiences from your childhood shaped your view of your worth?

2. What kind of person were you before you married? Have you changed parts of your personality or given up on your own goals—for this marriage, your husband, and his family?

3. What parts of your pre-marriage self would you like to rediscover? How can you reconnect with who you were before you married?

4. Do you believe you are a failure because your marriage has failed? What expectations or other factors have led you to feel

this way? Can you identify things your husband could have done differently to safeguard and strengthen your marriage?

5. Are you secure in who you are in the Lord, in your unique humanity? Do you know you have value as a person that is unfettered by any one man's view of you? If not, what lies has your heart believed along the way? Identify the things that make you unique and special and consider the hard times God has brought you through already. Do you trust God's plan to improve your life after divorce?

Resources

You Are Enough—Mandy Hale

Her True Worth—Brittany Maher & Cassandra Speer

Chapter Soundtrack

"Brave"—Sara Bareilles

"Mean"—Taylor Swift

"You Are Loved"—Stars Go Dim

"Just Like Fire"—Pink

"Stronger (What Doesn't Kill You)"—Kelly Clarkson

"Priceless"—For King and Country

5

Face Your Fears

Never be afraid to trust an unknown future to a known God.
—Corrie ten Boom

I 've been a big old scaredy cat most of my life. Scared of failure. Scared of getting hurt. Scared of missing out. Scared of rejection.

When I was in school, I would get really stressed out about a week before exam time or if a paper or project was due. I remember calling Daddy at times like these, to stew over all the upcoming deadlines, looking for encouragement more than anything. He would always tell me to stop worrying and start working. I now call it the Eddie Owens Formula for Success: Stop Worrying. Start Working.

This was sage advice. You get nowhere worrying about the future. Action is what is needed to drive out that fear. Have you ever noticed how making a little progress toward a task makes you feel a little less stressed with each step? As you move from one step to the next, attacking the task at hand, you start *believing* you will be ready to give your peak performance, be able to give that presentation, ace that exam.

I would hang up the phone with Daddy, pick up my pen or computer and start working on that paper, studying for that test, perfecting that project. And as I worked, peace would replace my fear, and confidence in my ability to get things done would replace my fears of inadequacy. I began to know that all would be well. All it really took was the initiative to stop procrastinating, stop talking about how stressed I was, and rather take action, working on the task at hand. It happened every time.

You can't allow fear of what people will say about you, fear of what will happen next, fear of backlash from your husband and his family, fear of losing control, fear of the unknown, fear of perceived failure, or any other fear keep you mired down and stuck.

Fear is Powerful Because It's Physical

Fear has the power to grip us, to paralyze us. But why is it so powerful?

Have you ever awakened from a bad dream, heart racing, hyper-alert, ready to fight or run? Cortisol and adrenaline are stress hormones that release into our bodies when something frightens us or upsets us, causing our heart rates and blood pressure to rise, and making the blood flow away from the heart and into the limbs for fight-or-flight mode, to equip us to run or to start throwing punches.[12] It's a protective mechanism God built into our bodies, meant for our good. According to Zachary Sikora, PsyD, of Northwestern Medicine, "fear is our survival response."[13]

This fight-or-flight response emerges in high-conflict interactions with combative people. If you have been in a high-conflict marriage, you know what I'm talking about. Your body tenses and prepares to defend you whenever your husband is around. Some

---

12 Northwestern Medicine, "5 Things You Never Knew About Fear." www. nm.org/healthbeat/healthy-tips/emotional-health/5-things-you-never-knew-about-fear.

13 Id.

women describe this feeling as a need to "walk on eggshells" to keep peace at home. Tense marriages, with their discord and constant strife, keep a woman's body in almost a constant state of anxiety as she worries about the next argument before it even comes. This is particularly true when arguments are physically violent. If this has been your life, your poor body is under constant stress trying to keep you safe, my friend. It needs relief.

This same response can continue post-separation from a high-conflict husband, as your body still hasn't figured out you're separated and safe. Don't be surprised if your body continues to react the same way it always has in response to your combative husband, even after a divorce case is underway, and often even after the divorce is finalized.

Laurel Leigh's Story

Chuck was such a charmer when we were dating and engaged. He was a little controlling—always wanting to know where I was and what I was doing, calling my phone constantly—but I chose to be flattered rather than concerned because he was so handsome and so much fun! The fun stopped soon after the honeymoon. He would hardly let me out of his sight. He made me download an app on my phone which gave him access to my location at all times. When the app's location map was a block "off" my actual location (it was still new technology at the time), he would accuse me of meeting another man, when I was actually at the store or in yoga class. He would tell me off when I got home, go through my purse, and accuse me of infidelity. He called me "Laurel Leigh the Whore" and other awful names anytime I put on makeup and perfume. Pretty soon, I was unable to do anything right in his eyes. I lived in a perpetual state of anxiety, worried when the next anger bomb was going to drop.

He would be so sweet and charming almost immediately after these blowups, apologizing for overreacting, blaming his ADHD for his behavior, acknowledging his irrationality, swearing he'd never mistreat me again. But I would only get three or four days of peace before the next irrational outburst. It was a roller coaster. I stayed for the good days, thinking he was just battling mental illness and I owed him a duty to stay with him in sickness and in health. It was brutal.

The bad days kept me fearful. The good days kept me stuck.

One day he got so angry that he headbutted me and shoved me into a wall in front of our toddler. This later escalated with him punching holes in our walls and doors, and ultimately slapping my face. I should have left long before then, but this was finally enough for me to seek out a divorce attorney. My family couldn't believe I had stayed so long. I still don't know why I did, either. Why did I not stand up for myself before I was physically abused? What was I so afraid of?

How Fear Keeps Us Stuck

When your body senses fear, the cerebral cortex, that area of your brain responsible for "reasoning and judgment[,] . . . becomes impaired—so now it's difficult to make good decisions or think clearly."[14] Have you ever noticed how discombobulated you can become during an argument? You think of all the things you *should have* said instead of the empty or foolish things you *did* say, in the heat of the moment?

Or maybe you tend to be quiet and withdraw in the face of hostility; that's what psychologists call your Freeze Response, which we will explore more later in the book. As game-changing Christian

---

14 Id.

business coach and cheerleader-for-all-women-entrepreneurs Jennifer Allwood explained, "Your brain is literally trying to save you from the pain of being uncomfortable. It's trying to save you from the pain of doing something you don't have experience with . . . But your brain lies to you. Your feelings lie to you."[15]

Blame your cerebral cortex. Fear can cause brain fog, a lack of clarity, a lack of direction about what to do or say.

If you want to think clearly, you have to get away from the unrelenting sources of your stress. If you stay stuck in the presence of the person creating the stress in your body, the person who evokes that fear response in you, you will never break free of this unchanging anxious state you're in. You'll never really think clearly about your situation. You will never get unstuck. Sometimes space is what you need for perspective.

Fear of Being Alone

The fear of being alone is a real thing. Married people become accustomed to being married. There's just something comforting about being part of a pair. Even if you're enduring abuse or your husband makes you feel unappreciated, at least you have a warm body with whom to go places, share the load of parenting children, and share financial obligations. No one wants to feel lonely. I meet women all the time who have lived in loveless marriages for years, frozen in fear that being single and empowered will somehow be worse than being married and abused.

Here's the truth: you were probably *already alone* to some degree in the marriage, whether or not you realized it.

---

15   Allwood, Jennifer. *Fear is Not the Boss of You*. Zondervan Books, 2020, p. 81.

Did your husband communicate with you? Did he share your hopes, dreams and fears, or even care what they were? Did he let you know you were honored, respected and loved? If you're reading this book, I doubt he did all these things to the extent he should have. His neglect and disinterest no doubt hurt you deeply, but it should also give you the confidence to know that you will be okay on your own. Being alone in your husband's presence, when you should feel the most supported, is worse than if your husband weren't there at all. I sure felt this way, for years.

Take heart, Dear One. You've been managing without his support already! You are capable of navigating the waters of Singledom. You *can* do life just fine without him.

Plus, Deuteronomy 31:8 tells us that we are never *truly* alone, even when other humans are not supportive, that the Lord himself goes before us, will never leave us or forsake us. Even women of faith fail to lean on the Lord when it comes to their marriage. That's what happened to Lorraine.

Joshua and Lorraine had a toxic marriage. Joshua, a stockbroker with an impressive book of business, spent his free time golfing with friends, while Lorraine donated her time to charitable fundraising and teaching Bible study. Life appeared good at their house, but they rarely connected or talked about anything of any importance. Each had their own interests, and interest in one another was not one of them. Lorraine can't stand Joshua, with his egomania and hot temper, and she feels alone. Every time she tried to discuss their marital issues, Joshua lashed out and told her she was ridiculous, that everything was fine, and why couldn't she just be happy?

He knows in his heart Lorraine is an amazing woman, beautiful and strong. He doesn't love her well, but he doesn't know how to change and doesn't want to make the effort. Fearful Lorraine will one day decide to leave him and take half "his" fortune and both their kids with her, Joshua often says things to keep Lorraine's confidence level in check. He tells her she's not aging well, that no one else will ever want her with her crow's feet and thunder thighs, that she's not smart enough to manage the bank account and won't have sufficient resources on her own, anything to knock her confidence level down a notch.

Believing she could do no better and afraid of being old and alone, Lorraine stayed married to Joshua, even while surrounded by all her dear friends who would surely be there for her if she decided to leave him. She was just too afraid to step out in faith and change her life, never knowing the true contentment she could be forfeiting.

There are many Lorraines in the world, unfortunately, who live in misery longer than they should. I also meet many women like Lorraine who do step out in faith, reclaim their lives, and find life abundant after divorce. I'm one of them.

Do not believe the lie that you will be abandoned or alone if you leave a toxic marriage. You have value, and the people who love you will come out of the woodwork to show you just how much. And your post-divorce life could bless you beyond measure.

Fear of Ruining Your Children

Another common fear I see among clients is that the children will go crazy, drop out of school, get pregnant, turn to drugs, or do some other unhealthy thing as a result of their parents' decision to divorce. This fear is born out of our lack of faith, and our failure to remember that God loves our children even more than we do, protects them, and sends his Holy Spirit to guide their decision making.

You also have to consider the long-term *negative* impacts an abusive home can have on children. Kids grow up to live what they were raised in, and toxic family dynamics can be generational. If children witness abusive communication so regularly that it becomes a normal part of their daily lives, they are more likely to abuse their own families in adulthood. The cycle needs to stop with you.

Fear of Not Having Enough Money

Are you afraid you won't be able to make it financially without your husband? Afraid of how your lifestyle will change?

When confronted with this concern in client consultations, I counter this question with another question: has God not provided for you throughout your life? What makes you think He will stop now?

To combat this fear, remind yourself of all the ways God has taken care of your needs throughout your life. And take the initiative to make a financial plan for your post-separation life. Your lawyer will help you petition the court for whatever support you need from your husband, and a good financial planner can help you plan a solid budget and wisely allocate your resources, both post-separation and post-divorce. Taking action drives out fear.

Fear of Embarrassment and Social Rejection

We fear man's rejection of who we are. No one likes being embarrassed or made fun of.

A divorce can put your family right in the middle of the fishbowl for all the world around you to analyze. It's one of the most unpleasant parts of the process, this feeling that all your friends are watching your life and forming an opinion about it. It sucks.

We worry that the Court of Public Opinion will judge us harshly, not understand our hurts or the reasons for our decisions. Like a middle schooler looking for a place to sit in the cafeteria, we wonder if no one will give us a seat at the table any longer. We tend to think filing for divorce will mark us with a giant Scarlet "D." That we will automatically become social pariahs.

But God's word tells us we need not fear public opinion. Proverbs 29:25 tells us it is dangerous to be concerned with what others think of you and admonishes us that if we trust in the Lord, we are safe. It's true. In Hebrews 13:6, we are taught to say with confidence, "The Lord is my helper; I will not fear; what can man do to me?" Your divorce is today's big story, but it will be yesterday's news by tomorrow. Find your identity in the Lord, and let any negative comments go in one ear and out the other.

You know your heart. If your conscience is clear and you're sleeping fine at night, ready to meet your Maker at any moment, do not let yourself be bothered by the idle chatter of a bunch of catty women you don't really like anyway. Your real friends won't talk about you.

One other comforting thought: folks are always going to want something to gossip about, and you can take solace in the fact that your divorce will be the top story only for a very short time. There is another divorce, affair or scandal right around the corner to take your place as the topic of conversation at the next book club meeting. Just sit tight for a minute.

It is more than likely that some people will disappoint you during your divorce season. Use this disappointment as fuel to drive you to a happier day. Prove the naysayers wrong by taking charge of your own destiny and getting through this divorce with flying colors, well-adjusted, poised, and ready for the future!

We Southerners love the movie *Steel Magnolias*. One favorite line is "an ounce of pretension is worth a pound of manure." There's nothing I hate more than the snobbery and judgment-passing from people who think they're better than somebody else. This sort of thing is still very much alive and well, at least in the South. Getting divorced, especially in a small town like mine, can draw attention to you in ways you never wanted or invited. People are quick to give their opinions, whether you asked for them or not. Onlookers' uninvited comments about your situation can and will hurt your feelings.

In the early days of my divorce, I avoided public situations when-ever possible, hoping that if people didn't see me out too much, they'd have less to say about me. Looking back on it now, I wish I had gone out more! Those people I was so fearful would judge me ARE NOT MY PEOPLE ANYWAY. Why did I care what they thought? Why do you? Dig deep and analyze what's driving this fear.

They could be judging you because they wish they had the cour-age to walk the path you're on. Or maybe because they don't like to think you're going to be happier than they are. Or perhaps your de-cision to change your life makes them uncomfortable because you're no longer sorted into your designated "married" compartment in their minds, and that is intimidating to them.

Also consider what's the worst thing that can happen if someone feels some kind of way about *your* marital status or decisions. Take heart, Dear Friend. Words hurt, but they're nothing to fear. They can't kill you. You will survive it, take stock of your relationships, and be blessed in the long run by the clarity it brings.

Fear of the Unknown

It is natural to be afraid of the unknown. No one in their right mind would jump off a cliff into darkness, not knowing what lies below. That's a lot of what divorce is—you're choosing to (or having to) leave your current "normal" in exchange for an unknown future. You're jumping off a cliff into a dark abyss, and you're terrified. I had that fear, and all my clients also have it to some degree. The trepidation over how life can ever improve, at a time when lots of days you may not even feel like getting out of bed, is very real.

What I've come to understand from watching my clients over the years is this: each one arrives at my office for her first consultation a shell of the woman she ultimately is at the end of the process. A bit of good news, progress in the case, encouraging words and practical advice from others who've been through it, and other little shots in the arm will help you along your divorce path. And when the process is over, you will have a better idea of what the future holds. You'll be able to plan and execute your next steps, and you'll walk forward with greater confidence. It just takes time, like all the older ladies always told us.

Think of your divorce like high school graduation . . . it's called "Commencement"—something is surely ending, but the real cause for celebration is that something even *better* is getting ready to COMMENCE! Your life is a great adventure, just waiting to be lived.

I wish I could go back and bottle the feeling I had as soon as my separation period began. My divorce wasn't final, but I had HOPE—for the first time in nearly two decades—that the future could be happy and bright! The trepidation of what exactly the future would look like was still there for sure, and there was sadness for the loss of what could have been, the adjustment to living as a single woman with three children, and the onslaught of being thrown for divorce litigation loops I didn't enjoy, but transcendent peace and hope were nonetheless ever present. Get excited and keep focused on that HOPE. God has a plan for you to go on to a great new adventure in your post-divorce life. You have to walk through this storm to get to it, but a glorious new day is coming. Remember this on the hard days.

Fear of Dating Again

Are you afraid of being alone for the rest of your life? This fear is natural, especially if your husband has abandoned you without warning and you've lost your bearings for the moment.

Let me tell you, you are not too old, and it is never too late to find happiness. Read that again.

As long as you're alive, it's not too late. I could tell you a hundred stories of midlife and later-life divorce clients who found their true love connection after being abandoned or mistreated by a first spouse. Age truly is just a number.

Middle-aged clients fear dating after divorce because "all the good ones are taken." Many say, "I'm too old to date again." It's NoNsEnSe. 😄 There is no shortage of kind, loyal, wonderful people who find themselves single for whatever reason and don't want to be. God could be waiting to bless you with your new love at any moment. He may have the most perfect person waiting for you when your heart is ready.

Psalm 147:3 tells us the Lord "heals the brokenhearted and binds up their wounds." He did it for me and He'll do it for you, too, friend.

It's a big world. There are plenty of people out there looking for love and connection—I know because I meet them daily in my office. You can date after divorce if you want to. Life is not ending!

And if you don't want to date, that doesn't mean you will be alone. Concentrate on loving your friends, children, and family well, and you will see all the meaning it brings to your life. Do not deceive yourself into believing you need a man in order to be happy!

Fear is Not from the Lord

2 Timothy 1:7 (NLT) tells us, "For God has not given us a spirit of fear and timidity, but of power, love and self-discipline." Notice how our *self-discipline* is juxtaposed here against the idea of fear in us. Being *self-disciplined* can help us overcome our fear, and that self-discipline was given to us by our Creator Himself. Claim this for your life, dear sister! You can overcome your fear with the right mindset.

God knows us, inside and out. He knows we have all that adrenaline and cortisol coursing through us. He knows what triggers it, and He is much, much bigger than our fears. This is why we are reminded so often in scripture that we should rest in Him, pray to Him and seek Him in anxious times.[16] We are reminded that with Him on our side, we have nothing to fear. He goes before us, stands beside us, and fights our battles. What sweet assurance for our scaredy-cat souls!

Try to remember these truths in your most fearsome moments. The Lord your God loves you, and He is going before you in this conflict. He is bigger than your husband. He is bigger than your pain. And He is in the midst of your life, working all things together for your good. Trust Him.

---

16   See Psalm 34:4-5, Psalm 23:4, Psalm 27:1, 46:1-3, Isaiah 41:13, Luke 14:27, Psalm 91:4-5, Genesis 50:21, Joshua 8:1, Isaiah 35:4, Isaiah 41:10, Jeremiah 42:11, Isaiah 43:1, and Lamentations 3:57.

Stop Worrying. Start Working

As John Wayne put it, "Courage is being scared to death . . . and saddling up anyway."

You know in your heart what must be done. Face it. Get busy. Schedule a meeting with a good lawyer. Do what that lawyer says. Gather the information and documents requested of you. Let the to-do lists focus your attention. You'll be amazed at how fear dissipates as you take ownership of the process and get it done, step by step. And before you know it, it will be behind you, and you'll be able to proceed with new confidence that you can handle anything life throws your way. You can do this! Turn those fears into your fuel, and let it drive you productively forward.

Questions for Reflection

1. What is your greatest fear, Dear One? What fears are keeping you stuck?

2. Do you know you are worth fighting for? Do you know God is there, fighting your battles for you? What battles has He fought for you before?

3. Are you afraid to leave your husband? What are you afraid will happen if you do?

4. What can you do to address and overcome each fear you just listed?

5. Do you believe God is greater than your worst fears? Do you believe He goes before you in battle? How has God's faithfulness to you manifested before? Consider examples from your life that let you know you can trust Him, even when you don't understand the big picture at the time.

Chapter Soundtrack

Age of Worry—John Mayer

Fear is a Liar—Zach Williams

Trust in You—Lauren Daigle

The Breakup Song—Francesca Battistelli

Fear of Being Alone—Reba McEntire

6

Healing Your Heart After Betrayal

It would seem that Our Lord finds our desires not too strong, but too weak. We are half-hearted creatures, fooling about with drink and sex and ambition when infinite joy is offered us, like an ignorant child who wants to go on making mud pies in a slum because he cannot imagine what is meant by the offer of a holiday at the sea. We are far too easily pleased.
—C.S. Lewis, *The Weight of Glory*

While Jonathan, Samantha and Sweet Wife are just composite personalities in a hypothetical scene, unfortunately Darling Boy and his mama are recurring characters in the lives of many women, especially in the South. Following is Sweet Wife's story, told from her perspective:

Sweet Wife Learns the Truth

"Wait. What? I guess I've known in my heart he was probably cheating, but now it's confirmed. He's been living a double life right under my nose, sleeping with my FRIEND. Someone I trusted and loved! Her?! Really?! Who is this man? Who is this person I'm married to? He's someone I no longer recognize. The lies and alibis all rush to my mind. He's been shamelessly deceiving me for months. I'm such a fool. A fool! How could I be so easily tricked? How did I get here after a decade of marriage? How many other women have there been? Is anything real? Is anything true?

Breathe. Stop and take a breath. Why is the room spinning? My children. Oh, God. Where are my children right now? I say, "I'm going to get the kids from your mother's." *I so desperately need to get to them. I grab my car keys from the kitchen counter and head to my car. He follows me, and all he can say is,* 'Please don't tell the children. What about them? I know you're upset, but you have to think about them.'

Exactly. What about them? Were you thinking of them when you were screwing HER? Why is he even talking to me right now? Why won't he just leave me alone, give me a moment's peace to process this bombshell?

But it's never really been about me or my feelings now, has it? Get away from me, you lying jerk! He won't let me close my car door, and my stupid, fancy car—the one he bought me for Christmas as a surprise so he could brag to his friends—won't start if the door is open—damn German engineering. It starts raining. I just need to get to my children. Let. Me. Leave! I yell at the UPS delivery man at the house next door to help me get him away from me. Being exposed to the man in brown is too much for him, so he finally lets me drive away. I drive like a bat out of hell to my mother-in-law's house, desperate to get to my kids. He chases me the whole way there. I'm crying out to the Lord as I'm driving, surprisingly calm in the face of this life-altering calamity. God, my God, You've set me free. Praise You, thank You for showing me the truth. I'm not crazy, after all. My gut was right all along! He always had a wandering eye, but now I know he's actually cheated on me. Thank You for revealing the truth.

I'm praying and driving, praying and driving, praying and driving in this thunderstorm that formed at almost the same time that my world just fell apart. Puddles of water splashing around my tires on the wet roads to the house. Praying and driving. Praying and driving.

He arrives on the front porch ten seconds after I do. I'm pounding on his mama's front door, out of breath, not sure what I'll say to her, but certain that I need to hold my children close to me, more than ever before. The children are my only True North, my compass in that moment.

Through the glass, I see her walking toward me, my dear mother-in-law, the one who has always had my back and shown great empathy with every struggle I've ever had with her Darling Boy, a woman of God I trust implicitly to be my safe haven this time just as she's always been when he acted out before. She opens the door, and without thinking, I say, "Jonathan has something to tell you. Go on, Jonathan, tell your mother what you've been doing!" Jonathan can't manage to speak (the coward), so I blurt out, "He's been sleeping with Samantha."

Her first reaction is to cry out, almost like a scene in a black-and-white movie, "My son! Oh, my son!" and to throw her arms around said Darling Boy, asking if he's alright, how could he ruin his life like this, how could he have no thought for his children, blah blah blah.

No thought, no words, no interest, no concern whatsoever for how this bombshell was impacting me. No word of comfort. No empathy. No safety. No offering of safe haven or solace.

That moment on the porch should have told me everything I needed to know about my life with these people, but I was still blind—perhaps willfully blind—because I wasn't quite ready to change my life. I was alone. I didn't make him leave that night.

The next day, I put on the most beautiful birthday party for my little girl at our home, just as planned. No one knew anything was awry. Like a good hostess, I put on lipstick and plastered a smile on my face. No one suspected a thing. As soon as the last guest left and the kids were settled, I shut the door to my bedroom, collapsed in my closet and cried for an hour. How did I get here? What would I do?

For some reason I still can't explain, I stayed with him another four years before finally finding the courage to divorce, thinking no one else would ever want me, a thirty-something woman past her prime, with three young children in tow.

From time to time during those four years, my mother-in-law would thank me for staying, acknowledging in her most honest moments that she'd always been sure I would eventually leave him and was shocked I hadn't, and expressing appreciation that I had stuck with him through it all and saying she hated to see my life wasted in a marriage where I wasn't being treated right.

And she was always kind to me in this way, right up until the day I finally told them all in no uncertain terms it was really over. I would be giving him no more chances. I could take no more BS. That's when I became her enemy. It was like I no longer existed. Like I had literally died. Never mind the fact that I'm the mother of her grandchildren and had never done anything but love her. Darling Boy was exposed, and no one exposes Darling Boy."

I love the quote from C.S. Lewis at the start of this chapter. Mankind has access to an ocean of God's goodness and blessings, a "holiday at the sea," but we miss the abundant life, choosing to play in a dirty mud puddle, "making mud pies in a slum" instead.

Darling Boy will choose the mud puddle every time. He wants to be a better person, a better husband. To truly have that abundant home life everyone thinks he has with Sweet Wife. But his unchecked sin is his demise. Sweet Wife and the kids are out there splashing in the beautiful ocean, waiting for him as he becomes more and more muddy in the slum. He never really comes to the ocean for that glorious holiday by the sea, and the family is collateral damage.

It always amazes me how some men can't be satisfied with the lovely, accomplished, kind, refined, sophisticated, beautiful women they married. It's a dynamic reminiscent of the verse in Proverbs about dogs returning to re-eat their own vomit, the very gross thing that has just made them physically sick and could just cause them to vomit again immediately, when they could be eating other food that is healthy, tasty and fresh. In the same way, some men betray their loving wives, the mothers of their dear children, for cheap thrills with other women—nasty, immoral, unprincipled women they barely know, exposing their wives to public humiliation, not to mention the dangers of STDs. So reckless. So thoughtless. So very, very selfish.

They Cheat Because Something's Wrong with Them, Not You

After seeing hundreds of adultery fact patterns play out in divorce litigation, I have come to believe that when a man cheats, it is because of some conflict within him, not because the wife did anything to deserve or cause it. Something in his ego needs to be fed, so he hires a hooker. Something in his childhood made him insecure, so he seeks praise from and pleasure with other women to make him feel "like a man." He shamelessly flirts with your friends, perhaps even in front of you, because their attention gives him some kind of adrenaline rush. He may even speak to you like his fraternity brother, telling you which of your friends he would most like to bed.

Friend, he is to be pitied, really. He just has some hole in his soul, bless him. He's trying to fill that hole with sex, but sex will never fill it. He's deceiving himself. It's something he must sort out for himself, with God's help, and fix if he's ever going to be a faithful husband. It's not the wife's job, or even within the wife's power or ability, to figure it out for him.

In my experience, many men are simply incapable of doing the work necessary to change course, and, sadly, the marriage has to end for the wife to get the relief and healing she needs.

Don't let him get away with telling you he cheated because of something *you* did. You must rebuke that very thought in the name of Jesus! You didn't make him choose to betray you. He must own his choices and be accountable for whatever consequences are coming.

It's time for Darling Boy to grow up and face the music.

Why Does Sweet Wife Stay Married After Infidelity?

1. **She's stunned and paralyzed**. The bomb of infidelity prompts a PTSD response akin to the reaction soldiers experience after warfare. Post-traumatic stress creates a physiological reaction in a woman's body. Discovering your husband's infidelity is, indeed, a trauma, and the stress that follows is overwhelming because you have to rethink your whole existence. It's an emotional explosion you were not prepared for, and it's rocked your whole world. Relationships you cared about are now forever altered, destroyed or lost. You don't leave him because you're stunned into "analysis paralysis" and frozen in fear that you can do no better.

2. **She is loving and forgiving**. She's heard in church all her life that love keeps no record of wrongs and is long-suffering, patient and kind; that God is glorified in our struggles; that evil can be overcome with good; that we should forgive others the way Jesus forgives us. She is determined to forgive him and trust he won't cheat again.

3. **She doesn't have enough support**. When Darling Boy cheats and is then propped up by his family, Sweet Wife is

often left totally unsupported. She can't tell her friends and family what she's dealing with or else they'll hate him, and she can't have them hating her husband if she's decided to forgive him and stay married. Alone and scared, she lacks the fortitude to do anything but be still—and despondent—dying inside, one day at a time.

4. **She blames herself**. Darling Boy is notorious for blaming Sweet Wife for not giving him enough sex, thereby causing him to stray. Let me tell you, Honey, no amount of sex can satisfy a man with a sex addiction. So many women report giving daily sex, only to find out later that Darling Boy left home to see his mistress right afterward.

   Darling Boy will also accuse Sweet Wife of not giving him enough attention, claiming *her* inattention—not *his* personal demons—is the real reason he stepped out. He'll say Sweet Wife was too focused on the kids or her career and not enough on him. You really can't win with a guy who will blame-shift like this. If you weren't taking care of the kids, he'd call you a bad mom! If you didn't work outside the home, he would resent you for putting too much financial stress on him, and he certainly wouldn't have that big truck in the garage or that fancy fishing boat in the backyard.

   If your husband uses such blame-shifting tactics on you, he's just trying to make you second-guess yourself and keep you stuck. And it's all a bunch of hooey. Do not be deceived. Do not waste your life with a guy like this.

5. **Her confidence is shaken**. It boils down to this: the betrayal of infidelity crushes a woman's soul, rocks her confidence, and makes her question all truth. You lose your footing.

What was once an unshakable foundation is now quicksand. You lose your sense of self and forget how to relate to the world. It's next to impossible to stand up for yourself and end your marriage when you're in such an uncertain state, and this is exactly why women forgive cheating men, at least with the first affair and sometimes after serial adultery.

Post-betrayal, Sweet Wife is no longer self-assured and begins comparing herself to the mistress, and to all other women. Why is she not enough for Darling Boy? Is she not pretty enough? Young enough? Good enough? When a woman lacks self-esteem, there's no way she's leaving her husband, and Darling Boy knows and exploits this to keep Sweet Wife trapped.

The trouble with this is that when a woman doesn't leave a man the first time he cheats, he is emboldened to think he can get away with cheating again. After all, if you didn't leave him the first time, surely you never will. "Once a cheater, always a cheater" is more than a saying; I've seen it play out in my clients' cases countless times. If you forgive him, great. But you must guard your heart, knowing full well that he's capable of hurting you again.

Be Jackie, Not Marilyn

Among my grandparents' generation, it was widely rumored that President Kennedy was involved romantically with Marilyn Monroe, the buxomest, sexiest, blondest bombshell movie star of their time. The scandal, explored in countless documentaries and biographies, has always intrigued me. Why would President Kennedy be so dumb as to forsake his amazing Jackie, who was the epitome of grace, quiet beauty, and sophistication, and the mother of his children? It's always struck me that while Jackie surely knew of her husband's affairs, you never read anything about her speaking of it or losing her composure over it. She had to be angry out of her mind and embarrassed beyond belief, but she didn't show her fanny over it like most women would be tempted to do. Her grace under the circumstances is beyond admirable.

I often bring up this illustration in my meetings with ladies whose husbands have betrayed them, to remind them that while they can't undo the trauma of the cheating, they *can* control their reaction to it. Do your best to stay classy and take the moral high road in the face of this revelation. You have nothing to be ashamed of, and you owe Marilyn none of your words. Let Marilyn see no reaction from you.

Be a Jackie, and let the Marilyns of the world be whatever they are.

And if you should ever happen to find yourself in the role of Marilyn, dear sister, apologize and leave those folks alone. That lady's husband is not your soul mate.

Ten Ways to Overcome Betrayal Trauma

To get your mind right as you head into your divorce case, it's essential to sort out the pain of his betrayal for *yourself*, even if he is not remorseful or repentant. Here are some things you can do:

1. **Pray**. You will need your relationship with God now, more than ever before. Pray without ceasing. Seek His wisdom and guidance in this moment.

2. **See a Counselor**. Betrayal trauma is a real mental health emergency. You need the help of someone trained in these matters to walk you through your recovery so that you don't spiral downward. There are psychologists who specialize in

trauma recovery therapy. Check to see if you can find one in your area. I will explore this in greater depth in another chapter.

3. **Confide in a wise friend you can trust**. You cannot shoulder this burden alone. Find a friend you can trust to help you process your emotions, to pick you up on days when you're down and

4. **Let yourself feel all the feels**. You can only heal by feeling the hurt and sorting through it. Don't try to suppress or bury your pain, or else it will only fester and make you bitter. This thing must be fully exposed, explored, sorted and compartmentalized if you're going to heal from it. It's okay to be angry. It's okay to cry. It's okay to have bad days. Give yourself permission to grieve the death of what you thought your marriage was, however that grief manifests. The most important thing is to work through the trauma so that "no root of bitterness" can grip you and cause you to fall out of God's grace. (Hebrews 12:15) You must guard your heart and not allow yourself to become bitter.

5. **Give yourself grace**. Do not be hard on yourself if you don't have it all together during this period. Give yourself a minute to regroup, knowing life won't be normal for a while. And that's okay.

6. **Set Boundaries**. Do not let your husband invade your space or have the access he needs to upset you. Don't answer the phone every time he calls. Better yet, stop speaking with him by phone or in person if doing so makes you cry or brings anxiety. Consider a ground rule that you will only communicate via email, and only about the children or

pressing financial matters. Guard your heart, dear friend. The one who broke you cannot heal you.

7. **Don't Allow Him to Blame You**. Hold your ground. You did not cause him to choose infidelity. Do not accept responsibility for his transgressions.

8. **Unplug and Take Time for Yourself**. It's amazing what a little time away in peace can do to quiet your spirit. Find a way to get away from the daily grind if you can. Plan a spa day. Attend a women's retreat. Go to the beach with your girlfriends. Take this time to recharge and heal.

9. **Gussy Up**. There's just something about feeling pretty that is good for mental health. Wash your hair. Shave your legs. Put on makeup. Buy a new dress. Try the Botox. Feeling like you have it together and looking your best can help you fake it 'til you make it.

10. **When You've Healed, Tell Your Story**. You went through a very hard thing, and God got you through it. He pulled you out of that pit so that you could go back and pull other ladies out, too. Use your experience to strengthen others. Do not keep it to yourself. Give God the glory and encourage others to trust Him in their struggles!

Questions for Reflection

1. Has your husband been unfaithful? How did you find out? What was your immediate reaction when you received the news?

2. What stage of the grief process are you in now? Do you feel you are processing your emotions in a healthy way? Why or why not? How can you manage things differently?

3. Do you feel yourself becoming bitter toward your husband? Have you prayed against any bitterness rising up in you?

4. Are you having a hard time forgiving your husband for his betrayal? Do you feel yourself becoming bitter toward him?

5. What are you doing to give yourself grace and opportunities to unplug and heal? Do you feel supported by your family and friends? Why or why not?

Chapter Soundtrack

"Lips are Movin"—Meghan Trainor

"Nobody"—Sylvia

"Your Cheating Heart"—Patsy Cline

"Need You Now (How Many Times)"—Plumb

"Better Than a Hallelujah"—Amy Grant

"Irreplaceable"—Beyonce

"Jolene"—Dolly Parton

"It Wasn't Me"—Shaggy

"Blame It On Your Heart"—Patty Loveless

7

Grieve It Like a Death

I sat with my anger long enough until she told me her real name was Grief.
—C.S. Lewis, *A Grief Observed*

There's no doubt about it: you are mourning a death. It's the death of a dream. Death of what could have been. Death of those parts of your daily life that will now change. Death of what you thought your future would be.

Margaret Atwood, author of *The Handmaid's Tale*, wrote, "Divorce is like an amputation. You survive it, but there's less of you."[1] One divorcing friend said something similar: "It's like my arm's been amputated and I have phantom pain. Pain from something that's missing." Your husband is no longer in your life, but the pain of his absence, the pain from lost familiarity perhaps, remains. It's the most foreign feeling, especially if you've been married a long time. You and your husband were united as one, and now you're losing a part of yourself. There's been a rift, a severance. It's a pain you can't fully understand until you've been through it.

What Dies in a Divorce

1. **Death of Your Dream**. On the day of your wedding, you believed this was it, that he was The One. Your dream of raising your family and someday rocking grandchildren

together on the front porch is not going to happen any-more. The expectation of being with your children every night of their lives is now impossible. The dream is gone, and a new reality is set to begin.

2. **Death of Relationships and Traditions.** Your relationships with your husband's parents, family members and close friends usually change or disappear with divorce. And all those holiday, birthday, baptism, and other family celebra-tions will not be the same going forward. They may actually be better, but they will not be the same. Your traditions cer-tainly will shift, as you cannot expect to be included in your husband's family gatherings any longer, and your kids will have to spend time away from you as you celebrate some holidays without them.

3. **Death of Identity**. You're going from married to single af-ter having settled into your identity as a married woman. You're feeling lost, like you don't know where you fit in the world anymore. You've lost your sense of security in who you are, of being grounded, as being a part of a couple was comfortable even if it wasn't perfect. Your marriage—along with your identity as a married woman—was supposed to be unshakable, and now it's over. Is nothing sacred and certain? Your foundation is shaken. The old identity is gone, and you've got to find a new one.

4. **Death of an Investment**. You invested in a relationship that is no more. All the energy, time and effort you ex-pended trying to build, then repair, salvage and restore this thing that's now dying now seems to have been a tremen-dous waste.

5. **Death of Idealism.** You once had so much faith in the kindness of other human beings, in their good intentions, but now that faith is diminished, if not gone entirely. If the guy who was supposed to love and treasure you above all others is capable of what brought you to a place of divorce, how is anyone to be trusted not to hurt you?

The Five Stages of Grief

Like me, you may have first learned about the stages of grief in your college psychology class. Every bit of that analysis applies to your divorce case. You will experience an array of emotions as you process your breakup and walk through a divorce. It's critical to your total healing—and your ability to fight for your legal rights with a clear mind—that you allow yourself to feel all the feelings rather than suppress or ignore them. Your lawyer needs you in a good frame of mind so you can contribute what is needed for them to make a compelling case on your behalf.

It's such a remarkable experience to watch my clients' transformation from the beginning of the grief cycle to the end. They begin the case with such uncertainty and need a lot of guidance as the emotions take over, but they typically progress quickly through the grief cycle as the divorce proceeds. But the stages of grief aren't always this linear, of course, as each of us experiences and processes pain and grief in her own way. As I explore a little later in the book, enlisting the guidance of a counselor can be a pivotal part of your healing.

1. **Denial.** The first stage is Denial, with its desperate hope for a possible reconciliation, incredulity that these tragic events are actually happening to you, and numbness to

what's going on around you. You're in shock, frozen, and unsure what to think or do. The world feels like it's spinning out of control, and you're not ready to face that yet, so you do nothing, hoping the situation will somehow resolve itself in a way that makes you feel better. It's the stage where false hope pervades your thoughts.

2. **Anger.** The second stage is Anger, that part where you might feel like screaming or breaking things because you're so mad about the injustice of your situation. You've been mistreated, and you're not happy about it one bit. You're angry at your husband. If he cheated, you're angry at the other woman and all the friends who kept his secret. Perhaps you're even angry at God. You're stressed to the max, and that stress is manifesting as all-out rage.

   They taught you in church to be slow to anger and to have control over your emotions, but this is unlike anything you've ever had to face.

   As an advocate for divorcees, I firmly believe in the power of righteous indignation. Just as Jesus was justified in turning over the moneychangers' temple tables, God does not expect you to be a doormat for anyone to mistreat you. You are completely within your rights to stand up for yourself and refuse to take further abuse. If your husband has abandoned or cheated on you, you are perfectly justified in being unhappy about that. More on this important stage below.

3. **Bargaining.** In the Bargaining stage, the self-doubt sets in, making you feel like maybe all of this is your fault, that you should change yourself, that maybe you could have done more to save your marriage, and if only you had worked

harder/taken more abuse/been more forgiving, the relationship wouldn't be ending. This is, in my experience with clients, almost always a delusional line of thinking. One party cannot save a marriage; it's got to have both parties' best efforts, and you wouldn't be in a divorce case if both of you had been trying your best.

4. **Depression**. The fourth stage, Depression, is that part where your stomach is in knots constantly, you're crying all the time, you're having trouble sleeping and lack motivation to do anything. You may go into hiding. Your family and friends are worried about you, with good reason. All of this is normal, okay and real. And there's no shame in getting medications to help you over the hump if your doctor agrees that you need them for a time.

Remember Elijah's story from 1 Kings 19 when you're feeling down. When Elijah was depressed, God sent an angel to comfort him while he rested, and then the angel woke him up and encouraged him to eat something. If you're depressed, Dear One, I'm praying over you now . . . that God will send you an angel to bring you comfort and hope, to encourage you to take care of your basic needs. I can tell you exactly who my angels were when I was walking through divorce, and I thank God every day for them.

This stage will pass, Dear Friend. It's okay if it takes you a minute. If you feel yourself slipping into a really dark place of deep despair or hopelessness, please get help from a trained mental health professional and tell a supportive friend.

5. **Acceptance**. The final stage is Acceptance. When I see my clients start to crawl out of the sadness, I know they've finally

come to accept their new reality: the relationship is over and will not be returning. In this stage, you start to have hope again that life can be good; you start making plans for the future; and maybe you even start getting excited about your post-divorce life.

Get Mad & Play Offense

Of all the stages of grief, the anger stage is where your lawyer can best use you. It is not sinful or wrong to insulate, protect, and defend yourself in your divorce case. You are not wrong to insist on a fair result. Moreover, you have a duty to your children to get the best possible outcome, the outcome that best meets their needs.

If your husband has mistreated you, your anger is justified, righteous indignation. Rather than suppressing it, the trick is to harness that anger into something productive to the litigation. Rather than lashing out in anger or raising your voice, let the emotions you're feeling propel you through the tasks your lawyer gives you to complete for your case.

When your husband's lawyer starts launching allegations against you in the divorce case, expect to be unnerved. In too many cases to count, the women I've represented have completely fallen to pieces when faced with their husbands' attacks, wondering how on earth this man they love(d) could now be tearing them down for all the world to see.

If this happens to you, remind yourself: YOUR HUSBAND SAYING SOMETHING DOES NOT MAKE IT TRUE.

As we read in Proverbs 18:17, "In a lawsuit, the first to speak seems right, until someone comes forward and cross-examines." If your husband is attacking your character, your parenting ability, or any other shortcoming you may have, don't cry over it. Get angry about it and use that anger like jet fuel for telling your side of the story.

Your lawyer needs your energy, not your tears.

As I often tell my clients, we want to play OFFENSE, not DE-FENSE in the case. We want our side of the story to carry the day. Instead of just trying to deflect the barbs coming at us from the other side, it's best to shift the focus to *your* claims, and be ready to back them up with evidence. Rather than crying about the allegations against you, focus on how to prove them wrong, while establishing the truth of *your own story*.

Retrain Your Brain

Putting yourself on offense is all in retraining your thinking. I've seen countless clients fall prey to their husbands' manipulation and start to second-guess themselves, questioning whether they are up for the challenge of going to court or following through with the divorce at all. After finding the courage to leave him or to take a legal hard line, so many women waver and forget their voice. Out of fear or fatigue, so many women sell themselves short in settlement—or worse, re-turn to their abusers—usually because they're so unaccustomed to considering their own needs and can't recognize the full extent to which they've been mistreated in the marriage. Instead of pursuing a new way of life in which her own needs are part of the equation, it's much easier to keep the abusive husband happy by not speaking up for herself. After years of living this way, many women become hard-wired to view themselves as unworthy of a voice, without standing to have an opinion, never daring to disagree.

I hear it all the time in client meetings. As I'm confidently explain-ing our strategies for presenting the case, my overall theories of how the client arrived at this place and is justified in her positions, the explanations for her choices and the faults of the other party in the relationship, the client will look at me and undermine my points in the most self-deprecating ways. Nine times out of ten, as I peel back the layers of the client's thought process, it becomes clear that she is merely regurgitating those lies her husband (and those in his camp ... more on the Flying Monkeys later in the book) has told her about herself.

When this happens, I usually stop dead in my tracks, confront the client and ask her why on earth she's saying such nonsense. And then I try to help her think through the situation from a new perspective, both to boost their confidence and to help her see how she's been controlled to believe demeaning things about herself. It usually goes something like this:

Here's the kind of analysis I go through with clients who are struggling to find their voice:

BSH (me): "Your husband cheated on you with his secretary, paid her utility bill and bought her expensive gifts. You have every reason to be hurt and disappointed.

Client: "It's really all my fault. I never was able to lose weight after our last child was born, and the secretary is much skinnier. He told me he wasn't happy with my looks when I was 15 pounds heavier, and I should have worked out more often. If I had, he never would have cheated on me."

BSH: "You are beautiful, kind and valuable. You're the mother of his precious children. There is no excuse for him cheating on you! Why are you making excuses for him? He spent your family's money on this disgusting other woman! Doesn't that make you angry?!"

Client: "Well, you know I don't work outside the home, so it's really all his money anyway. I can't tell him what to do with it since he earns it all. He's going to tell the judge I never made any money during the marriage. He'll say I was a worthless stay-at-home mom."

BSH: "He was only able to earn the money he gave to this other woman because YOU were taking care of the children, the dinner, the grocery shopping, the homework, the housekeeping, and everything else. Don't you see? That money he gave her was yours, too."

Client: "If I had done more, he wouldn't have cheated or left me. He always told me how I didn't do enough, wasn't pretty enough, didn't meet his needs. My shortcomings caused him to cheat on me. And then he felt sorry for the woman and started giving her financial support. He's just so generous. I can't believe I've lost such a great guy."

BSH: "He's NOT a great guy! Great guys don't destroy their families with infidelity and divert marital assets to their mistresses! How much money did he give her over time? When did this affair begin?"

Client: "It began several years ago, as far as I know. How do I find out how much money he gave her?"

BSH: "Do you have access to the bank records? If not, we can request them from the bank. We can also request the woman's utility bills to connect her account payment transactions to your husband's account."

Client: "Okay. I guess you can request those things."

Husbands say things like those illustrated above in an effort to undermine their wives' confidence and keep them trapped and controlled. They do it by framing the narrative in a way that makes the woman feel worthless, like she deserved whatever awful thing he did to her, like she can't possibly disprove all his positions, let alone formulate convincing arguments of her own. He wants her to have no confidence in herself. When representing a client like this, I do my best to empower her, to help her see how she arrived in this predicament, and to view the situation through a more offensive emboldened lens.

Remember: you have a story to tell about how all this went down! Be ready to tell it boldly and without fear. Find your confidence! Prepare to tell your version of the story in a way that is compelling and undeniable.

It is not un-Christian or unladylike to be righteously indignant over how your husband has wronged you or hurt your children. Get your head together and put on your game face! Your very future may depend on your willingness to defend yourself and tell your story in court. Pray that the Lord will go before you in battle and find that fire in your belly! Once you've accepted the situation and have fully healed, you will be able to look back on this time with such clarity, knowing the Lord set you free for a better life you never expected.

Questions for Reflection

1. Where are you in the grieving process right now?
2. How have Denial, Anger, Bargaining, Depression and Acceptance manifested themselves in your experience?
3. How quickly have you moved through the stages of grief? Have you reached Acceptance, or are you still angry, bargaining or depressed? Do you feel yourself healing more and more every day, or do you feel stuck in one stage or another?
4. What are your husband's most powerful arguments in the divorce case? What evidence can you obtain to refute his allegations?

5. What are your most compelling allegations in the divorce case? What evidence can you obtain to establish the truth of your story so that the judge will see it your way?

Chapter Soundtrack

"Everybody Hurts"—REM

"Split Screen Sadness"—John Mayer

"The Song Remembers When"—Trisha Yearwood

"I'll Be Over You"—Toto

"What Might Have Been"—Restless Heart

"Please Remember Me"—Tim McGraw

"A Little Bit Stronger"—Sara Evans

"I Hope You're Happy Now"—Carly Pearce and Lee Brice

"With or Without You"—INXS

Resources

Living Beyond Your Feelings: Controlling Emotions So They Don't Control You—Joyce Meyer

Cleaning Up Your Mental Mess—Dr. Caroline Leaf

Good Grief—Granger E. Westberg

Missing Pieces—a Bible study by Jennifer Rothschild

The Divorce Survival Guide Podcast

8

Take Care of Yourself

Self-care is how you take your power back."
—Lalah Delia, author and wellness educator

As you weather the tumultuous storm of divorce, moving from one stage of the grieving process to the next, it's very important to take care of yourself so that you are in top form to help your lawyer with your case. Don't neglect your mental, physical, or spiritual health during this time. There will surely be hard days, Dear One, but they will pass. This chapter is here to provide you with practical things you can do to keep a positive outlook and give yourself hope and strength for your future.

Be Attentive to Your Spiritual Health

Spiritual well-being is absolutely central to your healing journey.

I've often observed how clients return to their faith when the storms of divorce bear down on them, after years of having drifted away from their faith foundations. God promises that He will never leave us or forsake us.[3] If you were ever His child, you still are, and nothing can snatch you out of His hand.[4]

Your worship experience will likely be heightened as you cleave to the Lord in your desperation, sorting out your thoughts and pouring out your heart to Him more deeply than you ever have before. You're accepting He has a good plan for you, and you're seeking to discern that plan. There is such solace, mercy and transformation in that nearness. He wants you to cry out to Him in your distress,[5] to seek his presence and His strength continually[6] in times of trouble.

You need the fellowship of other believers during this transitional time. If you can do so without feeling too uncomfortable, try to stay connected to your local church body. If you can't bring yourself to participate at church as usual, either because you don't want to deal with people's questions or no longer know how you fit there without your husband, tune in online and stay immersed in the Word of God in private. The Word will be a lamp to guide your path and encourage your broken heart.

Your relationships with fellow church members could change with your divorce. You may be unjustly criticized and judged, and you will almost certainly be the subject of gossip. You'll likely have some fellow believers who brazenly approach you with their opinions about your marriage and divorce; they will try to talk you into staying married, preach to you about how "God hates divorce" even though they have no idea what's happened to you that got you to this place. Take their words with a grain of salt and stand in your truth. God knows your heart, and their words are spiritually abusive. You are bound to worship, serve and love your Lord, no matter what these other believers say or do. Don't allow their sins of judgment and gossip cause you to leave your church or lose your faith. God is bigger than all of it, and He is yours.

I didn't let anyone's opinion or ridicule stop me from serving my God, in my own way. We're told in Scripture not to judge someone else's servant, i.e., that God will judge His own servants, and we shouldn't go around deciding who's good enough and who isn't, who's behaving right and who isn't, who's doing the church thing better or worse than another.[7] None of us knows another's history or another's wounds, and you can never really know what's going on in a marriage unless you're the one living in it.

Throughout my divorce, I was closer to Jesus than I'd ever been before. It was a holy, intimate closeness; He was working in my heart and healing my wounds. I was resting in Him, sometimes on a breath-by-breath basis, trusting Him with my very life, with my children, with my future. Some people did their best to derail my faith and my resolve, but when you've got that kind of connection going on with the Most High, no human can break it. I am His, and He is mine. I could have done without the heartbreak, but I praise Him for it because it grew my faith so much to need Him so desperately during that season of my life.

It was uncomfortable, and it still is sometimes, if I'm being honest about it. But no judgy, snarky condescension from another believer was going to make me stop loving and serving the Lord where and how I wanted to love and serve Him. If you're struggling with where you fit in your church or sorting out spiritual questions, you might also consider consulting a Christian life coach. There are so many trained experts in this field who would happily be your go-to person when you need guidance on how to proceed in your divorce, ensuring you make the best choices for the glory of the Lord and for your own edification. As you stand your ground as a woman of God in the fight of your life against your husband, your primary focus should be making sure your spiritual life remains intact. There are many Christian life coaches out there offering virtual services if you can't find one in your local area. Accountability is key.

Above all, remember to pray.[8] Lay the desires of your heart at His feet. Pray that His will be done and that He will be glorified in your story. Pray for your departing Husband as you would pray for any enemy. Ask to be used by God in a mighty way in your singleness.

Corrie ten Boom, who endured persecution for protecting Jews during the Holocaust, wrote, "In order to realize the worth of the anchor, we need to feel the stress of the storm."[9] Storms will inevitably come our way, but we have a foundation on which to cling. Remind yourself when despair creeps in that Jesus wept, too. He knows our pain and meets us there. He'll turn your wailing into dancing and clothe you with joy in due time, and, as you're reminded in Psalm 30:11-12, your soul will sing His praises. Weeping may endure for a night, but joy comes in the morning.[10]

You're on a sacred path. Like Mary treasured her closeness with the Lord in her heart,[11] so you can enjoy the nearness that comes as you trust Him with your situation. Ironically, as your faith grows, you will come to see your suffering as the blessing it truly is.[12]

Believe it, Dear One. Claim these promises for your life and walk in the confidence that they will be true for you as they came true for me and for so many of my clients over the years.

As you heal and become stronger, you will find yourself becoming a dynamite force, ready to tackle your lawyer's task list head-on, get it done and embrace the next stage of your life.

Focus on Your Mental Health

Author Mary Kay Blakely aptly described divorce as "the psychological equivalent of a triple coronary bypass."

There will be times when it feels like your life is spinning out of control. It's the very unraveling of the life you've built, and you're looking at an uncertain future. You realize you're at the mercy of others (the judge for the ruling, attorneys for guidance, friends and family for moral support), perhaps for the first time in your adult life. It's a powerless, panicked feeling. Daily life is a battle. Getting through each day—sometimes each minute or even each breath—is a struggle.

It's okay to fall to pieces if you need to from time to time. It's a normal part of your healing. You're not going crazy.

The sadness is natural. It means your marriage mattered to you.

If you find yourself in emotional upheaval as you deal with the loss of your marriage, find a mental health professional to help you. During my divorce, my counselor became a go-to person in my life, and the help she gave me was critical to being able to process and manage what was happening. I would go to her office, cry and dump my stress on her couch for an hour, get sound counsel for how to proceed, and leave each time feeling a little better. It was a balm on my broken soul. Everyone going through emotional upheaval needs a safe, confidential, objective sounding board for unpacking and sorting out all the emotions.

Your lawyer may be very kind and compassionate, and I hope they are! But your lawyer isn't really there for or trained to provide therapy services, and a counselor's hourly rate is usually much lower. Moreover, your meeting times with your attorney are most wisely spent going over legal strategy and figuring out how to prove your case in court, rather than venting frustrations and analyzing how you arrived at this place in your personal relationships.

Friends are great, too, but there's a limit to how much you'll feel comfortable burdening them with your troubles. Let's be honest: even the most well-intentioned, selfless friends are busy managing their own families, often with little time to spare to help you deal with your personal problems. They love you, but they don't usually know much about mental health therapy or coping strategies. You will not feel guilty taking your paid counselor's time the way you might with friends. You can often be more transparent with a counselor than with friends. And the professional advice you receive from an educated therapist is almost certain to be more reliable than the counsel of a well-meaning but untrained friend.

A divorce is an opportunity to become more self-aware, to examine what went wrong in your relationship, to never have it happen again. It's a time for self-improvement. The faster you can get to a place where you're not blaming your husband for what happened, the faster you can get past the rage, jealousy and feeling of inadequacy, focusing instead on being your own best self, the faster you will be whole again.

I've been privileged to have a front-row seat to the transformation of hundreds of divorcing women, I firmly believe you won't be peacefully whole again until you are able to reach a place of genuine forgiveness for all the ways you've been wronged in your marriage and breakup. This usually doesn't arrive until the Acceptance stage of the grief cycle, so understand that it may take time to get there and give yourself grace as you work toward this goal.

We're warned in Hebrews 12:15, "See to it that no one misses the grace of God and that no bitter root grows up to cause trouble and defile many." In Ephesians 4:31-32, we're admonished to "get rid of all bitterness, rage and anger, brawling and slander, along with every form of malice. Be kind and compassionate to one another, forgiving each other, just as in Christ God forgave you."

Unforgiveness and bitterness will eat you alive, and that's why God doesn't want us to fall prey to them. As Marianne Williamson said, "Unforgiveness is like drinking poison yourself and waiting for the other person to die." She's right. Nine times out of ten, the person who wronged you is totally unaffected by how you feel about them anyway. You don't forgive them for their healing; you forgive them for your own. Don't waste years stewing over something when you should let it go.

You will know you have truly forgiven them when you're able to see how you've grown because of the experience. You will genuinely be able to thank them for putting you through the trauma that made you who you become after you've healed. It will take time, but you will get there eventually if you work on it.

It is my prayer for you, as it is for all my clients, that you reach this place of peace, forgiveness and acceptance, with renewed confidence and hope.

Physical Health Drives Mental Health

There's an old Gullah proverb to the effect that you must "take care of the root in order to heal the tree." Mental health is of paramount importance, the proverbial "root" of your life, and physical well-being significantly impacts mental stability. How your body feels and functions dictates how you cope with traumatic events, and your lawyer needs you at your best for the battle you're enduring.

Here are some practical things you can do to keep yourself feeling physically healthy, even as your heart is hurting:

1. **Eat right**. Divorce is often a marathon, not a sprint. Would a triathlete neglect her nutritional needs when training for a big race? Would a marathon runner forget to eat breakfast? Of course not! You need energy, and your body burns zillions of calories under the stress of divorce. If you don't feel

like eating (I call it the Divorce Diet), start with something you love to eat just to fill your stomach and keep up your strength, even if it's bad for you. Drink plenty of water, for you think better when your brain is hydrated. And when your appetite returns, make sure you eat balanced meals and healthy snacks. You'll feel better if you do, and feeling better is half the battle!

2. **Get enough rest**. Sleepless nights are a common side effect of divorce, unfortunately. Psalm 127:2 promises that God will give sleep to those He loves. You must be rested for battle, so consider this time-tested military method to clear your mind and relax your body to help you fall asleep in any environment:

   (a) clear your mind by envisioning something really boring (I typically think of a blank sheet of paper)

   (b) relax all the muscles in your face, including your mouth area,

   (c) drop your shoulders as far down as they'll go, then drop your upper and lower parts of your arms, left side first, then the right side;

   (d) control your breathing, breathe out, relax your chest, relax your legs from the top down, feeling the heaviness of your limbs on your mattress.

   This technique has worked for me many times when my mind was racing and sleep eluded me.

3. **"Alexa, play my Divorce Playlist."** Music has the power to soothe your very soul. Make a playlist of songs from a simpler, happier time, and include songs that bring hopeful feelings for the future (feel free to use mine if you'd like!).

Listen to it when you're getting dressed in the morning, in the car, at work, making supper and winding down for the night. During my divorce, I would float in my pool for hours listening to John Mayer on repeat, and it really helped.

4. **Stay home if you want**. There's no rule that says you have to be social to be happy. Solitude is sometimes just what you need, so don't feel bad declining invitations to go out when you just need to be alone. Sitting in silence with your thoughts is a form of self-care.

5. **Gussy up and face the day**. While there are some days you'll feel like being a recluse in your house, and that's fine, it's best for your mental health to get up most days and pursue some sense of purpose. There were definitely days during my divorce when I had to will myself out of bed in the morning. But once I was up and moving, drinking coffee, making the bed, putting on makeup and fixing my hair, my mental outlook would improve. I may have been a mess on the inside, but you wouldn't have known it to look at me.

6. **Take up journaling**. Some women find comfort in writing down their thoughts to sort them out. If this is you, get yourself a beautiful journal, your Bible for reference and a good writing pen, turn on some music and pour out your soul on the pages. Make lists of things you're thankful for, things you regret, things you're angry about, things that are troubling you, and then look for verses which speak to those things. It's so cathartic.

7. **Block out negative noise**. Give yourself permission to block, delete and unfollow those people who make you feel uncomfortable or less than. Doing so will help keep your

thoughts positive and, therefore, preserve and promote your mental health.

8. **Plan things to look forward to**. Your friends love you. Invite them over for wine and cheese to celebrate friendship for friendship's sake. Be sure to invite the ones who are most likely to make you laugh! Laughter is medicine for your heart.2 Plan a weekend getaway with friends or just schedule regular coffee or lunch dates at the local spots you love. Coffee dates with certain friends got me through my divorce, and we all know coffee is healthier than alcohol.

9. **Have a spa day**. Buy all the delicious bath salts. Fill up the tub. Light some aromatherapy candles. Turn on a mindless Netflix show or grab a book from your favorite author. Sit there as long as you want. A little escape may be just what you need. And oh, the power of a yummy facial or back massage to lift your spirits! Leave the kids with your mom, grab some girlfriends and take a day to pamper yourself and recharge, and perhaps for the first time in a long time, don't let yourself feel guilty about it. You are worth it.

10. **Exercise**. I've seen clients completely transform themselves with exercise during their divorce cases. Take the hurt you feel in your soul and take it out on dumbbells and treadmills! Go for a run! Your body will tone up, you'll feel more attractive, and the endorphins will propel your mental state to a healthy place. You may even meet some cute new fella at the gym!

Particularly if you, like many of my clients, are a victim of mental or physical abuse, you may have recurring fatigue, muscle pain, tension headaches, digestive issues which make it difficult to relax. These ten items will help with that.

Sweet Sister, you're at war, and you're physically exhausted. I pray God will minister to you in a palpable way—like Jesus washing his disciples' dirty feet, or strangers feeding and housing the disciples ministered to them—as you push to the finish line of your case.

Questions for Reflection

1. Are you taking care of your physical self? What could you do better? Do you have any unhealthy habits that need to go?

2. What are you doing to address your mental health needs during this time? What needs to change?

3. Is church weird for you now? What's going on, and why is it bothering you? How are you handling it? Are you allowing the weirdness to keep you from ministry?

4. Have you strayed from your faith? What can you do to get back on track spiritually?

5. Do you believe the Lord wants good things for you and works all things together for the good of those who love Him (Romans 8:28)? How are you sharing your anger, your questions, and your grief with Him, and how are you praying over them? Are you pouring out your sadness, praying for and believe there's joy to come?

Resources

Safe People: How to Find Relationships that are Good for You and Avoid Those That Aren't—Dr. Henry Cloud & Dr. John Townsend
Georgia Shaffer, Divorce Coach (www.georgiashaffer.com)
Walking With God Through Pain and Suffering—Timothy Keller
God Will Carry You Through—Max Lucado

Instagram: @divorcedchristian || @divorcetalkwithtwyla
It's Not Supposed to Be This Way—Lysa TerKeurst

Chapter Soundtrack
"Hold On"—Wilson Phillips
"Sweet Jane"—Cowboy Junkies
"Sounds of Silence"—Simon & Garfunkel
"I Guess I Just Feel Like"—John Mayer
"Thank U"—Alanis Morissette
"Gravity"—John Mayer
"Just Be Held"—Casting Crowns

9

Find Your Friends

Lots of people want to ride with you in the limo, but what you want is someone who will take the bus with you when the limo breaks down.
—Oprah Winfrey

In the Old West, circling the horse-drawn wagons was an essential way to fortify and protect a group of travelers on the wagon trail when robbers or enemies would approach. The round wall of wagons created a safe space in the center for the people to gather. If you're feeling attacked in your divorce litigation, your friends can similarly form an encampment around you to insulate and protect you from the artillery flying your way.

I love it when my clients bring their supporters to my office. Loyal and concerned, they often are able to help the client fill in the details of the story in a way the client is either too nice to relay, or too emotional to remember in the moment. Even the most independent women need their circle in uncertain times. I see it all the time in my office: a woman's friends are often more incensed at the husband than the client is! They help me talk the client into fighting for herself by sharing the infuriating details of how the husband abused or deceived the client. Those who love us give us gumption we wouldn't have without them.

We humans are hardwired for relationship. God recognized from the very beginning of human history that it wasn't good for man to be alone.[13] He knew we needed one another's support, and He has commanded again and again in the Bible to help one another. We support one another in times of hopelessness and despair. We encourage one another and build each other up.[14] Everyone needs friends. You never forget a person who came to you with a torch in the dark.[17]

I'll never forget how my people showed up for me in my darkest hour. They were the ones showing up with dinner on the day of my big settlement conference, the ones who gathered to celebrate my birthday and my divorce (what fun that was!), those who randomly texted just to make sure I was okay, the ones who helped me set up a generator at my house on the eve of a destructive hurricane, and those who housed my kids and me after said hurricane knocked out power to our house for a week. Those who invited me to their homes and fed me pumpkin pie on Christmas afternoon the first year my children weren't with me for Christmas afternoon. The ones who set me up on my first date post-divorce, the ones who got me out of the house for walks in the neighborhood or invited me on vacations. The ones who wrote affidavits on my behalf and let me know I wasn't alone in the struggle. The couple who came and jumped my car battery then followed me to the gas station to make sure I got there safely. The ones who prayed for me and hugged me when I cried. The ones who prayed for my children. The ones who sent me supportive articles and loaned me books. The ones who defended me when my name was disparaged. The ones who told me I wasn't

---

17   M. Rose (taken from an Instagram post by Mindful Christianity—
@mindfulchristianity).

alone. The ones who drove an hour to attend my second little wedding out in the South Georgia boondocks. The ones who are still there anytime I need them. Irreplaceable. Precious. Treasured. Ever so dear to my heart. Tried and True.

Sadly, some folks like being around only when you're down because they love drama, have a need to rescue you, or your hardship makes them feel better about their own domestic issues. Some just want the scoop on you so they can talk about your business with other people. But genuine friends are the ones who are there on your bad days and also on your good days, with you for all the highs and all the lows, just as you are for them. They celebrate your successes and offer true empathy when you're unhappy. May you be blessed with the right kinds of supporters in your life.

The Changing Circle

Did your circle change when you married? If so, was it because of the normal things like residential relocations or simply the fact that your new friends' kids play with your kids at school? Or was it because your husband made you abandon old friendships in favor of new ones he preferred for you, perhaps as a way of controlling you? Divorce has a way of bringing your true loyalists to the surface, as old friends return, and new ones emerge. Every divorced woman can tell you the people who stood by her during her divorce. Their ministry to you while you're despondent leaves a mark of affinity for them that you will carry with you forever.

Reconnect With Friends from Long Ago

The time your husband used to take up in your daily routine is now yours to spend a different way. Take the time to reconnect with those old high school and college friends, the ones who knew you when you believed all was right in the world, when you were that girl who lived big, the girl you were before life beat you up. They will reintroduce you to your real self, just when you think you've lost her. Those early bonds are some of the purest you've ever known. Reconnecting with them can bless your soul.

After my divorce was final, a dear college friend came to visit. We have the same birthday (same year and day!), and we were very close as sorority sisters in college. She was traveling through town to take her daughter on a college tour, so they stayed with us that night. Over dinner, we reminisced about our college days at UGA, sharing countless stories from long ago with our teenaged daughters. One thing she said to me that night has stuck with me ever since. She told me how my personality had changed after I met and married my first husband, how I started thinking and trying to morph myself into a different person to fit in with his family.

As she sat there describing to me her observations, I couldn't deny she was right. Over time, I became someone who no longer resembled the vivacious college coed I'd been before. My light—the very essence of who I was, of who God made me to be at my core—went out a little more every day I spent in that marriage. For many years, I lost a lot of my confidence, resigned myself to my circumstances, and did my best to get along, hesitant to step outside my husband's family paradigm. To please my husband, I neglected or even—in some cases—destroyed so many special friendships. I grieve those losses to this day, and though I have made amends with many of those friends since my divorce, the time lost will never be recovered, and the relationships will never be what they could have been had I remained invested in them.

If this has happened in your life, your divorce is a chance to set it right.

Social media gives us such a wonderful way to reach out to old friends, the ones who knew you when you were your most free, your most fun self, that version of you that lived before the world beat you up. Catch up on their lives. Share in their struggles and triumphs. Enjoy the catharsis of telling them your marriage (and divorce) story. Organize a reunion! Apologize for being out of touch and start doing better! Some old friends may have already been where you are, and their stories will embolden you and ignite your old spirit.

Make New Friends

You could very well find yourself spending time with people you never thought would be your friends at all. Women who have been through divorces tend to find and support one another in the most powerful ways. You may have never identified with some of them before, but now you do. You may form close bonds with those who take care of you—people like your hair stylist, financial planner, manicurist or even your attorney—as you rely on them for wisdom and guidance during this tumultuous season.

Emotional support may come to you in many forms, sometimes when you aren't even looking for it. Don't be surprised if you have a whole new friend group by the time your divorce is over. It will likely be a hodgepodge of those true-blue old friends mixed with all the new ones.

The Great Friends Cleanse

The wrong people will exit your life when they have to, and the right ones will find you when you need them the most. Trust the process. Find comfort in your timing, and let time decide who gets to stay.—R.M. Drake, author of *Something Broken, Something Beautiful*

Sadly, the old saying that you find out who your real friends are when you go through difficult times is absolutely true. You can expect to lose friends when you go through a divorce. I see it in almost every case I handle. And it happened to me.

Your relationships with members of your husband's family will likely be the first ones to change, if not totally sour. Blood is thicker than water. You should brace yourself for their backlash and clannishness; that way, you'll be pleasantly surprised if they remain cordial but not shocked down to your shoes if they turn on you.

Your new Scarlet D will be too much for some people. Some friends' husbands will dissuade their less-than-happy wives from hanging out with you, for fear that your singleness will make them want to try being single, too. These women will be nowhere to be found on those bad days when you need someone to show up. If they are too weak to stand up to their husbands and be there for you, they are not your friends.

Even without a domineering husband, some women in your circle may check out and avoid you merely because they are unable to handle chaos, and therefore want nothing to do with you unless all is copacetic. They're right there for the good times but run at the first sign of turmoil or turbulence. Bless them; they aren't wired to manage their own stress, let alone yours.

If a very close friend who knows all about your marital struggles suddenly ghosts you just as your divorce gets underway, without a phone call or even a text to check on you, this is a red flag. In experiences with my clients, I've observed that sudden changes in relationships usually mean either that suddenly absent friend has believed some lie your husband told her about you, she's sleeping with your husband, or both. Best friends don't just disappear like that unless something's up.

This may ruffle some feathers, but I'm going to say it anyway. Many women don't want other women to be happy. When you find happiness or get to a better place after your divorce, some will be jealous of your courage, good fortune and ability to take initiative to improve your circumstances. They are secretly miserable in their own abusive or toxic marriages and can't or won't do anything about it, so your progress makes them pea green with envy. Instead of cheering you on as all women should do for one another, these faux friends resent you for changing your situation while they are unwilling or unable to change their own. They especially hate it as you thrive in your independent, post-divorce life. Rather than sharing your joy, you'll hear they're gossiping about you in the community and trying to bring you down a notch in the court of public opinion. It will hurt your feelings. Have nothing more to do with them and thank God for showing you their true colors. Let them go.

At the end of the day, if you're like most of my clients at the end of their divorces, you'll have a handful of friends you know are the real deal. They're the ones who've checked on you randomly to make sure you're eating and sleeping enough. They're the ones who come alongside you to celebrate your post-divorce victories and also be right there if you need to cry.

Choose Friends Who Hold You Accountable

If you don't trust your decision-making ability at the moment, check in often with those friends with sound moral compasses to help you stay on your best behavior.

Trust the Objective Advice of Friends When Your Judgment is Skewed by Emotion

Find the friends who will tell you the truth, even when it hurts, for "faithful are the wounds of a friend."[15] Rather than letting it upset you, listen. Learn. A wise friend with your best interest in mind will give you sound advice.

There are times in every woman's divorce case when she lacks clarity and needs a good dose of hard truth from a trusted ally. A wise, objective friend can help you make rational decisions when emotions are running high.

Beware of Agendas

Everyone seems to have an opinion when you're going through a divorce. I caution my clients to consider the source of all the advice they're getting, and always be leery of the agendas from which others give advice on how the divorcing woman should proceed.

- ❖ Well-meaning pastors normally want to keep family units together, based on their genuine belief that divorce is not an ideal result.
- ❖ Marriage counselors go into mental health work because they want to make a difference in families. Their advice is often based on the hope that your marriage can be saved, but not every marriage should survive, and that therapist doesn't live in your house.
- ❖ Your in-laws may advise you not to proceed with divorce out of the selfish desire to avoid embarrassment and exposure of the family's internal issues. You may have loved and trusted them for years, but they are likely more focused

on protecting your husband and less concerned about you. Take everything they tell you with a grain of salt, and do not overshare.

❖ Your own parents may disappoint you with their agendas. Perhaps they fear having to help you financially in your post-divorce life, or maybe they just really like your husband or have believed the adverse things he's told them about you. Or maybe they disagree with your decisions or are simply unkind to you due to unhealthy family dynamics.

Remember: Your Husband is No Longer Your Teammate

Perhaps the one with the biggest agenda is Mr. Used-to-be-Wonderful himself.

Your husband can't be your friend right now, so do not share with him as if he is. You can cooperatively coparent, stay pleasant for the kids and all that. But when it comes to the legal conversation or financial negotiations, it's Plaintiff versus Defendant now, end of story. You mustn't trust a word he says to you or allow yourself to be lulled into a false sense of security. Make no mistake: he's trying to get out of this case with as little financial fallout as possible. And you can make things exponentially harder for your attorney if you allow him access to you for these kinds of conversations. We will delve into this again and again in later sections of the book; letting your husband remain inside your circle during separation and divorce negotiations is the worst mistake you can make. Please don't make your lawyer's job harder by doing this.

You're Not Competing With Your Husband for Friends

So often, friends close to a divorcing couple feel like they have to pick a side and be either "his friend" or "her friend" going forward, as if it's impossible to do both. You will be more content if you don't play this game, even if your husband does, and even if others choose him and start to exclude you. Just keep loving and treating people the same way you always have so that your conscience remains clear. Encourage those around you not to feel the need to choose sides.

Walk in your truth, wishing your husband well and encouraging his friends to continue to be there for him during the divorce in a healthy and supportive way. There are enough friends to go around for both of you; it's not a zero-sum game.

Questions for Reflection

1. Have you prayed and asked God to show you who your friends are? Have you asked Him to show you who they are not?

2. Who are those friends who have shown up for you in your time of need? How did they show up for you?

3. Have you experienced the alienation of friendships by husbands who don't want their wives to associate with you now that you're single? How did you cope with it, and how would you advise yourself concerning friendships if you could go back five years and have a talk with your younger self?

4. Has your husband's family changed how they treat you? How are you coping with this shifting dynamic?

5. Have you found new friendships in places and ways you never expected? How has each one blessed you?

Resources

Find Your People—Jennie Allen

Good Boundaries and Goodbyes—Lysa TerKeurst

We Saved You a Seat—a Bible study by Lisa-Jo Baker

I'll Be There (But I'll Be Wearing Sweatpants)—Amy Weatherly &
Jess Johnston

Made for This—a podcast with Jennie Allen

Balcony People—Joyce Landorf Heatherley

Chapter Soundtrack

"American Girl"—Tom Petty & the Heartbreakers

"Dear Marie"—John Mayer

"21 Summer"—Brothers Osborne

"You've Got a Friend"—James Taylor

"On the Way Home"—John Mayer

"I'll Be There for You"—The Rembrandts

"That's What Friends are For"—Dionne Warwick

"Take Me Home, Country Roads"—John Denver

"What About Your Friends"—TLC

"Wind Beneath My Wings"—Bette Midler

"Find Out Who Your Friends Are"—Tracy Lawrence

"Umbrella"—Rhianna

"Far Behind"—Candlebox

"Thank You for Being a Friend"—Andrew Gold

10

Watch Your Mouth

Speak only if it improves upon the silence.
—Mahatma Gandhi

Your Words Can Come Back to Bite You

The importance of discretion and self-control in your communications while your divorce case is pending cannot be overstated. Anything you share with another person could end up being discussed in front of the judge. Be very careful who you trust with private information.

Watch what you say to the kids, to your soon-to-be ex, and to third parties, especially in writing. A good rule of thumb is to communicate at all times as if you're being recorded. Or as my mama always says, behave as if Jesus is in the room, and hold your tongue if you can't say something nice.

We are reminded in Proverbs that "when words are many, sin is not absent, but [s]he who holds [her] tongue is wise" (10.19), and that "fools care nothing for thoughtful discourse; all they do is run off at the mouth" (18.2, MSG). You want your words to reflect wisdom, not foolishness. The goal is productive, thoughtful discourse rather than below-the-belt verbal attacks that derail progress in your case. Think before you speak, and measure your words carefully, especially when you're under oath.

Make no mistake: caustic talk does not play well in court. It's a pet peeve of several judges I know. One of them likes to remind litigants, "If you can't say something nice about the other party, then let your tongue cleave to the roof of your mouth." He's right. Saying nothing is always better than saying something ugly and later regretting it.

Common Communication Mistakes Divorcing Women Make

1. **Social Media Tirades**. It's generally a very bad idea to get online to air your frustrations. As much as you'd like to do it sometimes, nothing good can ever come from a mean or embarrassing post on your page about your husband or his paramour. It will most assuredly be Exhibit "A" against you at the courthouse. Social media posts are compelling evidence against you, for they are written in your own words. It's like handing him evidence on a silver platter! Don't post anything online you can't easily defend to a judge.

2. **Oversharing and Trusting the Wrong People**. Another common mistake is trusting the wrong people with your deepest, most private truths, and overexplaining yourself to too many people. You don't ever really know who will turn on you or who might be a double agent working behind the scenes for your husband. Pray for discernment on who you should trust. Surround yourself with wise women not prone to gossip. If they talk to you about others, chances are they will also tell others your private business. Choose wisely! And remember: you are not required to tell everyone your side of the story. It's none of their business, and it will all come out eventually—and organically—without your having to say a word.

3. **Taking the Bait**. One of the biggest mistakes a divorcing woman can make is allowing her husband to lure her into an argument. You may really want to tell him how you really feel about him, to really let him have it, but you must not let yourself fall into his trap. He could be drawing you into an argument just to record your reaction and play it for the judge. A good boundary to set for yourself is that you only communicate with him via email where you're less likely to misspeak or lose your cool. You should also make it a rule not to contact or engage with him if you're feeling emotional and more likely to say something you shouldn't. When you're upset, you are laid bare for all sorts of manipulation, more likely to say something you'll later regret and could easily make a strategic mistake that will harm your case. Unless it's an emergency concerning the children, it's safer not to engage. As the Instagram meme says, dance like no one is watching, but email and text like it may one day be read aloud in court.

4. **Chasing After Him**. Some clients have trouble letting their husbands go. They don't want a divorce, so they continue to pursue the relationship and communication with the husband in hopes that they can rekindle the romance. I'm all for reconciliation if it can be healthy and if it's possible, of course, but it's painful to watch an otherwise self-assured woman chase a man who doesn't want her. If this sounds like you, stop throwing him your pearls!

    Don't make a fool of yourself trying to get him back when he keeps telling you it's over. If you do, and then you go to court saying what a terrible person he is, his lawyer will be quick to point out how you still wanted him, so he must not be that horrible. In moments of weakness, call a friend who will keep you accountable instead of texting your husband. Retrain your thinking to focus on other things. Each day you're able to avoid contacting him, the closer you'll be to true healing. I always want my women clients to walk into court with their heads held high, ready to face their husbands with confidence and poise, and you can't do that nearly as easily if he knows you secretly want him back. Do not give him the satisfaction!

5. **Undermining the Lawyer**. More times than I can count, clients have discussed substantive legal matters or settlement terms with their husbands when they should have let me handle it for them, and in doing so gave away their legal strategies and bottom-line settlement terms to the detriment of the case. It's best not to try to negotiate with your husband without your lawyer's involvement. You hired your lawyer because she knows how to build and argue your case effectively for your most optimal outcome. Take her advice and let her do all your talking when it comes to the legal stuff. You make your lawyer's job exponentially harder when you give your husband insight into your settlement priorities, evidence or courtroom strategies. Always try to let your attorney run interference when it comes to these things.

The Art of the Canned Response

Judges hate it when divorcing couples bash one another in public, especially when children are involved. For this reason, it's important to practice in advance what you'll say when people ask you about your divorce, so that you will stay above board and classy and not undermine your case. Your friends can be subpoenaed to testify in divorce court, so you must watch what you tell them.

I often recommend my clients come up with a canned statement to have at the ready in such situations. It could go something like this:

Acquaintance: *"I heard you and Josh are going through a divorce. I heard how awful he has been to you. Is it true? What happened?"*

Divorcing Woman: *"I appreciate your concern. I'd rather not get into the details right now. No matter what happened in the past, I wish Josh well and hope he'll be happy. Please pray for both of us."*

Or, if you have children with him, it could be something like this:

Acquaintance: *"I heard you and Josh are going through a divorce. I can't believe he's got a girlfriend and took the kids around her. Is it true?"*

Divorcing Woman: *"Thank you for checking on me. I'd rather not get into the details right now. No matter what he's done, he's still the father of my children, and we have to coparent. I wish Josh well and hope he'll be happy. Please pray for both of us."*

Even if you don't really wish him well just yet and have no idea how you'll ever face him again, let alone coparent with him, saying something like what I've written above gives the impression that you are A-OK without him, and that is the image you want to portray. Your children don't need to hear through the grapevine that Mom is bashing Dad, and you don't want others to perceive you as bitter and spread rumors that you're a stereotypically bitter, angry, jaded ex-wife. Keeping it classy is always the best move, for the court of public opinion has a way of bleeding over into the court of law. There is no substitute for having the judge's respect.

Questions for Reflection

1. Do you struggle with keeping your feelings to yourself? Do you tend to speak before you think sometimes? When has this come back to bite you in the past?

2. Do you tend to overexplain or overshare? Are you active on social media? What can you do to ensure your words match your heart and good intentions?

3. How can you guard yourself against taking the bait and falling into unedifying arguments and cringy shouting matches with your husband which he will use to damage your case?

4. In your inability to accept the loss of your marriage, are you chasing after your husband, seeking out communication with him, while he's telling you he's done? What are some things you can do to keep yourself from initiating contact again?

5. Have you faced the questions of acquaintances about your situation? How did you handle them? How could you have handled them better? What is a canned response you can memorize for such occasions?

Chapter Soundtrack

"Roll It On Home"—John Mayer

"Don't Answer Me"—Alan Parsons Project

"Our Lips are Sealed"—the Go-Go's

"Found Out About You"—Gin Blossoms

11

Behave Yourself

It takes 20 years to build a reputation and five minutes to ruin it.
If you think about that, you'll do things differently.
—Warren Buffett

For optimal results in your divorce case, you must be careful to keep yourself under control and not let your upset feelings cloud your judgment. You must use your brain and make good choices, even as the emotions rage. Anything you do during this period of separation is fair game for the judge or jury to see, as your husband won't hesitate to present evidence of your bad behavior to support his child custody and other claims to be taken into account when the judge or jury rules on the issues of your case. You don't want to set yourself up to be embarrassed or, worse, to lose battles you could have won otherwise, due to poor decision-making.

Don't Act the Fool

When a client behaves foolishly with a divorce case pending, it makes my job much harder. Here's a sampling of what not to do:

Avoid the Party Scene

I get it. You're finally breaking free of an unhealthy home life, and you're wanting to sow some wild oats. But if you're out getting Cooter

Brown drunk or sleeping around every weekend, the community will talk, and they may even take pictures or make videos of you to share with your ex. In this day and time, cameras are everywhere. Hint: If you're going to make consistent or large alcohol purchases for whatever reason, use cash.

Don't cope with your emotions in unhealthy ways that turn you into someone you're not.

It is especially crucial that you keep your behavior on the up-and-up if you have children, because your choices could impact the court's decision with respect to your custody arrangement.

Wait to Start a New Romance if at all Possible

You are wise not to start dating until after your divorce is final. If you start seeing people while your divorce is underway, your husband and others will likely assume you cheated before the separation, and your new love interest could be dragged into court to answer awkward questions about when your relationship started and the extent of it. It's not exactly the best way to start your first post-divorce romance.

If you've already started dating online, delete those profiles until your divorce is final. It's never fun for your lawyer when your husband's counsel presents proof of your Tinder or Match account in open court. If you must join a dating site before your divorce is complete against your attorney's advice, for the love of Pete, please don't charge your monthly membership fees to the joint bank account. Not a good look when your spouse pulls out the records in open court.

There will be plenty of time to date after your divorce is behind you. Let your desire—if you have it—to move on drive you to do the work necessary to finish the case. Your lawyer will appreciate the help, and you'll be free sooner, with no one having any right to question your dating choices going forward.

Having said all that, I have to say the rules could be more lenient on this if: (a) Mr. Used-To-Be-Wonderful is already dating and/or (b) if your divorce is taking unreasonably long to complete. You should ask your lawyer if you've waited long enough. It will all depend on the totality of the circumstances of your case—and also the judge's usual view on the subject.

Avoid Being Provocative Online

Side-angle selfies when you're feeling pretty are just fine, but please, for the love of God, don't start an Only Fans page, and if you have one, do your lawyer a big favor right now and delete it. Judges—at least where I'm from—do not have a lot of respect for those who engage in the online sexual revolution. I've helped dads get custody of children from women who were selling pornographic content of themselves online, recorded when the children were in the home. If you need to make extra money, you can always find a respectable second job doing something that does not involve public nudity.

From time to time, I'll have a client who shares memes or photos on the Internet which are in poor taste. It's very important to stop and reflect further before posting anything that: includes keg stands or other alcohol consumption in large quantities, depicts a raised middle finger, glorifies illegal drug use, admits or reflects one's mental instability, encourages anti-government sentiment or promotes insurrection. Just trust me on this one.

Don't Leave Your Children at Home at Night

You don't need to leave your children at home to go out partying. If you do, you'll be accused of neglecting their needs in favor of your own, and it will undermine your custody case. It's best to lie low entirely and go out only rarely when you're in the middle of a divorce case, but if you must go out, try to do it when the children are with their dad or with a trusted relative. Hiring an occasional evening babysitter is also okay, but only if you've fully vetted the sitter for any criminal background or other concerns. Your husband could use your alleged "party lifestyle" and/or choice of caregivers against you in court as a reason to take your children away from you. I've seen it happen to my clients many times. You must not give him anything he can say to vilify you as a parent.

Guard Your Reputation

We're cautioned in 1 Corinthians 15:33, "Do not be deceived. Bad company corrupts good character." Do not allow your good character or your Christian witness to be altered by your associations. Be careful not to associate with those who will lead you into illegal drug use or other vices that could undermine your custody claim and other parts of your case. Your good reputation is your best asset, and you won't soon get it back if it's lost. Remember that "a good name is more desirable than great riches; to be esteemed is better than silver or gold."[18]

Don't Be a Jerk

Does your husband refuse to take responsibility for his behavior? Does he blame you for this breakup? Smear your name and spread a false narrative about you all over town? Steal or hide your most precious belongings? Hide money? Refuse to pay your bills as usual, purposely causing you to struggle financially? Abuse you so you'll bend to his will in some way? Already flaunt a new woman in public? Try to get the kids on his side, as if he and the kids are a team in a battle against you? Harass you by phone or text, or, worse, on social media? Maybe he's doing all of this and then some. How dare he treat you this way?

Remember the Golden Rule from Matthew 7:12? "Do unto others as you would have them do unto you"? This divorce is the greatest test of your faith you've ever faced. Your actions are your fruit, on display for all to see. What kind of witness are you going to be for your God in this struggle? It certainly isn't easy, especially when you feel as if you've given and given while your husband has only taken advantage of your kindness and forgiveness time and again. It hurts when you're the victim of injustice, and your natural human tendency is going to be to try to pay him back somehow, to make him feel some pain of his own. In your stress and frustration, it's tempting to lash out.

But in order to hold your head high without regret as you walk into a courtroom, you mustn't give in to the proverbial devil on your shoulder and treat your husband with the same vitriol he's slinging your way.

Here are some examples of things you shouldn't do without the judge's prior approval, unless your lawyer advises you otherwise:

- If your husband is covered by the health, dental and/or vision insurance plan you pay for through your employment or otherwise control, don't cancel his coverage. God forbid that he gets into an accident or gets really sick and needs that coverage. You wouldn't like it if someone did that to you, so don't do it to him.

- If you and your husband are living apart, don't allow the electricity to be turned off at his house if it's within your power to make sure it stays connected. If you can't afford to pay it, you should ask him to start paying for it or have your lawyer discuss some kind of resolution with his lawyer before just leaving him in the dark. Judges hate vindictive moves like this.
- Same goes for the cable, internet, and cell phone coverage. Don't just willy-nilly go and disconnect his services without some dialogue. Make an effort to reach some understanding in the matter, especially if your kids use his cell phone to call you or the internet and cable when they're in his care. The judge can settle the issue if you don't have an agreement before your hearing.
- Don't max out the credit cards in his name, deliberately placing him in financial distress. Unless it's your usual practice to buy those designer handbags or Christian Louboutin shoes on a regular basis, don't start now. The judge will think you're a selfish, heartless diva, and your husband will look like the victim of your flippant attitude.
- If the judge tells you to pay or reimburse some amount of money to your husband, pay it in a reasonable, convenient form of payment, and pay it on time. Folks have been arrested for harassment and held in contempt for paying with truckloads of pennies, for example. Common decency is always best.

I can always tell when emotional turbulence is getting the best of the ladies I represent. They come to my office crying, agitated, frustrated to the max, and with good reason. What I tell them is to let it all out in my office, with me, NOT to the husband or in the public eye, and certainly not in the courtroom. An understanding attorney will let you unload all the concerns in the privacy of a conference room and help you come up with healthy and productive strategies for how to deal with those issues in the context of the divorce litigation so that you (a) will feel heard in a safe place where venting can't come back to harm you, (b) can formulate a plan for addressing each issue in a controlled and nonviolent manner and (c) let you get it all out of your system and fully process all the emotions, well in advance of the day you meet the judge. A seasoned attorney will know how to speak with you to talk you off the proverbial ledge and help you make good choices.

Take Solace: What's Bad for Your Life is Good for Your Case

When my clients are struggling with a combative, underhanded husband or coparent, I remind them, "What's bad for your life is often good for your case." In other words, when someone is mistreating you, parenting poorly, breaking laws, harassing or trying to embarrass you, it usually backfires on them in court. His bad behavior is a pain in the fanny to deal with in daily life, but you can be thankful he's showing the world who he really is and giving you golden evidence to use against him in court. If he were able to restrain himself and be a fine, upstanding gentleman, carefully choosing to mistreat you in more subversive, unprovable ways, it wouldn't be nearly as useful in your case. Maintain your record of events, keep your attorney updated on what's happening, and say nothing of it to anyone else. As my mom has said all my life, "It will all come out on wash day." The truth will be revealed in due time. You need only be still. (Exodus 14:14).

Serve Your Spouse, Set the Tone

If you're the filing party, i.e., the plaintiff in the divorce action, you need to decide the most productive way to serve your husband with the petition. How you serve him can set the tone for the entire case. It can be an important consideration to discuss with your attorney from the beginning of the case.

Where I practice law, there are various ways to accomplish service. Perhaps the most courteous way to serve a defendant is to invite him to come into the office and acknowledge—or sign for—service of the summons and petition. I do not offer this option when I have reason to believe the Defendant will refuse to come to the office (thereby delaying our progress), or when I believe the Defendant may make a scene or be combative with our office staff. For safety reasons (as you never really know how someone will act when they receive divorce papers), it's usually best to serve the person via the sheriff's office or another independent, court-approved service agent. Your lawyer will know the right approach for your situation.

In my experience, I can tell you no one likes it when a law enforcement official with a badge and a handgun shows up at their place of employment, interrupts their workday, and hands them divorce papers in front of all their co-workers. It's horribly embarrassing and can make a man unnecessarily irate from the start of the case. For this reason, I try my best never to serve anyone at work unless we have no other address or way of reaching them.

Instead of serving him at work, I typically advise my clients to let me serve him at home during the early evening hours, at a time when service can be accomplished without unnecessary drama. We generally try to pick times to serve the Defendant when the children will not be there, too. To be served with a divorce petition in front of one's children is demoralizing and leaves an indelible mark on the memories of both the man and the children. It's just unkind, and there's no reason to make it harder than it already is. While you can't control exactly when the deputy or service agent will deliver the paperwork (all we can do is give it to them with our preferred delivery instructions), it's good to do your best to make the process as seamless and peaceful as it can be, in hopes that emotions can be kept in check and settlement can be reached sooner rather than later. Ask your lawyer the best way to handle service in your case.

Don't Destroy Property

Remember that scene from *Waiting to Exhale* where Angela Bassett throws all her cheating husband's clothes into his BMW, douses it with gas, throws a lit match on it and walks away like a boss, with flames erupting to the sky behind her? That was such a cool scene, right?

Uhmm...don't do that. It's a felony.

Don't take a Louisville to both headlights, either. Even if he cheated and deserves a good lesson, you don't want to wind up in jail.

No matter how awful your husband has been to you, try to remember the Golden Rule and treat him as you would like to be treated.

Don't break mirrors, write on anything with lipstick, or otherwise destroy the house. If he happens to get possession of the house, leave things neat when you vacate. Leave him some toilet paper and soap in the bathroom, and don't take the light bulbs from the lamps or the pine straw from the flower beds. Your husband will not hesitate to photograph the condition of the place and tattle on you to the judge for any mean-spirited behavior.

You can't throw away his family heirlooms or pawn his guns and taxidermy without raising the judge's ire. Same goes for throwing his clothes in the yard or cutting them up with scissors. I've had cases in which this sort of thing happened and believe me when I tell you it doesn't play well in court.

Don't Stalk Your Spouse

Is it eating you alive not to know what Mr. Used-to-be-Wonderful is doing since you separated? Do you find yourself wanting to jump into your car and try to stake out his location? Have you been trying to hack into his social media, email, bank and credit card accounts? Have you thought about hanging game cameras on some light pole near his residence so you can see all his goings and comings? Are your well-meaning girlfriends offering to follow him for you or fly a drone over his house?

Dear Sister, if this is ringing any bells, you must stop it right now.

It can be illegal to place other people under surveillance, and illegally obtained evidence is rarely admitted for consideration in a court of law, at least where I work. If you're just dying to know what your ex is doing, or if you feel there's a valid legal argument to be made in your child custody battle or otherwise because of his current behavior, handle it right. Talk to your attorney about how to obtain the evidence you need and find out if there is a good private investigator nearby whom you could hire to help you. A good private eye, if hired at the right time and sent to conduct surveillance at the right time, can bring great value to a case when they testify about what they saw. In court, it's always best for this information to come from an unemotional surveillance professional than from you or your bestie.

Aside from being illegal, consider what will happen if you get caught, dressed in all black staked out in your husband's new neighborhood? Do you really want to be known as a crazy ex? Don't give him anything to use against you, anything that will support his story (even if false) about your separation. You don't want people in the community talking about you that way, either. Plus, what happens if you stumble up in his space and find him with another woman? You can't know in advance how you will react to something like that, and you should never put yourself in a position to do anything irrational, criminal, or otherwise life-altering. Let a licensed investigator do the work, and you stay classy, friend.

From time to time, I'll have a client who is trying to hack into her husband's email account or social media accounts to look at his communications. First, doing this is illegal where I am unless you have his express permission, or he has a reasonable expectation that you would be able to look at his stuff (which can be arguable if he gave you the password or left the account "up" on a shared device he left in your possession).

It can be a close legal question, so my mantra is always that you shouldn't access someone else's accounts unless they know you're doing it and gave you permission. For example, what happens if you read your husband's private emails and stumble across his messages with his attorney, about your case, discussing litigation strategies and settlement proposals?

Yikes. This is the kind of thing your lawyer's nightmares are made of.

When you access and share your husband's confidential and/or attorney-client privileged information with your attorney, after you've obtained it illegally, you put your attorney in an uncomfortable ethical spot. Moreover, there are usually other (legal) ways to get the same information into evidence.

The Golden Nugget to take away: Have a talk with your lawyer before you read your husband's emails and other private communications.

Dear One, if you can keep yourself on the straight and narrow, all will be well. Give yourself grace if you've made mistakes as you grapple with your situation. No one really knows what to do when they're getting divorced. You can have fun but stay grounded in your faith and hold fast to your convictions. You will have a powerful testimony for other women after this is all over, if only you will be wise and remember Whose you are.

Questions for Reflection

1. Assess your choices. What kinds of things might you need to stop doing so that they don't come out in court?

2. Are men showing interest in you as word of your separation is circulating? What are you doing to guard yourself from moving to a new romance before your case is over?

3. Are you associating with people who, albeit fun, may not be the best influences on you in this time of transition? Do you feel yourself being pulled to misbehave because of their example? Do you no longer recognize yourself? If you answered "yes" to any of these questions, how can you change the situation to put yourself in a stronger position for your case to succeed?

4. Do you need to reassess how you're spending your time? How might you need to realign your priorities to set a good example for your children and to ensure your good reputation remains intact?

Chapter Soundtrack

"Better In Time"—Leona Lewis

"Bye Bye Bye"—NSYNC

"Free Bird"—Lynyrd Skynyrd

"Go Your Own Way"—Fleetwood Mac

"Harden My Heart"—Quarterflash

Resources

Uninvited: Living Loved When You Feel Less Than,
Left Out, and Lonely—Lysa Terkeurst

Breaking Open: How Your Pain Becomes a
Path to Living Again—Jacob Armstrong

Putting On a Gentle & Quiet Spirit: 1 Peter
(*A Woman After God's Own Heart*)—Elizabeth George

Instagram:

Proverbs Daily @proverbsdaily

The Christian Heart @thechristianheart

Faith Reel @faithreeel

Lauren Fortenberry @laurenfortenberrywrites

12

Let Your Kids Be Kids

Counselors, I've met in chambers with your children just now.
Do you know the one thing they all said that stuck out the most to me?
They said, "I don't care who's wrong or who's right.
I just wish they wouldn't put us in the middle.
—actual judges, in actual divorce trials I've handled,
more times that I can count

No one really knows what they're doing early after a separation; it's a learn-as-you-go, fly-by-the-seat-of-your-pants endeavor, especially right at the beginning, so don't be too hard on yourself if you make mistakes along the way. But if you have little ones or even teenagers, be aware that they are watching how you handle yourself during this time, and they are dealing with their own emotions as you grapple to make sense of yours. Being their mom is a sobering, sacred responsibility not to be taken lightly.

I've learned so much over the years watching my clients parent through divorce, some very well and others not so much. My own parents divorced when I was in third grade, and I drew from childhood experiences of living in two homes as I managed the inevitable bumps in the road that emerge as my children transitioned to life in two places. This chapter is to share some of the takeaways I believe will help you on this new parenting journey you're on, to make you think of ways to come alongside and support your little ones, and to have no regrets in court over how you've managed your kids.

You are Modeling a New, Better Way of Living

With each decision, conversation and action, you are teaching your children how to live, how to deal with conflict, and how to manage their emotions. Try to keep this guiding principle in the forefront of your mind: if you wouldn't want your child to behave/speak/respond in their own relationships and conflicts the way you are now behaving/speaking/responding, check yourself and change course. Many behaviors are learned and can carry forward generationally. When you stop and consider the impact that your actions today could have on your grandchildren and great-grandchildren, what perspective it brings!

Be a Safe Place for Your Kids to Land

I once heard a pastor speak about playing a game of tag with a group of kids and other dads in his backyard. The pastor spoke of his little boy running from place to place, trying not to be tagged "out" by another kid, before finally rushing up to his pastor/daddy, latching aggressively onto his dad's legs and yelling, "Safe!" He knew, with his arms wrapped around his father's knees, that he was untouchable. He was safe. He wouldn't be tagged, couldn't be touched or affected by the other kids. Isn't this every person's deepest human need? To feel that sense of safety and security, that we're okay, loved and insulated from being "taken out" by others who would do us harm? That someone has our back?

After a long day, doesn't everyone just want to come home, put on pajamas and feel the love and support of others in the household? Kids are just little versions of us, fighting their own battles in the world each day and coming home to sort them out at night. When you pile on the stress of their parents' divorce to the mix of the societal, educational, and other pressures on their little shoulders, it's even more imperative that your home be a safe haven for them to relax and know they're not alone.

Don't Rely On Your Children for Emotional Support

I always cringe when I hear people say, "my daughter/son is my best friend." Your child is not your BFF. You are the parent, and you need to act like it. Your little boy or girl is not your emotional crutch, and they are not equipped to be your confidant. It's not your child's job to support you through this divorce.

Children need you to be the adult. They are looking to you to know how to lead them through this transition, and you must rise to the occasion. They need to know you're in control so that they can feel secure, knowing without a doubt that you're still able to meet their basic needs.

Here are a few Do's and Don'ts I hope you'll find helpful:

1. **Don't tell them about your arguments**. Even if your husband does. Your kids are not your comrades in arms. Don't make them feel like they need to choose a side.

2. **Don't ask them to deliver messages to your ex**. I hear cringe-worthy stories from clients all the time of children relaying offensive messages from one parent to another. Be very careful not to put your children in this position. They'll never forget it.

3. **Don't involve them in your settlement negotiation**. Discussing such adult matters with kids can confuse them and cause them to question whether you're still capable

of meeting their basic needs. They never need to wonder where that football gear, prom dress or next pair of basketball shoes will come from.

4. **Fall apart in private.** It's totally normal to need to collapse from time to time and have a good cry. If at all possible, try to do this outside your children's presence.

5. **Don't obsess over them.** Your job is to provide a safe space for the grief, not to manage the grieving process for them. Having a life of your own outside of theirs brings your children security that "Mom has it together, and I'm okay."

6. **Dump your emotions elsewhere.** If you need an appropriate place to dump your emotions, find a counselor or a trusted friend, and don't vent to your kids. Doing so can put so much pressure on them, makes them feel the unhealthy need to take a side, advocate for you, or intervene with action of their own to help relieve your pain.

7. **Manage the messages your kids receive.** Do not hesitate to set anyone straight who disparages your ex in front of your children; the children need to see that you won't tolerate their **father being discredited, no matter what he's done to you.**

8. **Talk to other adults in your kids' lives.** It's usually a good idea to keep your children's educators, church youth group leaders, and coaches apprised of any big changes in your child's life so that those other adults can help you and the child manage any tumultuous days as they arise. Be reserved in what you tell these folks, as it's not a smear campaign on your ex but rather an effort to ensure other adults are watching and making sure your child's needs are being met during this season.

9. **Consider counseling, and parent each child as an individual**. A good counselor can come alongside your children and be a wonderful, confidential, safe resource for them to feel heard, a safe place for them to sort out their feelings. If you get a counselor for your children, respect your kids' privacy. Don't ask them to tell you what they said in their private counseling sessions. Let them have that space for their very own. The counselor will let you know if there's a particular concern you need to address at home, without your child having to articulate it to you. Consider having your children take the Five Love Languages quiz to identify how each one receives love. An easy and fun Enneagram analysis of each child's personality may also be helpful to your effort to meet each child's individual needs.

10. **Encourage the kids to love and respect your ex**. No matter your feelings about him. No matter what he's done to hurt you. Abuse situations are different, but you should encourage the children to have a relationship with their father to the extent that it's safe for them.

The Internal PR War

No matter how much you may now hate your husband, your kids still love him, and they're watching how you treat him, just like they're watching how he's treating you, their dear mother. Try to give, sacrifice and compromise for the good of your ex's relationship with the children whenever possible, and let the kids see you do it. Model kindness and cooperation. Show the kids your focus is on their well-being and adjustment, rather than using them to hurt your ex.

Even the worst husbands are sometimes the best dads. You must remember the children love you both, and that your ex has a relationship with the children that has very different dynamics than your relationship with the ex and different dynamics than your relationship with the children. Give your children the freedom to love and interact with their dad in their own way so that their paternal relationships can remain strong.

I majored in Journalism/Public Relations at the University of Georgia (Go Dawgs!). In our training, we were taught how to manage the public's perception of a given event or crisis facing businesses. It's commonly referred to as "spinning the story," and it happens in families all the time.

Divorcing families engage in an internal PR war of sorts. In an effort to build a "team" to gang up on the other parent, one parent will do their best to convince the children that the other parent is wrong, that all of this is the fault of the other parent. One parent tells the children too much about adult matters, looking to make them little soldiers in the war against the other parent. It takes great restraint not to set the record straight and tell the kids your side of the story when you're the victim parent in this scenario.

When you tell a child the worst things about the other parent, you are telling that child that half of them is defective. Children don't need this stress. Think about it; that other parent, once your lover and now your enemy, will always be the parent of your child. You should want your coparent to thrive! You are hurt, and I get it. I've been there myself. But your kids love both of you, and they came from both of you. Don't make a child choose which parent to love more. It's an impossible choice. With a little grace and self-control and a lot of prayer, it is possible to get your kids through your divorce so that they learn from it and emerge stronger and with greater empathy for others' pain than before.

Callie's Story

Callie and Kyle decided to divorce due to personal differences after sixteen years of marriage. While they were no longer compatible for various reasons, they had always agreed on matters related to the children's upbringing and had coparented magnificently to that point. They had already discussed it—they would NOT put the kids, Holden and Marie, in the middle of it, make them talk to lawyers, or bring them to court to give input on matters of custody.

When Kyle and Callie broke the news of their impending separation to the children sitting on the back porch of their home one warm June night, the children were upset, everyone cried, and Callie came away feeling that the kids were okay, that she and Kyle would be great coparents, and that the children would come through this transition with flying colors. She was relieved by their agreement not to put the kids in the middle of the litigation.

Over the next several days, the family had several good talks about how life was about to change, and the children seemed more at ease the more they understood what to expect. Callie was encouraged all the more by these talks that all would be well.

Then, about a week after that initial talk on the porch, all hell broke loose for Callie. Kyle and his mother secretly, and without telling Callie what they were doing, checked the kids out early from Vacation Bible School at their church, turned off the location service to the children's phones, and whisked them off to a private meeting with Kyle's lawyer in another town. Callie was at work that day, and Kyle told her his mother had picked up the children from VBS, so she didn't worry about them and assumed all day they'd been at their grandmother's house as usual.

Callie was taken to her knees when her lawyer called to let her know the children had signed some papers with Kyle's counsel saying they wanted to live with Kyle full-time. Callie's lawyer explained that these documents would certainly carry a lot of weight with the judge assigned to their case, that these documents could spell disaster for her chances of keeping custody of the children. Kyle, whom his friends had called "the cheapest man alive" for years, had figured out his child support may be lower—or that he could even get child support from Callie—if they resided with him most of the time.

Callie felt like she'd been kicked in the stomach. She felt so foolish to have ever trusted Kyle's promises of a positive coparenting experience, and now her sweet babies were squarely in the middle. Tearful and consumed with worry, she didn't sleep for days, and, unable to function, had to take a few days off work to collect herself. What was so unsettling was the ease with which Kyle had (a) lied to her face and (b) manipulated the children.

Just the day before going to see Kyle's lawyer, Holden and Marie had told them both they wanted to remain primarily in the home with Callie. The four of them had had an open, pleasant discussion about how the parenting rotation would work: the kids would stay with Callie most of the time and would visit Kyle for long, alternating weekends and for extended periods during their school breaks and holidays.

Kyle didn't show affection or speak with the children with kindness very often, and they were desperate for his attention. He generally found fault with most everything they did. Desperate for his approval, they had been coerced into signing those custody statements with Kyle's attorney, hoping he would show them some favor and love—there was no doubt in Callie's mind. The kids were in an impossible position now; they privately told Callie how their dad had pressured them with the lawyer, and explained how he hadn't given them any choice but to sign the papers. Holden said, "Mom, I just froze when they handed me that paper. I didn't know what to do, and Dad told me to sign it, so I did." Marie couldn't even speak of these events; all she could do was sob while her brother was speaking.

They didn't want to live with Kyle, but they just weren't able to speak up and plainly tell him that at this stage, let alone sign new statements in Callie's favor, without raising his ire. They were paralyzed with fear and didn't know what to do. It was clear: Callie would have to speak for and advocate for them, do her best to undo the impact of their statements. So that's what she did: she gathered all the medical and dental records showing she had been their primary caregiver over the years, got statements from witnesses at school, church and other social groups to vouch for her presence—and Kyle's absence—in the children's lives. Rather than shriveling in defeat, she put all her energy into proving why the kids should stay with her.

In the end, it all worked out for this family, as Kyle eventually lost interest in having the children the majority of the time (I see this scenario all the time...he didn't really want the kids, just control over the larger settlement conversation), and accepted Callie's offer of a more favorable financial settlement in exchange for giving her primary custody of the children. In Callie's estimation, it was a small price to pay, and she didn't mind sacrificing some assets and reducing her monthly support amount to get what was most important to her—the privilege of time with those sweet little souls she had brought into the world.

God entrusted you with these little ones' hearts, Sweet Friend. It's a privilege and a great responsibility you've been given to do your part in forming well-adjusted adult humans. If you're reading this book, that tells me your heart is in the right place and that you want to glorify God in your parenting. Keep at it and keep the faith! God loves your children more than you do, and He will make a way for you to parent them through this present time of turmoil. Pray for your children without ceasing. All will be well. You've got this, Mama!

Questions for Reflection

1. Are you tempted to speak with your children about your divorce in inappropriate ways? What kinds of things do you want to tell them? How can you be more mindful of the negative impact of doing this?

2. Is your home, and is your very presence, a safe haven for your children, or are you doing and saying things to increase their stress level? What changes should you make to make sure your kids know you're their safe place?

3. What are some things you can do to encourage and support your children during this time? Think about each of your children as individuals. What unique needs does each child have, and how can you meet those needs?

4. Are there qualified child counselors in your area? Have you asked your child's pediatrician for a referral?

5. Have you identified your children's "love language" and/or confirmed each child's Enneagram personality type? Check out resources referenced below and take the associated quizzes to ascertain how each of your children best receives love from others, and tailor your interactions with that child in that particular way.

Resources

Collateral Damage: Guiding and Protecting Your Child Through the Minefield of Divorce—Dr. John Chirban

@thecoparentingcollective and @ourhappydivorce on Instagram

www.enneagraminstitute.com—The Enneagram Institute

SPLIT: Divorce Through Children's Eyes (2013),
a documentary film by Ellen Bruno

The Five Love Languages of Children
—Gary Chapman and Ross Campbell

American Association for Marriage and Family Therapy—
www.aamft.org (articles on parenting children through divorce)

Childhood Disrupted: How Your Biography Becomes Your Biology, and How You Can Heal—Donna Jackson Nakazawa

Chapter Soundtrack

"Baby Mine"—Alison Krauss

"Hand to Hold"—JJ Heller

"I Hope You Dance"—Lee Ann Womack

"In My Daughter's Eyes"—Martina McBride

"Slow Down"—Nichole Nordeman

Part 2

Prepare for Post-Separation Abuse

1

Spotting and Breaking Abuse Cycles

Set me free from my prison, that I may praise your name. Psalm 142:7

Studies have shown that up to seventy-five percent of domestic violence homicides happen at the point of separation or after the victim has already left her abuser.[18] Rarely does abuse become physical until after other forms of abuse like coercive control, financial abuse, isolation and spiritual abuse have already manipulated and demoralized the victim. This chapter will help you identify whether you have been part of an abuse cycle, and help you break free from that abuse.

How Do Smart Women Get Trapped in Abuse?

Most abuse stories begin with a whirlwind romance that feels like a fairy tale. Prince Charming comes along, and you are reeled in and married before he lets you see the real him. You're stuck, maybe even with children, before he shows his true nature. His abusive tendencies start with small arguments and a lack of respect for your boundaries and then becomes increasingly more and more aggressive over time,

---

18   Kasperkevic, Jana. "Private Violence: up to 75% of abused women who are murdered are killed after they leave their partners." *The Guardian*, October 20, 2014, modified February 15, 2018.

culminating in your husband exerting more and more control over you, coercing your choices and behaviors to fall in line with his goals and agenda, to the exclusion of yours. He will become increasingly agitated, combative, mean, and harsh in his dealings with you, especially if you dare voice an opinion contrary to his or try to stand up for yourself or your children. Before you realize it, your real-life romance novel becomes a horror movie. You're now dealing with your husband's hatefulness, mental abuse, name-calling, and belittling, which often descends into destruction of your property; cheating; physical manhandling like shoving, headbutting, spitting and screaming in your face; and eventually even threats of an all-out assault and bodily injury.

And then, after all that ugliness, he'll bombard you with all the affection, gifts, quality time, kindness and whatever else he knows will win your heart back over to him. Experts call this "love-bombing." You'll get a few glorious days (or perhaps weeks) of his best efforts to make amends to keep you from leaving. Have you ever been wooed back to your husband with flowers, wine, fine dining experiences, exotic trips, jewelry, promises of counseling, promises to do better, perhaps even promises to have another child? Has he threatened to kill himself if you leave him, thereby making you feel a renewed obligation to stay and save him? This is the height of coercive control; after all, no one wants to be the reason another person ends his own life, or the reason children may lose their daddy. I can't tell you how many times I've seen my lady clients go back to guys after suicide threats like this. It's powerful leverage over an empathetic woman. This is abuse, my friend, and it is disgusting.

It's a true rollercoaster ride of ups and downs that leaves you to wonder which man is the real him. Is he Dr. Jekyll or Mr. Hyde? You're holding on for dear life, doing your best to maintain some kind of normalcy, confused about what is happening to you. You know in your spirit that something is very wrong, but you haven't the first clue what to do about it.

The National Domestic Abuse Hotline defines abuse as "a pattern of behavior in any relationship that is *used to gain or maintain power and control* over an intimate partner." The behaviors of the abusive partner typically involve "the intentional construction of a false perception of someone else's reality by an abuser for the purpose of controlling them."[19] All that meanness is designed to tear you down emotionally so that you then get a rush of relief and happiness when he's nice to you again. The chemical reactions in your body dictate your physical responses to how you're being treated, and it's literally an addiction. Over time, an abused person becomes physically addicted to the abuse! The experts call it trauma bonding.

When we're mistreated and perceive danger, cortisol and adrenaline are released as part of the fight or flight response. It's how God made us to get away from and survive in the face of things that don't feel safe. Each time you're mentally, physically or emotionally abused, it will trigger painful memories of childhood wounds of rejection, and your body will respond either with an urge to fight off the danger, flee from the danger ("flight") or freeze in your tracks. We are innately built for survival. Our bodies move us away from pain.

When you're used to living in a constant state of heightened alert because of your husband's abuse, your body naturally welcomes any opportunity to relax. When Mr. Used-to-be-Wonderful becomes temporarily wonderful again, showering you with pretty words, affection

---

19   Dr. Kirsten Milstead, *Why Can't I Just Leave: A Guide to Waking Up and Walking Out of a Pathological Love Relationship*, Author Academy Elite, 2021.

and gifts, your body releases all the feel-good hormones: oxytocin, do-pamine and serotonin.

Your body gets addicted to the rush these hormones give you when you're being love-bombed, so you eventually become pro-grammed to hang on during the abusive times, because you know the joys of the love-bombing are sure to follow. Your bodily functions override your ability to be logical about what is happening to you.

Smart women stay in these scenarios because hormonal balance in their bodies overrides reason. The breadcrumbs of love and affec-tion make it feel safer to stay with an abuser.

This is not the *real* marital love God contemplated. If you have to regularly suffer through days of your husband's abuse as you hold onto the day when he's nice to you again, something is terribly wrong. You are God's dearly loved daughter, worthy of love and respect. You should not be settling for crumbs, and you should not have to live in sustained fight-or-flight mode. My friend, marriage has its diffi-culties, but it shouldn't be like this. This is control, not love. Healthy love doesn't create anxiety. It relieves it.

Power and Control—Get out of the Monkey House

Some wise person once said, "Never make snow angels in dog parks." I love this quote. There are just some places where, no matter what you're trying to do to make something beautiful, it will never work, you'll never succeed, and you'll come out smelling awful.

Here's another animal analogy for you: a toxic marriage is like a house full of monkeys.

The next time you're at a zoo, go to the area where they keep the monkeys. You'll likely see monkeys everywhere, bouncing and swinging around, making crazy noises. They're fun to watch, but it's frenzied, loud, and smelly in there. I suppose the monkeys are used to the smell of the place, as it's just their usual environment. They're comfortable with the stink and the disorder.

We humans are sometimes like those monkeys. We get used to living in the smelly chaos of our homes, and we don't know how nice the air smells outside. We forget there's a better, cleaner, healthier way to live just outside the door. It's only when we leave the toxic environment that we can breathe clean air again. Once out of the proverbial monkey house after leaving a bad marriage, it's amazing how one's perspective changes. When you look into that monkey house from the outside, you'll say to yourself, "It's unlivable in there. Why did I live like that for so long?"

Abusers create disorder and confusion to control you. Abuse is all about power, control and manipulation. Check out this Power and Control Wheel created by the National Domestic Violence Hotline to help you analyze the reality of your situation:

Abusers choose empathetic partners who are prone to making excuses for bad behavior and allow it to continue rather than standing up to the abuser or calling him out.

It's a pattern I see repeated all the time among my clients: Abusers generally pursue Empaths, as Empaths are more likely to stay and endure abuse longer than someone who's naturally more assertive. Empaths are naturally (by personality) long-suffering, forgiving and full of kindness and humility. They think they can love the abuser into behaving better if they just stick it out long enough. We Christian ladies like to think of ourselves as "sanctifying our husbands" by our fine example as contemplated in 1 Corinthians 7:14. I've seen it countless times; women sometimes waste their best years chasing the false hope that their husbands will change. You can't change your husband, Dear One. He has to truly want to change.

Isolation

Isolation is just one tool an abusive husband will use to try to scare you into staying with him. By isolating you from friends, family and other support people, an abusive husband hopes to keep the abuse hidden from the purview of others. He's afraid he'll be exposed if someone else sees how you're being treated, and that they'll encourage you to leave him or assist your departure. Elizabeth's story is instructive:

Outgoing and others-focused, Elizabeth was always surrounded by friends and had a strong bond with her extended family before she married Edward. An avid community activist and volunteer, Elizabeth spent her free time ministering to the needs of the elderly and the poor, helping in various organizations however she could. As soon as Elizabeth and Edward returned from their Honeymoon, Edward gradually pulled Elizabeth from her volunteer work, telling her she needed to be home more and scheduling other things for them to do as a couple instead. Anytime she expressed interest in volunteering, he would come up with a scheduling conflict and dissuade her from going. He didn't like her going out with friends after work, either; he wanted her home in the evenings, so she obliged, happy to be married and wanting to please her husband. Edward told his friends to tell their wives to stop including Elizabeth in their gatherings, and they obliged. Over time, Elizabeth's friendships waned, and her circle shrank to be primarily Edward's family and co-workers. He was always present when she socialized, but Elizabeth was content just to be married.

Edward never let her forget that she hadn't been able to pass her nursing boards after college, so she didn't feel she could support herself apart from him, and she didn't think she was good enough or smart enough for anyone else to ever love her. She felt more secure as part of a pair, this *pair,* and she was willing to fight through the painful days when he made her feel unimportant because the good *days with him were* so good. She had been cut off from activities and friends she enjoyed, and her family missed seeing her as much as they had before, but it was okay because Edward loved her and needed her so much. And he always felt badly about the way he treated her, would apologize and promise to do better, and would plan an extravagant vacation or buy her jewelry when he really messed up. He was so cute when he repented, and she fell in love with him all over again each time he apologized. She was determined to be long-suffering and patient with him. Being his wife was her life's work.

About two years into their marriage, unbeknownst to Elizabeth, Edward began having a secret affair with a woman he met at work. Rather than tell Elizabeth about it and repent, he became combative paranoid, picking fights with Elizabeth and accusing her of adultery every time she went on an errand. She couldn't even go to the grocery store without being questioned about where she had been! None of this made any sense to Elizabeth. Where was this coming from? She hadn't done anything to deserve these accusations. It was so irrational that she didn't know how to respond. And the worst part was that she had no one she could speak to about it. All her closest friends had moved on, as she had declined so many invitations to get together that they had stopped inviting her anywhere. And she hadn't told her family about how she'd been treated, for they'd never understand if she decided to stay with Edward, and she wasn't ready to give up on him yet. Confused and anxiety-ridden, she felt more alone than ever.

Elizabeth secretly sought the help of a therapist, who taught her all about love-bombing and trauma bonds. She began reading every book she could find on narcissistic abuse trauma, and these books helped her identify the abuse patterns in her marriage. The therapist gave her coping strategies, and she remained committed to Edward and to his healing, determined to help him overcome his childhood wounds and be a better man. And even if he didn't get better, she now understood what was going on in her home.

And then, one day, the insurance company's Explanation of Benefits form came in the mail, and Edward found out she'd been seeing a therapist.

Edward hit the roof when he found out about the counselor and demanded Elizabeth stop going immediately. Elizabeth, for the first time in their marriage, stood her ground and refused to stop seeing the therapist, and the argument escalated quickly, culminating in Edward slapping Elizabeth across her cheek and putting a small cut just beneath her left eye. That was the final straw for Elizabeth; with the help of her therapist and an excellent attorney, Elizabeth broke free of Edward's coercive control, came out of isolation, and reentered her old social circle. His affair was exposed, and her friends rallied around her. It was hard to leave

Edward, but as she came to learn what Edward had been doing behind her back, walking away became easier and easier. She says she's forever grateful to have found a good mental health professional to expose the abuse cycles of her marriage. She never would have broken free without her therapist's encouragement, as she—by Edward's design—had been totally isolated otherwise.

Elizabeth's story is, unfortunately, all too common. Emotional and verbal abuse, stalking, intimidation and isolation can escalate to physical abuse in a hurry. Abusive men don't like being confronted or challenged, so when an abused woman stands up for herself, she is often met with more aggression.

If Your Husband is the Stalker Type

An abusive man who has lost control over you will often try to intimidate you into coming back. When intimidation doesn't work, he'll go crazy with jealousy at the first notion that another man is interested in you. Don't be surprised if he puts GPS trackers on or in your vehicle (check for these regularly, and if you have small children, check their bags for tracking devices, as well, being mindful that tracking devices can look like a writing pen or another common object to trick you into keeping them) after you've separated. And once you start dating again after your divorce, be sure to warn the new fella that he may also be a victim of intimidation and stalking. In my experience with clients, I've seen countless abusive men completely decompensate when they accept the fact that the relationship is really over. Guys like that just can't control their emotions, and those emotions can often lead them to do irrational, dangerous, sometimes even criminal things. Following is a sampling of common scenarios:

- ❖ The ex-husband waiting in a client's yard when she comes back from a date with a new beau;
- ❖ Game cameras[20] being placed on public light poles or trees near the woman's home so that her every move can be monitored;
- ❖ OnStar and other vehicle-monitoring subscriptions being maintained, post-divorce, for the ex-husband to continue to watch all the ex-wife's vehicle's movements;
- ❖ The ex-husband leaving the children at his home in the middle of the night during his visitation time to come and sit outside the ex-wife's house, and then following her new boyfriend, bumper-to-bumper, when the boyfriend leaves the property before daylight;
- ❖ The ex-husband hiring a private investigator to watch his ex-wife's every move; and
- ❖ Drones armed with cameras being flown above a woman's residence so that surveillance footage of her activities can be gathered.

Don't Fall Into Reactive Abuse

When faced with conflict, some people fight, others take flight or flee, and others freeze. If you're wired to fight back, you can create significant challenges for your case if you're unable to restrain yourself. Abusers love to push all your buttons, make you react, and then

---

20   In the South, our men post cameras in the woods to track wild game for hunting. And then they sometimes use the same cameras to stalk their women. Be on the lookout for these cameras around your homeplace. Head on a swivel, Sister.

use your reaction against you to paint you as the *real* abuser in the situation. Reactive abuse occurs when an abused person lashes out at her abuser, in response to gaslighting or abusive behavior, and is a highly effective tool an abusive person uses in court to confuse the judge and flip the roles of abuser and victim.

Reactive abuse is retaliatory in nature and can manifest as screaming insults at the abuser, crying uncontrollably, and (the worst kind to defend in court) physical counterattacks that injure the abuser or leave marks on his body.

Have you ever noticed how it's more acceptable in American culture for a woman to hit a man than for a man to hit a woman? Television and films popular during my formative years seemed to normalize the idea that it's okay for women to abuse men! Because of the TV show *Dallas*, I grew up thinking it was okay for Suellen Ewing to throw a bottle of red wine at J.R.'s head, that he deserved it because he was such a scoundrel. Scorned women on those shows regularly slapped men across their faces, pounded their fists on men's chests and hit them on the head with hard objects. These images desensitized us, and the collective American psyche forgives and is more tolerant of women lashing out at men while it condemns and demands justice for women who are subject to the same sorts of things. But in the end, it's all abuse. It's all unacceptable. And you can be arrested for all of it.

Where I practice, any physical assault against your spouse in the presence of the children can carry with it additional criminal charges in which the children are also named victims. The last thing you want is a charge for Cruelty to Children (or whatever it's called in your state) hanging over you when you're trying to win a custody battle. You must control your emotions and express yourself with words, not violence. Physical abuse is never okay.

When reactive abuse crops up in my cases, it's never pretty. The abuser gets the victim all upset and then, without the victim's knowledge, starts recording the interaction just as the victim is getting upset and begins to retaliate. The court isn't able to see what happened just before the victim retaliates, and the retaliation or reaction of the victim is seen as the abuse to be addressed. The victim is labeled "crazy" and the "abuser," and is often cut off from her children and significantly hindered in the litigation. Unless there is solid evidence to refute the real abuser's powerful false narrative, he gets away with his abuse, wins custody of children, and continues to abuse everyone in his life, unfettered and emboldened by the judge's support. A lying abuser with compelling evidence of your less-than-ideal reaction can truly destroy your life. I've seen it happen time and again.

The only way to avoid being accused of reactive abuse is *not to retaliate* when you are provoked, and it's easier said than done if you're the kind of person whose natural tendency is to fight back. In court, any kind of reaction can and will be used against you to support a claim that you are mentally unwell and unfit to parent your kids. An abuser loves nothing more than to take children away from a wife who's unmasked him and is ready to walk away for good. Children are powerful weapons in the game of an abuser because they mean so much to you.

If you tend to fight back in arguments, you must train yourself to leave controversial situations before they escalate. Fleeing is generally better than fighting, for it's hard to throw stones at someone for quietly walking away from confrontation. Every time you stay around and react negatively or unproductively to your husband's abuse, you give him the upper hand. The reaction can often be worse than the instigating event because, by the time you react, the argument has significantly escalated.

As challenging as it may be, you must try to keep your emotions and reactions in check. When you are able to control your emotions and restrain yourself from reacting, you can reclaim your power. And once the abuser no longer has power over your feelings, you have truly won the war.

How to Plan Your Exit

As you prepare to depart your marriage, the last thing you want is for your husband to see it coming. The element of surprise is your friend. You don't want him having any extra time to plot your destruction. You will need at least one safe person who knows your plan and supports you. Choose this person—or these people—carefully. Keep them on speed-dial should things become unsafe at home before you can leave.

Go ahead and copy all the important financial and personal documents (i.e., yours and the children's passports and Social Security cards, bank statements, retirement and brokerage account statements, contracts, Will, anything of value to you), save them electronically, and send them to safe locations (places like your lawyer's office, your mama's email, your safe deposit box) to be kept for later reference. You may not have access to these after your separation. As discussed in the Financial Abuse chapter, you'll need to squirrel some money away to fund life during your separation, at least until the first court date where you can ask the judge to award you financial support. You also need to have an overnight bag packed and ready in the back of your closet to grab and go should you feel the time has come for you to run.

Gather all your most treasured, irreplaceable possessions and put them in a new safe deposit box or at the home of a trusted friend or relative to keep him from destroying or "misplacing" them if he's able to access the house when you're not there.

If permitted in your area (ask your lawyer first), record his verbal abuse and outbursts, take photographs of damaged property and your injuries.

Log out of all online accounts, change all your passwords, and be aware that your husband could be seeing all your electronic and phone communications. Have trusted professionals check your devices and vehicle for location tracking devices and applications.

Assets can often conveniently "go missing" at the start of a divorce. If you know that your husband has stacks of cash on hand, count it and photograph it (with date stamp). If you have special jewelry, tractors, ATVs, boats, gun collections, or other expensive items, save the photos in various electronic places and send them to trusted members of your inner circle to ensure you can prove those assets exist should your ex claim they're gone.

Timing is everything in these high-conflict situations. It's best to handle the separation in a way that is as controlled, quiet and measured as possible, keeping the emotions down if you can.

Don't Let Your Abuser Woo You Back

It's been said that getting back together with a toxic ex is like taking a shower and then putting your dirty clothes back on. You can do it, but you'll regret it.

Diane's Story

My husband, David, and I had a small business together, which was great because we shared all the profits, and our little family had everything we needed. As the business flourished, we outgrew the office space we had rented and decided to build a bigger place. One afternoon, an argument ensued over the design of the building when I discovered how much smaller and darker my office was going to be compared to David's large, fancy, well-lit office with all the custom features. It wasn't about the office itself really. The office was a metaphor for our marriage; I had always felt less important than my husband. David's needs had always been more of a priority than mine were. The office design he had created with the builder reflected that I was not a priority, yet again. No one cared if my office was comfortable or not, and it was clear that David's office had been given much more thought.

When I asked him about it, David denied any knowledge of the disparity in our offices, saying he was just trusting the builder and the architect. When I asked the builder about it the next day, however, he confirmed that David had made a choice, that he had directed the builder to add upgrades to his office but not to mine. It deeply hurt my feelings, so I calmly confronted David about this later that day. David flew into a rage over being challenged about the office design. In front of our three employees and our children who also happened to be there, David threatened to slit my throat, called me a selfish b**ch, and proceeded to punch a hole in the rented office wall.

I quickly left the office with the children and went out of town for the weekend to see my family. David was despondent, texting and calling me constantly, incessantly apologizing and promising to start treating me better, and begging me to come back. The apologies felt nice, and he seemed genuine in his willingness to change, but I wasn't easily convinced.

I made him move out of the house for several weeks in hopes that a short separation period would heal us. He dropped fifteen pounds while he was away from me, and I started to worry about his mental and physical health. I didn't want to be the reason someone else was despondent, and I felt guilty for taking such a hard line with him.

His family wanted us to stay together at all costs, so they encouraged him to buy me some nice gifts and encouraged me to take and enjoy them, assuring me they'd never let him treat me like that ever again. David invited me out on a date, and it felt so good to be pursued again that I gave in and accepted the invitation. My husband showing me what seemed to be genuine affection and care, after years of meanness, manipulation and thoughtless criticisms, was my kryptonite. He was wooing me back.

I finally let him move back into the home when he said he was going to have to get an apartment, and that if he got an apartment, he didn't know if he would be able to avoid cheating on me. The thought of him being with another woman was just too much for me to bear at that time. I was so insecure and just knew he would have a better post-divorce life than I would, plus I had these children to raise and was sure no other man would want me. Looking back now, I see how stupid I was to let fear cripple me like that. He knew that comment would manipulate me to take him back, and I allowed myself to be manipulated.

And he was right back to his old abuse patterns, plus the flirtations with other women, within a matter of weeks.

Do not be fooled, my friend. Once you break off the relationship, it's best to limit your contact with an abusive husband except as absolutely necessary to manage your children. You must erect healthy boundaries and unwaveringly enforce them. Your husband knows you as well as you know yourself, and he knows how to manipulate you into doing what he wants you to do. He loses all his power if you refuse to engage with him. If he has limited access to you, he can't woo you back easily. Pray for him from afar. Remember the good times all you want. Just don't go back. Don't let the same snake bite you twice, Friend.

Physical Abuse

I always caution against allowing an abuser to woo you back because going back to him makes him think you'll never leave, no matter what he does to you and no matter how unsafe your home becomes. It often happens that a woman will hit a breaking point with her husband's abuse, will bring a supportive friend with her to see me, will hire me to file her action, full steam ahead, only to change her mind shortly thereafter and tell me to dismiss her case. She stays with her abuser, seduced by his promises to change and treat her better. Seduced by his love-bombing wiles, she so wants to believe it will be different. She so wants to believe this is her fairy tale ending, her happily ever after. But it rarely is.

Those same women are inevitably back in my office filing a *second* divorce case just a few months later, only this time the abusive husband is better equipped to defend himself and has had time to get his litigation game together because he knew it was coming. The psychology of the case is always different the second go-round. At the time of the second filing, the credibility of your story can be diminished by virtue of the fact that you took the abuser back. Moreover, the parties' circumstances have often changed by the time of the second filing; evidence of abuse may not be as fresh or available as it was the first time, and older evidence is generally less probative. The abuser's counsel can argue that all those things that happened before last filing are water under the bridge now, and it's hard to refute after you've voluntarily let that crazy person back into your house and bed.

Giving your husband a litigation advantage, while significant, is the least of your worries if you let him woo you back. Much worse is when your post-reconciliation life with the abuser escalates into physical abuse. I've got hundreds of photos of women's bruised, broken, bloody body parts in my computer from cases where women reconciled with a high-conflict man. My biggest fear every time a woman returns to her abuser is that she will be physically harmed.

When an attorney or police officer or other concerned person in your life tries to protect you from further abuse, please let them, Dear One. Let them give you restraining orders and take other available measures to make you safer. If your physical safety is in jeopardy, you might also consider adding some small but mighty, $3.00 slide locks[21] to the inside of the doors of your home to keep him out long enough for you to call for help.

 These locks, with their two little screws, require someone to break down your entire door to get to you. I recommend them to all clients whose husbands have been violent before. It could be what saves your life or the life of your child!

21   https://www.amazon.com/National-Hardware-N183-608-V808-Brass/dp/
B000LNMUW2/ref=asc_df_B000LNMUW2/?tag=hyprod-20&linkCode=df0&
hvadid=168556243666&hvpos=&hvnetw=g&hvrand=16375509438281499171&
hvpone=&hvptwo=&hvqmt=&hvdev=c&hvdvcmdl=&hvlocint=&hvlocphy=
9011409&hvtargid=pla-304992868799&psc=1

Abuse is Generational. Be a Cycle Breaker!

Abuse cycles are often generational. A grandparent models abuse in the home, their children think it's normal, so they mistreat their own spouses and children, and then those children continue abusing their families. You don't want your little boy or girl growing up to be an abuser or—worse—the victim of domestic abuse because you set an example that living that way is normal. How will you feel if your grandchildren are abused because you allowed abuse in your home? Or if your son or daughter ends up in a divorce because abuse was normalized during their childhood? Do your best to break the cycle when it's within your power to do so.

The first step will be the hardest, Dear One. Take it and then just keep walking.

Questions for Reflection

1. Have you been caught in a cycle of abuse in your marriage? How did your husband love-bomb you after being abusive? What percentage of your marriage was good, and what percentage of the time was he abusive? Do you see a pattern? Do you think you're trauma bonded to him?

2. Are you a person who fights, flees or freezes in times of conflict? What is unhealthy about the way you typically respond, and what do you do well when managing times of discord? What can you do to keep yourself calm during times of abuse so that you don't retaliate or make poor choices that could be used against you?

3. How has your husband isolated, threatened, intimidated or physically abused you as a way of controlling you and keeping you with him? How did it start? Did you challenge

him, or let him isolate you from others? Why did you handle it the way you did? What could you have done differently? What can/will you do about it now?

4. How has your husband manipulated you to keep you under his control?

5. Read and reflect on Isaiah 61-62. When God offers freedom and a better way of living, we can sometimes refuse His help and choose our own way because we are afraid. If you're praying for a breakthrough in your abusive marriage, I encourage you to consider these passages. Is God answering your prayers for relief with a way out, and you're just refusing His help for whatever reason? Consider also God's promises to rescue and honor you found in Psalm 81:7 and Psalm 91:15. Do you trust Him to do it? Do you believe His promises?

Resources

Generations Deep: Unmasking Inherited Dysfunction and Trauma to Rewrite Our Stories Through Faith and Therapy—Gina Birkemeier (www.generationsdeep.com)

Domestic Violence Hotline: 1-800-799-7233

The Emotionally Destructive Marriage: How to Find Your Voice and Reclaim Your Hope—Leslie Vernick

Danish Bashir, Narcissistic Abuse Expert— @narcabusecoach on Instagram

Lisa A. Ramano, Breakthrough Life Coach— @lisaaromano on Instagram

American Murder: The Family Next Door (Netflix, 2020)

A Journey through Emotional Abuse: From Bondage to Freedom—Caroline Abbott

Why Can't I Just Leave: A Guide to Waking Up and Walking Out of a Pathological Love Relationship—Dr. Kirsten Milstead

Something Broken, Something Beautiful—R.M. Drake

Something's Not Right: Decoding the Hidden Tactics of Abuse— and Freeing Yourself from Its Power—Wade Mullen (2020)

Out of the Fog: Moving from Confusion to Clarity After Narcissistic Abuse (audiobook)—Dana Morningstar

Chapter Soundtrack

"Wasting Time"—Collective Soul

Ghost"—Indigo Girls

"Two Dozen Roses"—Shenandoah

"I Will Survive"—Gloria Gaynor

"We Are Never Getting Back Together"—Taylor Swift

"Hit The Road, Jack"—Ray Charles

"Just Like a Pill"—Pink

Counter Parenting • Legal Abuse • Stalking & Harassment • Isolation • Smear Campaign • Financial Abuse • Coercive Control • Spiritual Abuse

POST SEPARATION ABUSE

@lawyerbree

@lawyerbree
@crushyourdivorce

2

What is Post-Separation Abuse?

When people think of domestic violence and abuse in relationships, the first thought is of physical abuse—the kind that leaves scars, bruises, broken bones and other bodily injuries. But I've come to realize over my decades in law practice that the worst wounds people receive in their intimate relationships are the emotional ones, the ones that often don't heal quickly. The ones that aren't as visible or obvious to other people.

The National Domestic Abuse Hotline more broadly defines "abuse" as:

> *a pattern of behavior in any relationship that is used to gain or maintain power and control over an intimate partner. Abuse is physical, sexual, emotional, economic or psychological actions or threats of actions that*

influence another person. This includes any behaviors that frighten, intimidate, terrorize, manipulate, hurt, humiliate, blame, injure, or wound someone. Domestic abuse can happen to anyone of any race, age, sexual orientation, religion, or gender. It can occur within a range of relationships including couples who are married, living together or dating."[22]

An abusive husband often uses things like coercive control, isolation, mental and verbal abuse to keep the abuse victim trapped in the marriage. And eventually these forms of abuse escalate to include physical violence, as well.

Abused women often think, "If only I can get away from my abusive husband, I'll have peace." They think the separation itself will stop the abuse. But it's usually not that easy.

While separating from an abuser is a pivotal first step in improving your life, you shouldn't be surprised if his mistreatment, manipulation, mind games, stalking, and other efforts to control you persist after you've left him.

Abusers often have untreated (and often undiagnosed) mental health challenges. Labeling everyone who misbehaves a "narcissist" is now en vogue, but I'm not a mental health professional, and I'm not qualified to assign clinical labels. In the end, the labels and diagnoses don't matter as long as you know how to deal with high-conflict behaviors. In this section, I'll call those exhibiting abusive behaviors "high conflict" and leave the diagnosing to the professionals. A high-conflict husband will often ramp up his tactics even more once you've had the courage to leave him, for he's losing control over you, he knows it, and he will pull out all the stops to punish you and deter

---

22   https://www.un.org/en/coronavirus/what-is-domestic-abuse.

you from staying the course. I deal with this with clients every week in my practice.

We will explore various forms of Post-Separation Abuse in this chapter. I prepared the Post-Separation Abuse Wheel above to guide our discussion. The goal of this section of the book is to help you:

1. identify Post-Separation Abuse as such;

2. learn techniques for becoming emotionally indifferent to the abuser's attacks, for your finally learning not to care what he thinks or says is the only thing that will finally strip the abuser of his power over you; and

3. gain strategies for standing your ground, holding fast to your convictions, protecting your children, and responding with grace and class when post-separation abuse rears its ugly head.

Resources

Runaway Husbands—Vikki Stark
The Covert Passive-Aggressive Narcissist—Debbie Mirza

Section Soundtrack

"Luka"—Suzanne Vega
"A Broken Wing"—Martina McBride
"Because of You"—Kelly Clarkson
"Big Girls Don't Cry"—Fergie

3

Understanding Financial Abuse

I can live without money, but I cannot live without love.
—Judy Garland

What is Financial Abuse?

Financial abuse is when one partner in a relationship uses financial resources to control the other partner. The financial abuser restricts the victim's ability to access, use, and save financial resources, all as a way of controlling the victim's ability to leave the relationship or have a voice in how decisions are made in the household. When one partner controls the financial resources, he controls the whole relationship.

Molly's Story

Meeting Shane felt like a fantasy. It was a whirlwind romance right from the start! He blew me away with all his romantic gestures . . . the roses delivered to my office, the fancy dinners, the fabulous trips to exotic locations . . . it was intoxicating and so much fun. He was everything I'd seen in the movies all my life. He was handsome and charming, confident and smart. Sweet and attentive, he seemed to have genuine interest in making me happy. He made me feel beautiful and special. In no time at all, I was totally head over heels in love with him.

The day we returned from our tropical honeymoon, Shane insisted that I sign over my paychecks to him each week so that he could take care of all the bills. Thinking what a nice load off my plate that would be, I gladly began signing over my paychecks to him, and he would put the funds in a bank account in his name only to which I had no access, and to which I didn't think I needed access. I would charge anything I needed on a credit card he gave me, but I was just an authorized user on that card account and not an accountholder. The other credit cards I'd used before the wedding were closed, for Shane didn't think I needed them anymore.

Shane began making comments about my weight and appearance almost immediately after we were married. He would complain if I ate dessert, saying it "would go straight to my hips," and he would ridicule me in front of our friends if I misspoke, broke something, or didn't perform perfectly in social settings. I got appetite suppressants and promptly became anorexic. I stopped being so outgoing for fear of humiliation. My confidence level waned.

He would compare me to other women on television, and even sometimes to my friends, saying I should be working out more to be thin like Madelyn, or get on the same skin care regimen as Lisa, for she had such beautiful complexion. It became obvious that Shane was looking at my friends and comparing me to them. In his most honest, drunken moments, he would even speak of the sexual things he'd like to do with my friends, as if I were his fraternity brother or something.

The whirlwind romance was over, but I convinced myself that this is what everyone went through early in marriage, that this is what people meant when they said, "marriage is hard." I was horrified over the possibility of ever being divorced and didn't feel I had any real reason to leave him. After all, he hadn't cheated on me, and he didn't beat me. Surely he was just joking around and didn't mean the hurtful things he said. Surely it was just the bourbon talking.

About six months into the marriage, Shane said his business was going so well that we didn't need my income anymore, and that he'd really like me to be at home to take care of the house, meals and laundry. I was a successful medical sales rep at the time, and I loved my work, but it was a stressful job, and I could see how joining a daytime tennis team and a book club could be a nice change of pace, so I agreed to quit my job as Shane requested. Shane didn't like me being around all those male physicians all the time, and I'd never been one to rock the boat, so I called my boss and resigned my position.

About three weeks after I quit my job, my credit card—my only credit card—was declined at the mall. Embarrassed, I returned the items to their shelves and quietly left the store. When I got home, I told Shane about the card being declined, and he explained quite flippantly, "Oh...that must be because you tried to charge over your limit." I was incredulous as I choked out the words, "My limit? What do you mean, my limit?'" He then explained that the card I was using for all my expenditures had a daily cap on the amount I could spend, and that he got a notification on his phone each time I used the card.

What in the actual . . . WHAT?! Was this guy for real? It was a Twilight Zone moment.

But I told myself I shouldn't complain because it was good to follow a budget, and all my needs were met, so there was nothing to worry about. I could spend less and still be happy. It was good to be disciplined, and I needed to be a better steward of our money in obedience to the Lord anyway.

Anytime I got birthday money from my parents, I would keep it a secret from Shane so that I could use it to buy myself clothes or something else I wanted. If I dared buy something without his permission, I would race to throw the shopping bags into the back of my closet before he got home, and I would wait to wear new things for a few months so that when he asked where it came from, I could honestly say I'd had it a while. But if Shane wanted a new TV or golf clubs, he went and bought them, and I didn't dare raise any objection since he was the one making the money.

Shane chose a home for us shortly after our first anniversary. Shane handled the closing without me, surprised me with keys one afternoon, and we moved in the following weekend. The house was nice but not at all what I would have chosen. I was hurt that Shane didn't even ask me what kind of house I would like. But I was also thankful to have a place to live, so I didn't complain.

He always gave himself the best and gave me the leftovers. When I needed a new vehicle, he gave me his hand-me-down SUV and bought himself a new one. I always used old cell phones when he traded up to the newer model; I never got the new one. He would spend to bless himself, but never to bless me. Again, I didn't complain, for I had a car and a cell phone. All my needs were met, even if I clearly wasn't my husband's top priority.

When our first child was born, Shane refused to pay my obstetrician what was owed for the delivery. As a result, that doctor wouldn't see me when I became pregnant for the second time shortly after the first child was born. I had to find a new doctor to take me as a new patient. Shane wouldn't pay that doctor, either. Both doctors' offices put my bills in collections, and my credit score took a nosedive, as both bills were in my name only because I was the patient.

I incorrectly assumed Shane was also keeping to a strict budget. It wasn't until my divorce lawyer got his credit card and bank statements that I realized how Shane was spending on lavish meals (with other women he knew from work), gifts (for the same women) and hotel rooms (*you guessed it*) *while I was pinching pennies at the grocery store. He had been cheating on me for years. He had deliberately convinced me to stop earning my own money, to give up my financial independence, to become reliant on him.*

I never saw or signed a tax return during our marriage. I never knew Shane's income. All his bank statements, credit card statements and financial account information came to his office address. We only got thank-you notes, catalogs and junk mail at home. I was completely in the dark on our finances and living expenses.

When the kids were little, I busied myself with their playgroups, school and extracurricular activities. I bonded with other moms like me, never talking about what I was going through at home. I considered myself happy at the time, thinking it was everyone's dream to be a stay-at-home mom, and that I was so very lucky to be able to be home with my kids all the time.

But when it came to light that Shane had been living a double life, actively engaged in an affair with his secretary that had been going on for years, I felt an utter terror unlike anything I'd ever faced before. How would I leave this marriage? How would I afford basic necessities? How would I support the children? And I had all these financial matters to consider while also trying to sort out the despair I was feeling over Shane's infidelity. Part of me just wanted to die, but I knew I had to persevere for my little ones.

But a dear friend gave me the money I needed to hire a great attorney. I called my old boss, and she connected me with an industry associate who happened to be hiring, and I got an entry level job to support myself and the children. That job has led to two promotions since then, and I'm earning a nice income now. The court awarded me use of the home and custody of the children, which also required Shane to pay child support to me each month. I set up a bank account for the first time in years and made a budget. My divorce was very painful and tumultuous because Shane fought to avoid paying me anything, but the judge saw through his schemes and awarded me a fair division of assets, alimony and child support. The best part was being able to breathe again and regain my confidence when it was over.

Getting away from Shane's control was the best thing I ever did. It's nice to make financial choices for myself again, and I'm happier today than I've ever been.

Women often abuse men in this way, as well, and I do not mean to assert that men are always the perpetrators. Because this book is for women, I'm focusing on how men abuse women but in no way mean or allege that any form of abuse is one-sided or gender exclusive. Time and again, I've observed men financially abusing their wives in the following ways:

- Wife is prohibited from working outside the home for compensation.
- Wife is given an allowance like a child, even being reduced to the humiliation of having to ask for money for things like feminine hygiene products. The abusive Husband revels in being begged for money.
- Wife's spending is controlled and restricted. She's required to account for every penny she spends, while Husband can spend as he pleases.
- Wife is prohibited from having a separate bank account or any savings of her own.
- Any funds Wife receives from family or any other source is immediately confiscated or controlled by the financially

abusive Husband. Husband feels entitled to the Wife's inheritance and gifts from others.

- Wife is not allowed to build her credit or own any asset in her name.

- If Wife *is* allowed to have household accounts or debts in her name, the abuser orchestrates the demise of her credit score by maxing out the credit cards in her name and then not paying it.

- Husband creates debt by forging Wife's name to loan obligations without her knowledge.

- The woman is financially punished (put on "spending restriction," as one client put it) for perceived bad behavior or, conversely, rewarded with treats or temporary spending power for behaviors pleasing to the abuser.

- Husband controls and manages the finances, and the Wife is not permitted to see bank statements or pay bills for the household. The Husband in this scenario will often have all household mail sent to his office or post office box to keep the Wife in the dark.

- Wife is not allowed to pursue educational or training opportunities that would make her more employable.

- If Wife starts working outside the home, Husband pressures her to quit, refuses to help with the children so she can work, or may intentionally sabotage her ability to work by disabling her vehicle or hiding/breaking the equipment she needs for the job.

- Husband harasses Wife at work with disruptive texts, impromptu appearances at the place of employment, or incessant phone calls.

- Husband constantly threatens to cut Wife off financially anytime she disagrees with him.
- Husband makes big purchases without Wife's input or knowledge.
- Husband uses the children's savings without Wife's agreement or knowledge, thereby reducing the family's wherewithal for supporting the children through college.
- Husband becomes physically abusive in anger over Wife's spending choices.

These may seem like extreme cases, but I see some form of the items listed above in many of the cases I handle. You would be amazed how many women are suffering in silence.

Financial abuse is the most powerful form of domestic abuse because it keeps the victim trapped in other forms of abuse. Even if she's brave enough to leave, the financially abused wife will often return to the abuser when she finds she can't support herself and her children on her own.

Financial Abuse Before Separation

During initial divorce consultations with prospective clients, I go all-in—I ask pertinent conduct and financial questions to get the lay of the land so that, if hired, I can jump right into the case and start drafting court documents immediately. As I work through the pages of my questionnaire, it's amazing to see how little some people know about their own financial picture. They've trusted their spouses to manage the income and investments and pay all the bills each month. Some women think that's just what marriage is supposed to be, that the man should be in charge of the money and the bills.

I would estimate that about fifty percent of my clients allow their spouses to handle all the family finances. This is unwise even if you never get divorced because the death or mental disability of your spouse would leave you lost in the wilderness as to how to manage day-to-day affairs. But it's especially unwise when one is faced with divorce.

Quite often, one party's handling of all the financial matters of a household starts as a service to the other party. Intending to take on the stress of the role, one spouse handles it all with no ill intent whatsoever. But in other cases, control over the household financial management is a means of abusing the other party by limiting that party's access to funds, by design. People who don't understand their financial situation are almost always more hesitant to leave their spouse, even while suffering abuse, because they are afraid (a) that they can't make it without that spouse handling day-to-day household financial management tasks or (b) that they won't be able to access the funds necessary to leave.

Financial abuse takes many forms and is a factor in nearly ninety-nine percent of domestic abuse cases in the United States.[23] You read that right. Ninety-nine percent. In one Swedish survey, married women were asked, "If you weren't financially dependent on your husband, would you stay married?" Thirty-seven percent of them said no! That's a lot of unhappy women out there feeling stuck. Based on the cases I see, I would submit the percentage is even higher in the United States.

---

23 https://centerforfinancialsecurity.files.wordpress.com/2015/04/adams2011.pdf [University of Wisconsin @ Madison study—2015].

According to data published by the Pennsylvania Coalition Against Domestic Violence (PCADV) in 2022:[24]

- ❖ Seventy-eight percent of Americans don't recognize financial abuse as domestic violence.
- ❖ Fifty-three percent of financial abuse victims have lost a job due to an abuser.
- ❖ Seventy percent of financial abuse victims were not able to have a job.
- ❖ Fifty-nine percent of financial abuse victims' credit was harmed by their abuser.

A 2016 Avvo study[25] of American women similarly found that seventy-five percent of women said they'd rather be alone, successful and happy than unhappy in a relationship.

The abusive husband orchestrates a self-perpetuating cycle. By restricting Wife's access to financial resources and credit she needs to secure necessities for independent survival, the abusive husband knows his wife will be less likely to leave him, no matter how awful he is to her, even if he is physically violent. It's a terrible quagmire. While she is increasingly vulnerable to continued violence the longer she stays, she has no choice but to stay if there are no resources available to fund her exit, or to obtain safe and affordable housing, food, clothing, transportation and other necessities for her children. With inconsistent employment history or a long lapse in time since

---

24   https://www.pcadv.org/financial-abuse/

25   https://stories.avvo.com/media-resources/press-releases/women-failing-marriages-less-likely-regret-divorce-yet-likely-place-blame-spouse-avvo-study-finds

her last employment, the abused woman is unattractive to employers and unable to support herself and the children, post-separation. The fear of financial instability keeps countless abused women stuck in unhealthy homes. The abusive husband's whole aim is to demoralize his wife, make her feel worthless apart from him, thereby making her more likely to stay.

What to Do If You're Contemplating Separation But Haven't Left Yet

Abuse or not abuse, anyone planning to leave a marriage is wise to consider the financial picture and make certain preparations before leaving. If time allows and your physical safety is not in jeopardy before separation, consider doing the following:

1. **Squirrel Some Money Away**. You need to start trying to save every nickel you can as you prepare to depart. Borrow from family members if you can. Get a part-time job (if you can do so without being beaten and without exposing the children to danger) and open a separate bank account, ideally in a new bank neither you nor your husband or his family has ever used, for your earnings.

2. **Run a Credit Report**. Visit Equifax, TransUnion or Experian online and run a credit report on yourself to ascertain all the debts in your name. You need to know all the debts in your name in order to prepare to divide them in your divorce litigation. Your credit information is your private information, and you're entitled to see it. I've never known a client whose online request for a credit report resulted in the credit reporting agency alerting the husband to the request, but online platforms and search criteria are ever

changing. Therefore, you should be very careful when you request your report to confirm that your husband's identifying information is not included in the request and that he will not receive any kind of notice that you're gathering this information for yourself.

Your lawyer will need a list of the debts you need your husband to pay, and if he's committed fraud, forged your name on loan documents, or otherwise stolen your identity, your attorney needs that information so that he can be held accountable for it. While you're at it, go ahead and run credit reports on your children, as I've also seen abusive parents open credit accounts and max out credit cards in the names of their children! You have to know how bad it is in order to fix it, so get that report right away, and start addressing issues one at a time.

3. **Gather Your Tax Returns**. Joint income tax returns are often e-filed by the abusive husband without the wife's authentic signature or approval. The good news is that if your name is on a tax return, you are entitled to a copy of that return (and all the financial information it includes), even if your signature was forged. Ask your lawyer how to go about ordering copies of all tax returns if you don't have possession of them or if you're afraid asking the CPA will alert your husband to your plan to divorce him. If you don't have legal counsel or if you plan to represent yourself (usually bad idea, but I digress) you can call 1-800-908-994626

---

26   This is the phone number to call as of the date of this writing. Check online to confirm the number hasn't changed before calling.

or send in a request by mail to request the returns using IRS Form 4506. Tax returns are treasure troves of financial information, especially in cases where there is a family business or complicated investments.

4. **Make Copies and Secure Your Valuables.** When preparing to separate from your abuser, it's important to make copies of all financial documents you can get your hands on, just in case they disappear later. Make copies, scan and save credit card statements, bank statements, tax returns, life insurance policy information, retirement and stock brokerage account statements, annuity statements, appraisals, loan statements, deeds, vehicle titles and purchase documents, documents received at real estate closings, business documents and any contracts signed by you or your husband If copies of the documents do not lie in your possession, consider requesting them from courthouse personnel, mortgage companies, stock brokerage companies, retirement plan administrators, life insurance agents, and other third party custodians if you can do so without raising suspicion or alerting your husband to your plans. Email copies of these documents to your mama, your lawyer, and your best friend to ensure they are preserved. Get a safe deposit box and put all your most special jewelry and other irreplaceable belongings in it. All of these items could be hard to recover after your separation.

5. **Get to Safety.** First and foremost, you must establish physical safety for yourself and your children When news of your decision to separate reaches your husband, he may lash out physically, so you will need to be someplace he cannot get to you or have a judge's order in place keeping him from coming

to your location in a rage. You are most certainly more likely to suffer physical abuse upon separating if your husband has ever manhandled, choked, hit, struck, pushed, or otherwise laid hands on you before, or if he has threatened you with physical violence in the past. If you are not physically safe in your home or know that you won't be safe once the separation/divorce cat is out of the bag, you must get to a safe location or make a plan for where you will be when your husband learns of your decision. Your lawyer can help you petition the Court for an order of physical protection in your jurisdiction. Leaving an abusive husband can be life-threatening, and while sometimes abused women are forced to flee in pajamas with only their children, it's best to have a thoughtful plan before you leave, if time allows. Check for a shelter for victims of domestic abuse in your area and ask their trained professionals for counsel on how best to make your escape. They may even have a temporary housing option for you and other resources you'll need to survive on an interim basis.

Post-Separation Financial Abuse

Getting away from an abuser is only half the battle, as the abuse is almost certain to continue—albeit in new forms—after you are separated as the abusive husband continues to do everything he can either (a) to make you feel like you can't make it without him so you'll come running back and he will "win," or (b) to punish you for exposing his abuse, embarrassing him and making him look bad as you thrive apart from him. This abuse takes many forms. Here are a few examples so you'll be able to identify and overcome it if/when it happens to you:

1. **He refuses to get the kids.** In an effort to coparent cooperatively, you establish a parenting time schedule and do your best to follow it. He, however, does not. Instead of getting the kids during his allotted time, an abusive husband will opt out of visitation with the kids so that you won't have the childcare you need in order to work and earn an income. He'd rather see you struggle than enjoy time with the children because he hates you more than he loves them, wants to punish you more than he wants to parent them.

2. **He hides money.** We'll get into this more in later chapters, but abusive men are notorious for concealing their wealth during divorce proceedings so that you can't claim your part of it. They just don't think the rules apply to them. If your husband isn't transparent with the finances or if he's disposing of property or shuttling assets to his friends or family members for hiding, a good lawyer will be necessary to force his compliance.

3. **He won't pay child support.** Until there's a court order, many financial abusers will refuse to give their wives any funds for the support of the children, let alone funds for her own support. Some guys still refuse to pay child support or alimony even after a court order is in place, and if they do pay, they wait until nearly a full month after the due date to pay, just in time to avoid an enforcement filing to compel their cooperation but placing the woman in extreme hardship in the meantime. Any father who purposely puts the mother of his children in financial distress is abusing not only the mother but also the children. It's despicable.

4. **He pays the debts in his name, but not the debts in your name**. Financial abusers often endeavor to put you under further financial duress by not paying the bills in your name while keeping their own debts current. It's just another part of the scheme to make it hard for you to find financial independence away from him.

5. **He abuses the legal system**. Another thing abusers do is try to drain your resources by raising silly issues with the judge to keep you in court, thus creating legal expenses he knows you can't easily afford. Sometimes an abusive husband will seek custody of children based on the housing and other financial instability the husband has created on purpose, arguing to the court that you cannot support the children's needs. Many of the men who do this are simply trying to (a) hurt and punish you, and/or (b) get out of paying child support. Rarely do they have any real interest in parenting. More on legal abuse later in the next chapter.

How to Plan Your Exit

Don't let financial abuse defeat you; let it FUEL you toward independence! It's much easier to leave an abusive husband if you have a way to support yourself. If you can make yourself employable, you're much more likely to thrive in your post-separation life. It may take a little time, so the sooner you can get to work on the steps necessary to establish financial independence, the better off you'll be. Here are some practical things to begin thinking about:

1. **Update Your Education**. It's never too late to go back to school! Federal grants and loan programs are available to

women with limited resources who are wishing to pursue or complete their higher education. Start researching degree programs available to you online and in your local area. What are you good at? What kind of work would you enjoy? What kind of education or degree do you need in order to have the job you'd love to have?

2. **Train on the Job for a New Career**. Find someone who's doing what you love to do and offer to work for them to learn what they know. Update your resume and get it out there to potential employers for consideration. Check to see if there are government or technical college training programs near you in your preferred field.

3. **Start a Side Hustle**. Are you artistic or a maker of beautiful things? Be thinking about a way to parlay your creative talents into a business!

4. **Become an Entrepreneur**. Do you have a business idea? Dropship boutiques and online stores are a great way to make money in the online space right from your home. The Small Business Administration also has programs for women entrepreneurs. Check to see if there's an SBA Women's Business Center in your area.

Questions for Reflection

1. Are you financially dependent on your husband? How did you become dependent? How can you articulate and prove this reality in court?

2. How has your husband prohibited you from working outside the home? How has he restricted your access to money, credit and other financial resources?

3. What are you naturally good at doing? How can you parlay this gift into a way to make money?

4. Do you have a safety plan or a plan for escaping the home should your ex become physically violent? Have you told anyone of the kinds of abuse you're enduring in the home? What are the resources available to abused women in your area? How can you access and utilize these services to get yourself to a better, healthier place?

5. What financial support do you need from your ex to ensure your and your children's survival while you get back on your feet, post-separation and post-divorce? Have you started working on a list of requests for the judge? Have you spoken with your attorney about how best to present your claims in court?

Resources

U.S. Domestic Violence Hotline—800-799-7233
(www.thehotline.org)
www.WomensLaw.org—legal information and
protection resources, sorted by state
The U.S. Small Business Administration—Women's Business
Centers—https://www.sba.gov/local-assistance/resource-partners/
womens-business-centers
FreeCreditReport.com—check your credit exposure and score
Custody Peace—resources and education on all forms of coercive
control / financial abuse / impact of abuse on child custody
litigation https://www.custody-peace.org/
www.studentaid.gov (Federal Student Aid—
information on educational funding options)

Chapter Soundtrack

"You Don't Own Me"—Lesley Gore

"Respect"—Aretha Franklin

"Just a Girl"—No Doubt

"You're So Vain"—Carly Simon

4

Objection! Legal Abuse and How to Handle It

You never really know a man until you divorce him.
—Zsa Zsa Gabor

Before We Dive In, a Word of Encouragement

The warnings of this chapter are to prepare you for a worst-case scenario in which your ex manipulates and uses the legal system to do you harm and cause you extra pain and frustration. Legal abuse does not take place in every case, but it does take place often enough in the cases I see that it's worth the space I've given it in this book. I see women all the time who deal with this form of abuse and are totally unprepared when it happens to them. That's the thing about manipulators...they're able to lull you into a false sense of security, only to attack when you least expect it and are least equipped to mount a counterattack. They use your kindness against you. They perceive your trust as weakness.

You may be shocked and disturbed as you read this chapter's stories of the ways a legal abuser abuses our legal system and could use it to abuse you, but let not your heart be troubled, Dear One. Knowledge is power. The more you understand about legal abuse, the more likely you are to have a good plan for how you and your lawyer will deal with it, well in advance, should it happen.

What is Legal Abuse?

Legal abuse is a tactic whereby one party uses the legal system to harass, coerce, intimidate, and exhaust the financial and emotional resources of the other party. To the legal abuser, your divorce is a zero-sum game. In his mind, there can only be one winner and one loser. You are his *possession*, and losing you is a big loss, and losses of any kind are unacceptable to a person like him. This is the heart of why he could make it so hard to finalize your divorce case. A controlling, abusive husband generally wants it to be super hard for you to make your official exit.

Divorce cases can be, and often are, settled by the parties without aggression or turmoil. Rational, well-adjusted adults can negotiate reasonably and treat one another with fairness as they reach a final settlement of their marital issues. They part company gracefully and peacefully. If only every case could go that way!

As with all other forms of domestic abuse, legal abuse happens because one party is emotionally or mentally unwell. An angry or hurting person will misuse court proceedings and litigation procedures as weapons to control, harass, intimidate, coerce you into giving them what they want or behaving in a certain way.

I. **They'll Tell You Not to Get a Lawyer.** The first thing an abusive ex or soon-to-be ex will do is try to convince you not to get a lawyer to represent you. They'll suggest you "use one lawyer" (impossible, as every lawyer can only represent one party, and that party would be *him*, not you, in this scenario) or that you just sign the papers he has his lawyer prepare for you. "Just trust me," they'll say. Dear Friend, <u>do not trust him</u>. You are now his adversary. The divorce case will be officially styled "You versus Him." "Plaintiff versus Defendant." Get your own lawyer.

2. **He'll Expand the Legal Proceedings Unnecessarily**.
    Once a divorce case is underway, legal abusers will often
    file multiple, frivolous motions with the court, seeking
    extraordinary and unreasonable awards from the court
    that would not be in your family's best interest. They will
    argue you have violated a court order in some way, which
    requires you to incur the legal expenses and emotional
    energy to respond by the court-imposed deadline or even
    prepare for a hearing to defend yourself, to prove a nega-
    tive—that you did *not* do what is being alleged. They will
    also abuse the discovery process, asking you to produce
    documents and items they already have in their possession
    and making you answer irrelevant questions in deposition,
    among other things.

3. **He'll Seek Sole Custody of the Children**. There is no lit-
    igation more costly than a child custody battle. The legal
    abuser will often seek custody of children even when they've
    never been all that interested in or involved with the chil-
    dren before, just to hurt you as deeply as possible, just to
    keep you incurring legal costs you can't afford, and just to
    gain power over you in the litigation.

4. **He'll Make Mountains Out of Molehills**. He will call his
    lawyer to tattle about every little thing that puts a silly little
    bee in his bonnet, things we in the South refer to as "yaah-
    yaah" (soft "a" sound) that don't amount to a hill of beans
    when you really get down to it. Legal abusers know what
    they're doing in driving up your legal costs with such non-
    sense, and a whole lot of it must happen before the court
    will see it as the legal abuse that it truly is.

5. **He'll Violate Court Orders and Do Whatever He Wants**. The legal abuser thinks he's special and that the rules don't apply to him. He doesn't respect judges or the legal system generally and will intentionally thumb his nose at court orders and refuse to follow them.

6. **He'll Make False Reports**. As part of the larger false narrative he's creating for the community, prepare for him to make false reports to law enforcement personnel, child protective service workers, your employers, your children's teachers and medical providers, and therapists just to create new issues you must address, often at great financial and emotional cost to you. He will threaten you with baseless legal action to scare you into submission or make you less likely to voice your own concerns in a legal forum.

7. **He Won't Negotiate in Good Faith**. Rather than engage in good faith settlement negotiations, the legal abuser will make you believe he can be reasonable, only to refuse every term you offer or continually change the terms instead of letting the litigation (and its costs) end. Legal abusers know how to frustrate settlement efforts; they either refuse to negotiate by not responding or saying, "I'll see you in court," or they waste your time with false promises they never make official, just to preserve the tie between you, just to keep you in the conversation with them. The legal abuser will often play the victim, telling people "I don't want this divorce. I want counseling and reconciliation. She's the one pushing for divorce," as an excuse for refusing to cooperate in discovery or engage in meaningful settlement discussions. Legal abusers drag out divorce cases for as long as the court

will allow, often because they know they'll have to ante up and give you some money in the final resolution.

Sometimes the legal abuser will drag them out indefinitely just to have a reason to talk to you, even if it's only through legal counsel, as he is addicted to having your attention and energy, and he wants it even more now that you've walked away. This is just another means of control, another way of keeping you trapped, all at your expense.

Legal abusers love litigation. It's like mud-wrestling a pig; soon into the contest, you realize the pig is enjoying the dirtiness of it all, while all you want is to get out of the muck and take a shower.

How Abusers Reverse Your Roles to Confuse the Court

The abuser is driven by two primary desires: (1) to win and (2) to preserve his reputation. In order to do so, he makes every effort to silence the victim and assume the victim's role so that others in society and in the courts will believe him and sympathize with him.

Legal abusers are masterful at reversing the victim/aggressor roles when their tactics are exposed, and this intentional reversal of the narrative in an effort to confuse the court has come to be known as "DARVO" in legal circles.

DARVO:

<u>D</u>eny the behavior. When his bad behavior is exposed, the abusive ex will summarily deny the allegation.

<u>A</u>ttack the person raising the issue. Along with denying and dismissing the allegation as untrue and ridiculous, the abuser will go on offense against anyone brave enough to expose the truth about him. The abuser will launch personal attacks

and make up whatever false narrative about the speaker fits the abuser's purposes.

Reverse roles of <u>V</u>ictim and <u>O</u>ffender. Denying and dismissing the allegations and turning the story around on the accuser with false allegations of the accuser's wrongdoing lead to a reversal of the narrative to make you the offender and him, the true abuser, seem like the victim in the situation.

DARVO is especially prevalent in the child custody battles I handle. In my experience, abusive fathers are more likely to seek sole custody of children than non-abusive fathers, as taking a woman's child from her is the worst way to break her spirit, which is often the abuser's ultimate goal. The legal abuser is typically the type who must win at all costs, and winning the children is just one part of their game. It's not about his bond with the children or a genuine desire to love and care for them. The children are just pawns in his strategy to bury and beat you in the contest. No tactic—not even hurting your children—is off limits. Nothing is sacred to a man like him. If your husband is high conflict, prepare for your children to be used to advance his cause. Most often, the legally abusive father reverses the roles of victim and offender in a custody battle by accusing the mother of parental alienation, i.e., of trying to poison the child's mind against the father. What often starts as a legitimate allegation of the father's abuse (sexual, physical, or verbal) of others in the household, reported by the mother or even by the child, results in the father playing the victim, claiming he has been unjustly accused, and arguing that the mother is perpetrating an alienation scheme. Women think they're doing the wise thing by reporting abuse to child protection authorities and others, but men in these scenarios can convince judges that the child should be placed with him, and he ends up with custody of the child. A 2022 study from Professor Joan Meier at George Washington University Law School revealed what I've seen for some time now. This study found that when a mother claims the father sexually abused the child, and the father then claims parental alienation, only *one in fifty-one* children's claims of sexual abuse are substantiated or validated/accepted as true by investigators. The study further found that when a mother is accused of alienating the child against the father, she is *twice as likely to lose custody of the child* than if she had just stayed quiet. Meier's study, which examined two thousand (2000) custody cases involving child abuse and domestic violation in the United States, also noted that when the court believes the mother is alienating the children from the father, her claims of child abuse against the father are never found to be true.[27]

Stats like these are enough to scare you to death.

Kelly's Story

After twelve years together, Kelly and Garrett's marriage was in trouble. They seemed to be having the same argument repeatedly. Garrett controlled the family finances and made Kelly ask permission anytime she wanted to buy anything other than groceries or do anything other than go to work. When Kelly would stand up for herself, tell him he wasn't being fair, and lobby for the funds she needed for the children and for the proper running of the household, Garrett would become enraged. His unloving reaction and unwillingness to share financial information and

---

27   https://wamu.org/story/19/08/19/fathers-are-favored-in-child-custody-battles-even-when-abuse-is-alleged/. According to this article, Meier's important research is expected to be published soon by the National Institute of Justice.

resources with her made Kelly feel like he loved his money more than he loved her. Kelly would start crying, and Garrett would call her ridiculous, slam doors, and destroy property in the house in anger. He hated nothing more than when Kelly challenged him like this. He had been raised with that old-school view that women were to submit to their husbands and do what they were told. Kelly's assertive streak did not sit well, so he was always looking for ways to squelch and subdue her.

Kelly loved being a schoolteacher in their small town, as her schedule was the same as the children, and she had them with her all the time. Garrett had to travel out of town overnight regularly for his sales job, so Kelly did the lion's share of the work at home. Garrett loved the kids, but he didn't spend a lot of his free time with them.

One afternoon as Kelly was working the carpool line at the school, loading the last few students into cars and onto buses, a man about her age walked up to her and asked if he could speak with her for a minute. Assuming the man was a parent of one of her students wanting to discuss some school-related matter, Kelly said she was happy to speak with him. Tears formed in his eyes as he began to tell Kelly that his wife has been cheating on him with Garrett in one of the towns Garrett covers for work. With a pit in her stomach and a shaking voice, Kelly questioned, "How can I be sure this is true?" The man then showed Kelly photos of Garrett and another woman cozied up in a restaurant corner booth, which had been taken earlier that same week by the man's private investigator. Kelly's world began to spin as she immediately recognized the location depicted in the photo—it was the restaurant in the hotel where Garrett always stayed when he was working in that town, the same hotel where she and Garrett always stayed when she went with him on work trips before the children were born. Kelly felt like she was going to vomit right there on the school sidewalk.

Kelly looked up just then and saw her kids approaching. Kelly and the man quickly exchanged contact information so more details could be shared later, outside the children's presence. In the days that followed, Kelly never let on to Garrett that she knew anything but began gathering all kinds of proof of Garrett's double life, carefully saving every bit of it to cloud-based storage. She wasn't sure yet if the marriage could be saved or not, but she knew she had to be able to prove Garrett's infidelity before she confronted him about it. She wasn't ready to give up on her marriage or file for divorce without a solid financial plan for the future, so she told no one what she knew. She ran the household and did her best to keep her interactions with Garrett as normal as possible.

In my experience with clients, the typical woman will confront her cheating husband immediately upon hearing about his affair, as it's such traumatizing news that she must naturally have an answer from him right away. They let their emotions get the best of them. But Kelly in the story did all the right things; she kept her composure, didn't go off half-cocked, and gathered evidence with a plan to expose his deception when the time was right, trying to get a post-separation financial plan together in the meantime. As you'll see as you continue reading Kelly's story, she made one crucial mistake which shifted the whole trajectory of the conflict.

A couple of weeks later, Kelly's world turned upside-down when the school principal called her over the intercom and asked her to come to the front office immediately. Kelly was greeted by a sheriff's deputy when she arrived in the office, who handed her Garrett's divorce petition. The petition was accompanied by an order giving Garrett full custody of the children and possession of the family home "until fur-

ther order of the Court." Kelly's name was removed from the children's school pick-up list, and while she was still able to see them at school, she was no longer allowed to take them home with her. She called her mother and made arrangements to move in with her, as she couldn't go back to the house. Garrett had told a judge that Kelly was crazy, showed the judge photos of the damage to their home, and claimed Kelly had been the one who had done that, not him, and that she was a danger to the children and to him. Garrett had, of course, not told the judge he had a girlfriend in another city or how he'd treated his wife like a second-class citizen for years. He didn't tell the judge of Kelly's limited access to funds or how all her paychecks were direct deposited into his separate bank account.

Kelly was more afraid than she'd ever been in her life. How could she afford a lawyer? How could Garrett have pulled this off? There was so much to show the judge to undo this mess, but how could she do it without access to her home? Would anyone believe her when she told the truth of her situation? Why was Garrett trying to destroy her? Did he plan to take the children from her so the other woman could raise them? Why would he have her served with the custody order at work, to embarrass her in front of all her colleagues and students? Kelly was so overwhelmed by it all that she just wanted to give up.

Garrett had found Kelly's evidence of his affair on their synced iCloud database. She had no idea he could see these items when she saved them there. She also had no inkling that Garrett had installed spyware on her phone that allowed him to see all her communications, including her communications with Garrett's girlfriend's husband. When Garrett discovered Kelly knew of his activities, he beat her to the lawyer's office, made up a false narrative of events, and turned the tables on her to gain advantage in the litigation from the jump.

Kelly's mother cosigned with her for a bank loan for the lawyer's retainer fee. The lawyer was amazing and presented the case masterfully. When Garrett deleted the iCloud evidence of his affair, Kelly's lawyer spent hours building the case against Garrett in other ways; he obtained the report and testimony of the private investigator and of the other woman's husband, all at great cost to Kelly, of course. Kelly's lawyer obtained records from the children's medical providers and obtained witness statements from the community to confirm Kelly's good character and great reputation as a friend, educator and parent. She had a costly psychological evaluation to disprove Garrett's allegation of mental instability. After Garrett prolonged the trial court's proceedings, appealed the ruling to a higher court with no good legal grounds, and refused to work out a fair final settlement at mediation, the court finally saw through his schemes. It just took tens of thousands of dollars in legal fees for Kelly to prevail, and she operated in a constant state of fear for over a year as new and baseless legal bombs were regularly dropped on her; she lived in constant anxiety, anticipating Garrett's next frivolous demand. She lost 15 pounds from the stress of it all.

Garrett never thought Kelly would be able to fight the legal battle in her weak financial position. She came out of her divorce in debt to relatives and credit card companies, but she was awarded primary custody of the children, her home, and a solid alimony award. The judge awarded some, but not nearly all, of her attorney's fees and litigation expenses.

Unfortunately, Kelly's story is all too common. The spouse with access to funds typically gains the early advantage in a case like this, and evil prevails over good for a while. It's easy for the abuser to play the smoke-and-mirrors game because they're used to deceiving and charming other people to get what they want. Once the abused party gets an attorney, shares her story and supports it with hard evidence of the abuser's lies, however, I generally see good prevail over evil in the end.

Anyone who's been through a divorce like Kelly's will tell you it's nothing short of excruciating. You just have to walk through some very hard stuff to get there. It's like the old saying goes ... "if you're going through hell, just keep going." If you can focus on building your case with facts and evidence and present your side clearly, you will eventually get out of hell and reach the other side. There is always hope for a brighter future after going through something like this, and you'll appreciate the good days even more after the battle is done. If this is happening to you, just keep walking, Sister. I promise it won't last forever.

The Perils of Being Labeled "High Conflict"

When courts receive motion after motion and have to engage in multiple conversations in a case, that case is often unofficially labeled "high conflict." I've seen it many times. No judge wants to sit through hearing after hearing or make multiple rulings on what are perceived to be trivial issues with the same divorcing parties, again and again and again. Cases where this kind of thing happens become hot potatoes in the legal system, with judges eventually trying to avoid being assigned to handle them.

A particular divorce action can get a bad reputation around the courthouse in a hurry.

When lots of motions are filed in a case, or if there's a lot of chaos and confusion in the case which the lawyers cannot resolve without a judge's intervention, the "high conflict" label (often unspoken) starts to attach. It's a shame when this happens, for it only takes one party being difficult to make a case "high conflict," and the legal abuse victim ends up having to prove, at great financial cost and often in the face of the abuse perpetrator's quite convincing lies, that *she* isn't the one creating the chaos. I've seen judges check out and paint with a broad brush when cases involve high levels of conflict, throwing up their hands and doing less and less to intervene, with resignation that the parties "just have to learn to get along" and that there's little the court can do to make them behave. I recently had a judge tell me the parties' situation was just "unfixable" because there was so much dysfunction, and I knew right then he wasn't interested in dealing with the parties' disagreements much longer.

As your abusive ex abuses the litigation process, the case can be increasingly minimized as a lost cause, as a squabble that can't be resolved. You don't want to frustrate your judge if it can be avoided, so my recommendation is to save up lots of issues for the same motion and hearing rather than presenting your grievances in a more piecemeal, repeated basis. Saving it all for one proceeding where you present a large volume of evidence at once is typically wiser (and is certainly cheaper) than calling multiple judicial conferences or hearings.

The court is your only hope for stopping legal abuse, and you must work within the parameters of the legal system you're given. You and your lawyer should do everything in your power to avoid being viewed as the one *causing* the conflict, so it's important to prepare your legal counsel if you believe your husband is the kind who will engage in legal abuse. In my experience, someone is more likely to manipulate legal systems if he does any of the following things:

❖ He isn't honest on his tax returns.
❖ He lies in business dealings, always trying to gain the upper hand or beat the other guy in a negotiation instead of seeking mutually beneficial terms and being willing to compromise.

- ❖ He's always trying to "game the system" and get something without paying for it.
- ❖ He has sued people frivolously (or threatened frivolous legal action) when they made him angry or didn't give him his way.
- ❖ He will lie to his mother for financial advantage. He manipulates and charms his parents, while lacking respect for them, in order to get money and financial benefits, perhaps even to the unfair exclusion of his siblings.
- ❖ He has no respect for law enforcement or anyone in a position of authority. He thinks he is smarter than they are.

Staying one step ahead of your ex, preparing for his schemes, and documenting his underhanded acts are the keys to overcoming this kind of abuse and getting you to the finish line unscathed.

How to Handle Legal Abuse

As Kelly found out, you cannot beat a legal abuser at his own game because he doesn't play fair. You must, therefore, play your own game, your own way.

Ethical humans like you come into divorce litigation ready to negotiate in good faith, with an eye toward resolving the dispute in a way that is fair to both parties. Your heart is in the right place, but your legally abusive ex does not share your ethics. You deal in altruism, while he deals in trickery and unjustly plots your demise. Justice is not the legal abuser's goal for his divorce case.

Here are some tactics for you and your lawyer to consider as you prepare to litigate with a legally abusive ex:

1. **Protect Your Privacy**. I've seen so many cases where the ex-husbands accessed my client's emails and texts with me

and saw our litigation strategies. If you don't keep your communications private, you're handing him an advantage in the litigation. Legal abusers will use any advantage they can get in the case, and you don't need to help him.

❖ Make sure you change all passwords on your email, social media and cell phone accounts, and set up two-step verification so you'll be notified via text anytime someone tries to log in.

❖ Make sure you're not logged into any such account on any of the devices in your ex's possession.

❖ Don't make the same mistake Kelly made. Un-sync your phone from the shared cloud platform and other shared digital albums and platforms. You may even need to get a new phone if your old one is inextricably tied to him.

❖ If necessary, set up a new email account dedicated only to communications with your lawyer and witnesses about your divorce, and pick a new password you've never used before, one your ex would never be able to guess.

❖ Have your phone checked for spyware.

2. **Stay Focused on Your Story**. Every divorce case has two narratives: yours and his. The ultimate aim is for the judge to believe your version of the facts rather than your high-conflict ex's version. Do not allow him or his lawyer to rattle you or question what you know to be true. Tell your story to the judge with conviction and be ready to back it up with evidence. If he makes outlandish claims, be sure to point out repeatedly that he has no proof of anything he's saying. Judges and courts deal in proof and evidence, not conjecture.

3. **Be Careful In Negotiations**. When negotiating with a high-conflict ex, we deceive ourselves in thinking the ex will reciprocate in good faith if we demonstrate genuine compromise and try to meet halfway to settle. A high-conflict husband only knows how to take. There is no giving from him in the give-and-take process, only taking. He just wants to get you in a conversation to feel your energy coming in his direction. Keep this in mind as you and your lawyer negotiate with him and be careful not to give up too much too early in the discussion. We explore this in greater detail in the next section of the book.

4. **Do Not Diagnose Him**. In trying to help others understand your struggle, you may be tempted to call him names like "narcissist" or "bipolar." You've read all about these terms online, and you are probably correct in your feeling that your husband has an undiagnosed condition like this. But in the end, the labels don't really matter; judges only care about his behavior and how it impacts you and your children. You shouldn't call your ex a narcissist in court unless you have a clinical, admissible diagnosis by a licensed mental health professional in hand. You are not qualified to throw around mental health labels, and you'll be ripped to shreds when cross-examined if you try to do so without anything objective to back it up.

5. **Don't Take the Bait**. Do not engage in arguments with this fool. He has no interest in your opinions or explanations, he doesn't want to reach consensus, and you will never change his mind. He wants you to get in the weeds and argue with him, so don't do it!

- ❖ He just wants to feed off the energy you contribute to the argument, as it makes him feel important. Silence demonstrates your indifference, and your indifference will show him he no longer has any control over you or your emotions. Your silence is the only thing that takes away an abuser's power.
- ❖ Do not respond to every single attack he launches your way.
- ❖ Do not feel compelled to argue over nonsense or try to defend yourself against ridiculous allegations.
- ❖ Choose your battles, focusing only on the allegations that, if believed, would truly impact your case, and let your lawyer do your arguing.
- ❖ When circumstances force you to respond, state your truth politely, cordially, reasonably, and—most importantly—succinctly. Keep your words few.
- ❖ Rising above the back-and-forth and refusing to participate in foolishness demonstrates to the court that <u>you</u> are the voice of reason here, while he is the one ranting nonsense.

6. **Expect Him to Lie**. Abusers will lie, and their lies are often convincing and believable, as he truly believes his own narrative. The breakdown of your marriage has to be your fault, anyone's fault but his own. They don't fight with facts or deal with evidence, just hyperbole and wild accusations. In response to this nonsense, you must be armed with facts and evidence to refute his claims. Focus your energy on gathering your proof rather than trying to convince him to see things your way.

7. **Request and Enforce a Restraining Order**. If your lawyer agrees your ex's abuse rises to a level that warrants a restraining order under the laws of your jurisdiction, go get one. Don't back down, make him come to the hearing, and enforce the order if it's granted.

8. **Erect Boundaries and Enforce Them**. It's okay and empowering to erect boundaries. If your lawyer approves, block your ex's number if his texts and calls rise to the level of harassment, and communicate only via email or coparenting applications (I like Our Family Wizard or Talking Parents) when necessary to discuss matters about the children only. Make him go through your lawyer. You'll be amazed at how your quality of life improves when you're not subjected to the attacks of a narcissist on an incessant, constant, daily basis. Use the tools available to you to build your fortress.

9. **Attend Regular Therapy Sessions**. DARVO and other legal abuse can make you question yourself and your sanity. You need mental health support to help you cope with and process the legal abuse being perpetrated against you. It's important to keep your mind and spirit calm during the storm of divorce litigation.

10. **File Protective Motions If Needed**. Check with your attorney for advice on whether your ex's abuse of legal process warrants the Court's immediate intervention. If you file such a motion, ask your attorney to seek recovery of your fees if the law of your jurisdiction permits it. Courts usually will not tolerate the unreasonable expansion of legal proceedings as a way of abusing the other party. Your lawyer will know how it works in your area.

Prepare for Post-Divorce Legal Abuse

If your Mr. Used-to-be-Wonderful is legally abusive while your divorce case is proceeding, don't expect that abuse to cease when the judge finalizes your divorce, especially if you bested your ex in the case and received a favorable ruling that makes him look bad. If your ex feels that you unmasked him or that the result of your case was unfair to him, he very well may not be able to let it go and move on. I've seen it a hundred times; losers in divorce cases remain obsessed with taking you down, destroying your reputation, and "getting back at you" or "making you pay"—using the legal system as a tool—in the months following the entry of the court's divorce decree. When the watchful eye of the judge is removed with the finalization of the case, the abuser's behavior can become worse than it was when the litigation was pending.

This post-divorce legal abuse can manifest in the following ways:

❖ He will file petitions seeking to take the children from your custody or control how you parent the children when they are in your care. New custody litigation will ensue, with great financial and emotional cost to you, just as you are trying to regroup following the divorce.

❖ He will bombard you with letters from his attorney or personal emails and texts taking issue with your parenting style, your romantic relationships, and any decision you've made for the children, threatening court action if you don't comply with his preferences on these matters, or making such poor decisions when he has the children that you have to take him back to court to correct the behavior and insulate the children. Your lawyer's work concerning these issues can be extraordinarily time-consuming and expensive.

- He will refuse to return the children at the end of his allotted parenting time, just so you'll have to call (and pay) your lawyer for assistance in making him comply.
- He will refuse to pay court-ordered financial obligations, so you'll have to pursue legal action against him. When abusers do this, they often pay what they owe you in full just before the court date so that you won't take them all the way to court, but by that time you will have already incurred substantial fees for making him comply. When this happens, it's often best to force the hearing to seek recovery of your fees; otherwise, he won't learn the lesson and will continue to make you sue him.
- He stalks you and your new love interests, creeping you out, making you fear him, and causing you to seek legal assistance, all at great cost.
- He harasses you on social media, via friends, via phone and via text. Your lawyer tries to make him stop, and that costs you money.

It's generally a good idea to keep your attorney on retainer for a while after the divorce is final, just to deal with new residual issues and to insulate you from the sorts of antics outlined above. Talk to your lawyer about how the ongoing nature of the representation must be communicated to put your ex on official notice of your lawyer's ongoing involvement. If you are represented by counsel where I practice, it's much, much harder to deprive you of your rights without involving your lawyer, and this layer of protection can be invaluable if it also applies where you live.

Questions for Reflection

1. Consider these verses in the context of legal disputes with an unreasonable opponent. How do they apply in your case?

   a. Proverbs 29:9: "When a wise man has a controversy with a foolish man, the foolish man either rages or laughs, and there is no rest."

   b. Proverbs 25:8: "Do not go out hastily to argue your case; Otherwise, what will you do in the end, when your neighbor humiliates you?"

   c. Proverbs 19:5: "A false witness will not go unpunished, and he who breathes out lies will not escape."

2. Has your husband provided false testimony about you to a judge? Do you fear that he will? How will you respond if this happens to you? Do you have evidence ready to disprove any false report he may make against you?

Resources

How to Annihilate a Narcissist: In the Family Court—Rachel Watson

https://www.1800respect.org.au/legal-abuse || 1-800-RESPECT

Legal Abuse Syndrome: 8 Steps for Avoiding the Traumatic Stress Caused by the Justice System—Dr. Karin Huffer

@RebeccaZungEsq on Instagram || www.rebeccazung.com

Chapter Soundtrack

"You're No Good"—Linda Ronstadt

"Virginia Woolf"—Indigo Girls

"Shut Up and Drive"—Chely Wright

5

Spiritual Abuse

I give them eternal life, and they shall never perish; no one will snatch them out of my hand. My Father, who has given them to me, is greater than all; no one can snatch them out of my hand. John 10:28

Why I've Included this Chapter

I've seen so many women be rejected and suffer spiritual abuse from fellow believers and church leadership when going through divorce, and I recognize the need to prepare you for this possibility and equip you with coping skills should this happen to you. In no way am I issuing a broad indictment against the Church in general, as churches can be places of great solace when someone is walking through betrayal, abuse, and divorce. I'm a proponent that hurting people should continue to worship during the storms of life and need fellowship with other believers, especially in hard times. My own church was a wonderful support to me when I went through my divorce; I would not have made it without them.

After studying human nature in my law practice for over two decades, I've come to believe that humans are wired with a need for connection with and support from other humans, and church is a great place to find that. But Sister, when humans fail to protect the vulnerable or expose the weak to further abuse at the hands of a cruel husband, while purporting to have the backing of God Almighty, something is terribly wrong.

I've included this chapter to comfort and encourage the divorcing woman for whom the Church has not been a safe haven, the sister in Christ who's been unlovingly rejected or unfairly judged by fellow believers. To let her know she's not alone, and that God loves her and will continue to pursue her heart, even as those claiming to represent Him and speak for Him have let her down. To give her the tools she needs to defend herself and hold her own should Mr. Used-to-be-Wonderful use her spiritual convictions to manipulate her.

What is Spiritual Abuse?

"Spiritual abuse is using a person's religious convictions to keep her in a toxic relationship when the offending person shows no true attempt in changing their behaviors."[28]

Spiritual abuse manifests as:

- ❖ using the Bible to shame a Christian woman for leaving an abusive husband.
- ❖ condemning a woman as a heretic or calling her a lesser Christian for getting out of an abusive marriage.
- ❖ calling her an adulteress or telling her she's lost her salvation because she's not staying with an abusive or adulterous husband.
- ❖ telling her she's not enough for God to love her anymore, that she is unfit to worship or serve in her church because of the state of her marriage.
- ❖ shunning a woman and excommunicating her from church circles and service because of her relationship decisions.
- ❖ condemning a woman for getting clinical help from secular (but credentialed and licensed) mental health professionals

---

28 Shannon Thomas, www.southlakecounseling.org

or telling her it's a sin to take prescription drugs for mental health, telling her that she should be satisfied with Christian counseling services only.

❖ manipulating a wife by using her faith and false Biblical interpretations as tools to keep her trapped in abuse instead of leaving his sorry self.

After looking into the eyes of so many hurting women who've been unfairly judged by their fellow believers to the point that they no longer felt welcome in church and having studied the teachings of Jesus since my childhood, I just cannot believe my Jesus—*our* Jesus— condones any form of spiritual abuse.

In some faith circles, it's always going to upset the apple cart whenever a woman stands up for herself and doesn't "stay in her place." You must do it anyway, Dear Friend. Jesus never intended for you to be abused.

Consider the New Testament interactions of Jesus and the Pharisees. Jesus called out the Pharisees for using religion to control the masses and enrich themselves. That's why the Pharisees hated him and pushed for him to be crucified. He challenged their power structure, and he, therefore, had to be squelched. People have been using religion to control people for centuries. Wars have been fought, revolutions have happened, and much blood has been shed over challenges to this kind of power.

Even today, in many American churches well-meaning believers genuinely believe divorce is the evil to be avoided. They do not defend the abused or help them find safety, opting instead to fight for all marriages to be saved, no matter the circumstances, no matter the abuse that may be involved, often giving the abuse perpetrator chance after chance instead of holding him accountable. When women stand up for themselves and make the courageous decision to get out of an abusive relationship, those in opposition to her choice, often not knowing the full extent of the story, are quick to give the husband the benefit of the doubt while judging and denouncing the wife, when they should be offering her kindness, support, and assistance.

I've learned in my decades on this planet and in law practice that people don't like it when they can't control you, when you refuse to fit into the neat little category they have for you. Think about it. It's an uncomfortable threat to church leadership's control over the marriages in a congregation, a threat to their control over their *own* marriages even, when women leave oppressive, cheating or abusive men, for when other women see one woman courageously change her life via divorce, they are more likely to believe they can make the same move. While I believe the spiritual abuse inflicted on divorcing women in churches is usually born out of fear rather than sinister intent, the abuse is harmful, nonetheless.

A good spiritual leader, even a husband endeavoring to lead his wife spiritually, should try to encourage your behavior in positive ways without trying to take away your ability to make your own choices or superimpose his own will over yours. We all need positive influences and wise counsel in our lives! It's a service to us when friends give sound advice to help us avoid errors in judgment. That's why God gave us friends, and I certainly hope my friends always feel free to set me straight when I'm doing something I shouldn't be. That kind of Christian admonition is sanctifying, necessary, and life-enriching.

But when someone close to you uses the Bible to try to control your choices instead of recognizing your free will, that can become spiritual abuse. As teacher Mark Ballenger wrote,

Really, spiritual abuse is all about control. A good spiritual leader should influence our behavior in positive ways. As Paul said in 1 Corinthians 11:1, "Be imitators of me, as I am of Christ." They should teach, instruct, and discipline us when we need it. But even God himself allows us to sin. God gave us choice and he respects our right to choose even if we are choosing wrongly. A spiritually abusive person will need to control you all the time.[29]

Power, Control, and Submission in the Church

I've noticed this dynamic especially in denominations and faith traditions in which men have historically been dominant, limiting the role of women's service and preaching that women should be submissive to men.

<u>Your Husband Will Rule Over You, Eve</u>. Those who would oppress women and keep them in abusive marriages have a warped view of the Bible's teachings on marital submission. Scripture must be taken in context with other Bible scripture, and it's ever so dangerous to take particular verses in isolation. Abusive husbands tend to focus on the parts of Scripture which, taken in isolation, seem to give men dominion over women. These scriptures include:

1.   God's *curse* on Eve, after she and Adam had eaten the forbidden fruit, when He told her childbirth would be painful and her husband would "rule over her";[30] and

---

29   Ballenger, Mark. "What Does the Bible Say About Signs of Spiritual Abuse?" https://applygodsword.com/what-does-the-bible-say-about-signs-of-spiritual-abuse/

30   Genesis 3:16.

2. Ephesians 5:22, where wives are instructed to "submit to [their] husbands."

Those who use these verses to justify paternalism and misogyny totally forget that the curse of Genesis was just that, a *curse*, and never what God intended for women when he created us. The "curse verse" recognizes that women will be oppressed by men *now that sin has entered Creation,* but this does not mean God *approves* of men mistreating their wives. This isn't God giving men a license to rule, any more than His giving men dominion over the animals[31] was a license to abuse animals.

Husbands who tout Ephesians 5:22 as a license to exert power and control over their wives fail to consider the entire passage, which *begins* in verse 21 with an overarching theme of *mutual* submission in marriage, as we are instructed to "submit to *one another* out of reverence to Christ." Men are to love their wives as Christ loves the Church, and women are to respect their husbands. Submission, love and respect are not a one-way street. The Biblical ideal in marriage is that *both* partners defer to *one another,* placing each one's own needs and self-interests secondary to those of the other partner, out of love for one another. If submission is not mutual, it leads to the husband dominating and abusing the wife.

Imagine how many epic marriages we would have if everyone understood this!

---

31   Genesis 1:26.

Misogyny in the Early Church

Unfortunately, there's a long tradition of chauvinism throughout church history that still persists in the oppression of women in some churches today. Consider these quotes:

❖ *God maintained the order of each sex by dividing the business of life into two parts and assigned the more necessary and beneficial aspects to the man and the less important, inferior matter to the woman.*—John Chrysostom, Archbishop of Constantinople, 397–403 A.D.[32]

❖ *For good order to have been wanting in the human family if some were not governed by others wiser than themselves. So by such a kind of subjection woman is naturally subject to man, because in man the discretion of reason predominates.* —Thomas Aquinas, Latin theologian, 1225–1274 A.D.[33]

❖ *. . . woman was given to man, woman who was of small intelligence and who perhaps still lives more in accordance with the promptings of the inferior flesh than by superior reason. Is this why the apostle Paul does not attribute the image of God to her?"* —Augustine, early Latin church leader, 354–430 A.D.[34]

❖ *For woman seems to be a creature somewhat different from man, in that she has dissimilar members, a varied form and a mind weaker than man. Although Eve was a most excellent and beautiful creature, like unto Adam in reference to the*

---

32 "The Kind of Women Who Ought to Be Taken as Wives," translated by Elizabeth A. Clark. https://christianhistoryinstitute.org/magazine/article/women-archives-wifes-domain/

33 Summa Theologica, Question 92, Art. 1, Ad. 2.

34 De Genesi ad literam *Book 11.42.*

image of God, that is with respect to righteousness, wisdom and salvation, yet she was a woman. ***For as the sun is more glorious than the moon, though the moon is a most glorious body, so woman, though she was a most beautiful work of God, yet she did not equal the glory of the male creature.***"
—Martin Luther, 16th century theologian and priest, father of the Protestant Reformation[35]

❖ *On this account, all women are born that they may acknowledge themselves as inferior in consequence to the superiority of the male sex.*—John Knox, Reformed theologian, founder of the Presbyterian Church of Scotland, advocated for violent revolution[36]

Now, praise Jesus, we've certainly come a long way since the days such small-minded views of women were openly preached and widely believed. But you can see where modern-day abusive men in the church got their warped perceptions that promote abuse of women in marriage. You can't tell me this pleases the Jesus described in my Bible.

The Bible contains no compelling argument for staying with an abuser, and there are, conversely, countless arguments from Scripture that you are precious to God, and that He is against any messaging that tells you otherwise.[37] Divorced mom and blogger Leslie Tovato reminds us that Jesus, while he walked the earth, treated women in a way to show us we are:

---

35 *Commentary on Genesis*, Chapter 2, Part V, 27b.

36 *Commentary on 1 Corinthians*.

37 Instagram post. @leslie.trovato. January 20, 2022.

- ❖ *Worthy of tenderness*[38]
- ❖ *Worth the time*[39]
- ❖ *Worthy of forgiveness*[40]
- ❖ *Worthy of belonging*[41]
- ❖ *Worthy of grace when she makes a mistake*[42]
- ❖ *Worthy of being heard*[43]
- ❖ *Worthy of being believed*[44]
- ❖ *Worthy of real love*[45]

You are not someone's possession to be controlled and mistreated, Love. You are God's special creation, unique and precious. And you're just as important to God as your husband is.

----

38   Mark 5:25-34 and Luke 8:43-48 (healing the woman with the hemorrhage).

39   Luke 10:38-42 (Jesus with Mary and Martha).

40   John 8:1-11 (Jesus forgives the woman caught in the act of adultery, delivers her from being stoned).

41   Mark 15:40, Matthew 27:56, John 19:56, Luke 23:49 (Mary Magdelene as an early disciple supporter of Jesus' ministry).

42   John 8:1-11 (see above); Luke 7:36-50 (Jesus forgives sinful woman who anoints his feet with perfume).

43   1 Peter 3:7 (husbands are to be considerate of their wives and treat them with respect); Mark 16:1-8 (women were the first to discover the empty tomb and tell others).

44   Matthew 28:1-10 (women telling others of Jesus' resurrection).

45   Ephesians 5:25.

Churches Fail Women by Pushing Them to Marry Too Young

I see it all the time in the stories of women and men I represent. The couple has married super young, and five-to-fifteen years later, after a few children are born, the marriage is in shambles. Tempers flaring. Abuse erupting. And nine times out of ten, adultery is actively underway or about to start because one or both of them (a) are miserable and (b) never sowed all their wild oats or dated anyone else before tying themselves down in this marriage. They now realize that they got married out of obligation, to please their parents, to have a big, fancy wedding to impress the town, or because it was "just time to get married." They realize they never really had much in common, and now, years later, they have even less in common than they did when they were young.

A lot of the problem is that churches push young people—those good kids seeking to glorify God in their bodies who don't want to fall into the sin of premarital sex—to marry too early, without truly knowing each other. Fueled by a mixture of pheromones, the natural desire to be settled in a comfortable, committed relationship, and the euphoria of all the attention of well-wishers in society, young Christians often rush their courtships to get to the wedding night. It's not until after the Honeymoon (and sometimes even during the Honeymoon) that they relax and reveal their true selves, and issues emerge as the parties' true selves don't mesh as well as the false-perfect selves each one portrayed before the wedding. And I won't even speak about the issues that come with sexual incompatibility.

Once married, I believe most people just accept their situation and do nothing about it, living in misery, toxicity, and sometimes abuse rather than seeking a change. They don't want to be perceived as failures. They like the look of being a cute married couple. They like the acceptance of society that comes with being married. They figure everyone has problems, and this is just the set of problems they've been dealt.

Of the brave ones who *do* seek the help of counselors and the Church when they face marital issues, so many of them are, sadly and tragically, encouraged to stay in abusive situations when they shouldn't be. The Church must do better.

Brenda's Story

Brenda grew up in a Christian home and attended church every Wednesday night, and Sunday morning and Sunday night. She was active in her youth group, made the purity pledge in high school that she would not have sex until she got married, studied her Bible daily, sang in the youth choir, shared her faith as often as possible, and generally did her best to live in a way to bring honor and glory to God. She was her parents' pride and joy, the quintessential American good girl. Brenda met Ben during her sophomore year at her all-female college. Ben was a graduate student at another college nearby and checked all her boxes for a husband. He was a lifelong Christian and active in his church, having been president of his hometown youth group. He, too, had taken the purity pledge and appeared to be a nice young man. His professors loved him, his parents thought he hung the moon, and all the good girls wanted to marry him. Brenda felt so blessed when Ben focused his attention on her. They fell in love quickly after starting to date at Christmastime, got engaged by Easter, and were married before football season. It was a big church wedding with all the necessary hoopla.

Twenty years old and filled with optimism for the future, Brenda left her studies in early childhood education to move back to Ben's hometown. They had lunch every Sunday at Ben's parents' house, which Ben's mother always made sure was delicious, Southern perfection. Brenda joined Ben's family's church, and it wasn't long before she was recruited to work with the youth group, mentoring teenaged girls and leading them in Bible studies. Ben and Brenda were everyone's favorite young couple. Small town celebrities.

Ben seemed like the perfect guy. He'd finished his MBA and landed a great job as an executive in the largest company in the area. Ben ran their beautiful home like a military squadron, giving Brenda checklists of tasks to complete while he was at work each day. So each day, Brenda would get out of bed, make the bed just the way Ben liked it, make Ben's coffee and breakfast, clean the kitchen, clean the house, buy groceries, do the laundry, cook a balanced dinner, and have herself showered and in full hair and makeup when Ben got home at 6:00 p.m. sharp. This was her daily routine every day except Wednesday and Sunday, as church attendance and service were her only real break Ben allowed her to take from her household duties.

When he arrived at home every afternoon, the first thing Ben and Brenda did, after Brenda met him at the door with a Crown and ginger, was go over Brenda's task list for that day and evaluate her performance. He even gave her a daily report card, something that had started as a joke but eventually became something very serious to Ben. Then, while Ben watched T.V. or checked his stock portfolio on the computer, she would finish making dinner. By the time dinner was done each night, Ben would be deep in his cups. And as she cleaned the dinner dishes, Ben would tell her all the ways her cooking could be improved, about how she should change how she did the laundry and point out all the errors she was making in the way she kept the house.

Brenda didn't mind his criticism at first, as she understood that Ben had high standards for himself and also for her, and she wanted to be the best wife she could be, both to honor Ben and to honor God. Brenda had always been an overachiever in school and sports, and she didn't mind being pushed to be her best self. Ben hadn't treated her like this or shown her his picky side when they were dating; that part of his personality only emerged when they returned home from their honeymoon. But even so, Brenda intended to honor her vows and love him well, even if he rarely gave her any compliments. Ben was stressed at work, and she felt it was her duty to make his home life as pleasant as possible. She knew God loved her, and she was serving Him—not just Ben—with her acts of service. She would submit to Ben in obedience to God. Surely, she thought, he would start to love her better... if only she showed him enough submission and respect. She had read The Excellent Wife[46] and was determined to live out its principles.

But then, one Monday night, everything changed.

One of the girls from the youth group had called Brenda around 2 p.m. that day, crying and in need of a listening ear. Brenda invited the girl over to the house and spent the afternoon with her, comforting the girl and giving her sisterly support over several cups of coffee. The girl didn't leave until 5:30 p.m. When Brenda realized she'd lost track of the time, panic gripped her. She jumped into action trying to get all the task list items done before Ben came home. She had forgotten to start the dinner, so she

---

46   Peace, Martha. *The Excellent Wife: A Biblical Perspective,* Focus Publishing, 1999. This book was published the year I got married and heavily promoted in conservative congregations and Christian marriage conferences since that time. I heard the author speak to a women's group as a newlywed. Its teachings only work in the context of a healthy marriage where the husband is not abusive. The book does a disservice to women caught in abuse, as it leaves the reader with the impression that she should stay and continue striving for excellence in her marriage without addressing her needs as much as her husband's.

*called and ordered pizza, hoping it would arrive at the house by 6:30 p.m.,
their standing time Ben expected dinner to be on the table.*

*She couldn't do her hair or makeup in the time allowed, but she man-
aged to throw on some clean jeans and was brushing her hair just as she
heard Ben's car in the gravel driveway. A curse word escaped Brenda's lips.
She knew Ben wouldn't be pleased.*

*When Ben entered the house, a very discombobulated Brenda was still
mixing the Crown and ginger. As he grabbed the double old-fashioned
from Brenda's shaking fingers, Ben took one look at the condition of the
house—cups and crumby plates still on the coffee table, sofa pillows di-
sheveled, no dinner cooking in the oven, bathroom untidy—and became
visibly irritated. As he went over the incomplete task list with Brenda, he
became angrier and angrier by the minute, and as he finished the last of
his second Crown and ginger, he let Brenda know she'd earned an "F" on
that day's report card.*

*When she told Ben she'd ordered pizza, Ben was already working on
his third drink. His handsome face turned a shade of bright red Brenda
had never seen, and he began to raise his voice, the anger visible in his
eyes, following her from room to room in the house just to mercilessly
berate her: "You stupid [expletive name]! You only have one job—to keep
the house and make my [bleep beeping] dinner! Are you really this incom-
petent?!" and other demoralizing comments.*

*Brenda's dad and brother had never behaved this way, so Brenda was
profoundly confused by Ben's rage. She couldn't understand why he was so
upset over such a silly circumstance. She'd realized early in the marriage
that Ben was high-strung, Type A, and maybe a touch controlling, but
now she was seeing that Ben obviously had a dark side he'd kept carefully
hidden. One that his family surely knew he had but had never warned her
about. One that made her feel very unsafe.*

Brenda began to cry hysterically, and, thinking she could reason with this madman, apologized profusely and tried to explain the events of her day, thinking Ben would calm down if only he understood she'd been helping that young girl all day.

But Ben was unfazed by her explanations or her tears, and the confrontation only escalated as Ben shouted at her, "Shut up! I don't want to hear your excuses!" He threw his glass, and it shattered against the wall, leaving a dent in the sheetrock next to the China cabinet. Then, as he went to make himself another drink, cursing Brenda under his breath, Brenda ran toward the bedroom to get to her cell phone so she could call her mother. When Ben saw her headed toward the bedroom, he ran after her, arriving just in time to stick his arm and foot in the doorway to stop the door from closing, and grabbed Brenda by the wrists. He then threw her on the bed and held her down by her throat, spitting as he spoke to her nose-to-nose, telling her she should "stop making excuses for complacency," that she wasn't good enough, that she would never be good enough, that he never should have married her, that he should have married Joy, his high school sweetheart.

As Brenda gasped for air and begged him to stop, the doorbell rang. Jarred back into reality by the sound of the chime, Ben stood up, smoothed his clothes and hair, walked calmly to the door, gave the pizza man a friendly greeting as he paid the tip and grabbed the pizza, and returned to the bedroom where Brenda was still lying on the bed in shock, afraid to move.

Acting like nothing had happened, Ben smiled and said, "Come on and let's eat." Brenda had never been so afraid in her life. It was like Ben had two personalities.

Brenda and Ben sat and ate their pizza in silence as Ben pounded his fourth drink. As Brenda ate, she considered how she could escape the situation and get to safety. Her hometown and family were a five-hour drive from there. Not wanting to call law enforcement authorities and expose Ben and his family to public embarrassment, and not being able to get home to her family quickly, she resolved that she would seek help from their pastor and his wife when the time was right.

When Ben finally passed out for the night, Brenda quickly packed an overnight bag, grabbed her keys and her phone, put on some flip-flops and a jacket and drove across town to the church parsonage, where the pastor and his wife allowed her to stay in their guest room for the evening.

When Ben realized Brenda had gone to her parents' house the next day, he called her apologizing, begging her to come back, promising never to act like that again. Then, the elders of the church began calling her and encouraging her "not to be a wayward wife" and to come home to Ben, for he was sorry for what he'd done and had promised never to do it again. Besides, he hadn't hit her, so it wasn't abuse, and he hadn't cheated, so she didn't have any Biblical grounds to leave him. He was so very repentant, they said.

Brenda's parents and brother wanted her to file for divorce. But Brenda didn't want to give up on her marriage. She believed in forgiving people like Christ had forgiven her, so she went back to Ben after a six-week separation.

When Brenda returned to town, Ben's mama quietly thanked her for staying with Ben, in a single, hushed conversation in the kitchen one day, and they never spoke of the matter again. Ben's family wanted to act like Ben's problems didn't exist. They weren't a family that addressed their issues.

At first, Ben really seemed to be better, and the fun of their engagement period reentered the marriage. Ben took Brenda on dates every week and acted like the adorable, exciting Ben she fell in love with. He did away *with the task list, and he cut back on drinking, blaming alcohol for his violent outburst. But this good behavior only lasted a short time, and pretty soon Ben was back to his condemning comments and heavy consumption of Crown and gingers. And vodka shots. Mixed with painkillers. And when he drank, especially while also taking painkillers, he got mean, and his controlling, violent side came out.*

Brenda, ashamed she had gone back to him and too embarrassed to tell her mom she'd been right, just continued to endure Ben's verbal abuse and combative aggression. He could usually string together about three fun days of flirtation and love-bombing, but they were always followed by a week or more of what she called the Dark Side of Ben. He would usually pass out drunk before their arguments became physical, so Brenda was able to manage most days without fearing he would harm her. For a while, Brenda just accepted that this was normal, that this is just what her marriage would be. She was determined to hold on for the good days and hope he didn't hurt her on the bad ones.

But Brenda could keep peace only for so long. The final straw came one night when Ben got drunk and baselessly accused Brenda of having an affair with a single guy at church. When Brenda defended herself and called Ben "ridiculous," Ben was triggered, grabbed a chef's knife from the kitchen, held it to Brenda's neck and threatened to slit her throat. Brenda managed to get away, but this time she ran to a neighbor's house and called 911. Law enforcement came to the house and arrested Ben, and Brenda filed for divorce immediately.

Much to Brenda's surprise, the church leadership believed Ben when he told them Brenda was lying, that he had never threatened her life. They encouraged Brenda to take Ben back, citing his "genuine remorse for his behavior," his "willingness to quit drinking, go to counseling and rehab, and save the marriage." They were quick to point out to her that he hadn't actually harmed her physically and hadn't cheated on her, so she didn't have "Biblical grounds" to divorce him. They told Brenda she was no longer allowed to lead the church youth group now that she was seeking a divorce, but they allowed Ben to remain in his church leadership position. The older ladies in the church, friends of her in-laws who'd watched sweet, charming little Ben grow up, suddenly didn't know how to interact with Brenda, and they certainly didn't offer her any support or solace as the divorce was underway. Ben had been perfect in their eyes. They'd never seen him misbehave, and he was so utterly friendly and delightful from what they could see, so his wife must be fabricating all these crazy stories about him. Several ladies in the community came to Brenda to encourage her to take Ben back, telling her things like, "marriage is always hard the first year, Honey," and "you have a Scriptural duty to submit to your husband, and you don't have Biblical grounds to leave him." And Ben's third grade teacher was downright rude to Brenda in the grocery store.

Brenda felt like she was in an alternate universe; didn't these women understand that Ben had threatened her very life? Did the Church really care more about men being in control than whether she lived or died? Was it really more important for men to be in charge than for women to be safe? Brenda knew their advice was not coming from the God she knew. Not from the God who loved her and wanted her best.

Ben's divorce lawyer made Brenda sit for a deposition, and Ben used the proceeding to torment and spiritually abuse Brenda even more. Ben's lawyer, all WASPy and self-righteous like Ben, pulled out a Bible and mercilessly grilled Brenda for three solid hours, running up her legal fees and making her read scriptures through tears and defend her decision in Biblical terms. As if that had any relevance to the lawsuit, the division of their property, her alimony claim, or anything else the judge would be deciding.

Ben dragged out the litigation as long as he could, just to keep Bren-da trapped and to prevent her from moving on. Brenda gave up claims to assets and support just to get the case to end without a public trial.

Ben went on to marry several more times, fooling each new love just long enough to get her to marry him, only to change his personality soon after each honeymoon. But he remained a church leader all his days, and no one ever called him out about the way he treated the women in his life.

What To Do About Spiritual Abuse

If you're a victim of spiritual abuse, here are some ways to cope with it:

1. **Put On Your Armor.** If you are experiencing spiritual abuse, you are in the midst of spiritual warfare. It's a supernatural attack on your faith and your spiritual health. When I was a little girl, my mom would pray the "Armor of God" passage from Ephesians 6:10-17 over me on the way to school in the mornings:

The Armor of God

[10] *Finally, be strong in the Lord and in his mighty power.* [11] ***Put on the full armor of God,*** *so that you can take your stand against the devil's schemes.* [12] *For our struggle is not against flesh and blood, but against the rulers, against the authorities, against the powers of this dark world and against the spiritual forces of evil in the heavenly realms.* [13] *Therefore **put on the full armor of God**, so that when the day of evil comes, you may be able to **stand your ground**, and after you have done everything, to stand.* [14] *Stand firm then, with the **belt of truth** buckled around your waist, with the **breastplate of righteousness** in place,* [15] *and with your feet fitted with the readiness that comes from the gospel of peace.* [16] *In addition to all this, take up the **shield of faith**, with which you can **extinguish all the flaming***

arrows of the evil one. *¹⁷ Take the* **helmet of salvation** *and the* **sword of the Spirit, which is the word of God.**[47]

This powerful text reminds us that we're fighting a spiritual battle bigger than humanity and its judgment. Bigger than human meanness. Know Whose you are and call on the name of the Lord as you confront those who would wound your spirit and your walk with Jesus. The New Age folks are always talking about "manifesting" good things into your life by believing them and speaking them over yourself. This is kind of the same concept, but in the Christian context.

As a little girl, I would visualize my spiritual armor—the breast-plate (the feeling that I was one of the *good guys*, one of the *righteous*), the sword (the *Word* and all its promises that God had a plan for my life), the helmet (*salvation*, that feeling that God had me and wasn't letting me go), the shield (my *faith* in something bigger than humans), being put in place as my mama prayed it over me. Pray that God will put this armor on you every single day, girl. You're going to need it as you walk the hard road of divorce.

2. **Use Discretion.** Don't go around telling everyone your story, no matter how good it makes you feel to get it off your chest and gather supporters. It's best to keep your marital issues discreet. Trust few with your story and your plans. And, for the love, be careful about adding yourself to people's prayer lists; prayer groups are notorious for using your story as their excuse to spread gossip down the prayer chain while feigning genuine concern. Not everyone is genuine, and not everyone wants your best. Choose your prayer warriors carefully.

----

47 Emphasis supplied.

3. **Do Not Disparage the Church, But Consider a Short Break**. Christians are notorious for giving Jesus a bad name. Everyone falls short, and people disappoint one another every day. But please do not allow your disappointment in a particular Christian or set of Christians make you hate the Church in general or assist in its demise. Don't let their callous treatment cause you to lose your faith or stop serving and loving others the way you know Jesus wants you to. Do not let your heart be hardened against your faith.

Consider taking a break from that particular congregation. You may need to find a new place to serve if you're not going to be allowed to use your gifts to God's glory in this particular place, or if you're being judged and made to feel unwelcome.[48] It's okay to break ties with people who don't understand, love, support, and protect you.

4. **Tell the Judge**. There's nothing more off-putting than a self-righteous litigant passing personal judgment on another and hitting below the belt. Attacking someone's spiritual life to demoralize them and gain advantage in a lawsuit is never well received. Do not be afraid to tell your lawyer this part of your story if spiritual abuse is happening to you. See what your lawyer thinks about incorporating the abuse story into your case presentation. Judges are normal people

---

48   Gretchen Baskerville, "Nearly 6 in 10 Christians Switch Churches When They Divorce". November 23, 2021, Christians and Divorce, For Pastors, Safe Churches and Friends, www.lifesavingdivorce/switch, citing a LifeWay Research study.

who see all kinds of folks in court. When good people like you are attacked without justification, judges don't like it.

5. **Pray for Wisdom and Discernment**. Be careful to pray for wisdom and discernment from the Lord on how to manage your situation, keeping your duty to love your fellow humans paramount in your mind. Keep your responses to spiritual attacks laced with grace.

Sweet Sister, you'd be amazed to know how many people you are inspiring and encouraging by how you are responding to your struggle. Do not let spiritual abusers derail your departure from abuse or stop your progress toward God's best for your life. Keep going!

Questions for Reflection

1. Do you see yourself in Brenda's story? How is your story similar? Did you handle your situation like Brenda did, or did you do something different?

2. What is your understanding of marital dynamics? Were you raised in a church that preached submission? Were you taught submission was the woman's job only, or were you taught marriage involves mutual submission? How has your view of this concept shaped your marriage and how you and your husband treat one another?

3. What is your husband's view of your role in the marriage? Does he behave as if you are an equal partner to be respected and loved, or does he try to control you? Does he demand that you "salute the uniform" and show him respect even when he's wrong, or does he allow you to speak your mind freely?

4. Have you endured any of the kinds of spiritual abuse outlined in this chapter? How did you handle it? How would you handle it if any of these things happened to you after you separated from your husband?

5. Do you know how much God loves you and values you as a human being? Go back and read all the biblical accounts of Jesus' interactions with women cited in this chapter and note the kindness with which he treated them all. How do you think Jesus feels when he sees one of his daughters being spiritually abused?

Resources

Leslie Trovato ~ @leslie.trovato (Instagram) || @leslietrovato (Twitter)
"Church Shaming: A Deeper Look Into the Truth of Divorce for One Southern Woman"—Ashley Holt[49]
"How the Church Causes Unnecessary Hurt for Divorced Women"—Connie A. Baker, MA, LPC[50]
"(Divorced Women) Shunned by the Church"—Jen Grice[51]
Redeeming Power: Understanding Authority and Abuse in the Church—Diane Langberg

---

49 Holt, Ashley. https://styleblueprint.com/everyday/church-shaming-a-deeper-look-into-the-truth-of-divorce-for-southern-women-living-secret-lives/. StyleBlueprint Editors (2018).

50 Baker, Connie. https://conniebaker.com/how-the-church-causes-unnecessary-hurt-for-divorced-women-2/, November 8, 2019.

51 Grice, Jen. https://jengrice.com/divorced-women-shunned-by-the-church/, 2021.

Chapter Soundtrack

Lion and the Lamb—Bethel Music

Head to Toe (The Armor of God Song)—Christy Nockels

The Kingdom Is Yours—Common Hymnal, JonCarlos Velez, Dee Wilson, Jamie MacDonald

6

Haters Gonna Hate:
Surviving the Smear Campaign

The Lord will fight for you; you need only to be still.
—Exodus 14:14

Prepare To Be Smeared

A telltale sign that you're dealing with an abusive ex is what I call a "smear campaign." Post-separation, the abusive ex will carefully and strategically use lies and exaggerate or twist facts to raise suspicions and foster a negative public opinion of you. A few examples might be:

❖ After you show your best friend the broken door frame he destroyed during an emotional outburst, he'll swear you're the one raging in the household, not him.

❖ After you discover he's cheating on you, he and the mistress will both tell everyone they know how delusional you are, that you're really the one who's been cheating on him all along, and that you're a mastermind trying to throw everyone off the scent of your own affair. The worst abusers even make up elaborate false stories about your bizarre sexual preferences, expose private details of your sex life, or lie and say you have STDs you don't have . . . all just to humiliate you, and so you'll stop telling people about the other women in his life.

- If you say the smallest thing about being so unhappy you could die (or something similar), he'll twist your words, call 911, report that you are suicidal, put a camera in your face and try to have you put in a mental health facility for observation, feigning concern for you all the while and looking like Mr. Caring and Concerned Husband.
- If he's financially abusive and withholds money and resources from you when you need them, he will blame you, saying you're a spendthrift who can't be trusted with money. To bolster and perpetuate the lie, he may even accuse you of being a gold-digger who "married him for his money."
- If he's isolated you from friendships, he'll deny it, telling people how truly anti-social and weird you are.

This is a concerted effort to ruin your good name, destroy your credibility, and punish you for daring to step away from his abuse and control. Claiming to be long-suffering, forgiving, and heroic in their purported efforts to "help you" with whatever behaviors they falsely attribute to you, the smear campaigner endeavors to make others—sometimes even your own family—empathize with them and turn on you. These men are often master manipulators, skilled spin doctors, wolves in sheep's clothing—masterful at convincing people of both your instability or immorality and their own altruism. Instead of seeing the smear campaigner's vindictive trickery, the public perceives him as concerned about you, having done all he could do to help you or convince you to turn from your sinful ways. He will come off as the victim in the scenario, while you look heartless, crazy, or worse. While you may be the victim in reality, you are the villain in his narrative.

Your ex may be just crazy enough that he believes his own lies, which is what makes men like him so convincing.

The smear campaign is pretty pathetic when you boil it down. An abuser cannot handle it when he loses control, and you having walked away from him to start a new life away from his manipulation is too much for him to handle. The thought of you happily moving on to new relationships, new opportunities, and new experiences, without him and wholly unaffected by what he thinks about it, sends a guy like this into a tailspin. He wants you to pay for leaving him, and he finds solace for his torment in the empathy he gets from others, and that third-party empathy increases with each shocking, hurtful tale told about you. You used to be his emotional supply, but now you're gone, and he has to find a new supply to feed the emotional hole within him. That's the whole purpose of spreading a false narrative about you—to garner all the emotional pandering he can get. It's not at all about you. It's all about him and his need to be fed. He doesn't feel whole unless someone is feeling sorry for him and providing him with a steady supply of affirmation keeping him pumped up.

Bottom line: you cannot prevent your ex from lying about you if he's bent that way, but you can control how you respond if it happens to you. This chapter is designed to get you thinking about what you can do to combat your ex and his smear campaign.

Beware of Flying Monkeys

An abusive ex will often deploy other people to help him spread disparaging misinformation about you in your community in hopes of discrediting you and destroying your reputation. These people will believe the abuser's false narrative and join his team in your divorce battle. Like the minions of the Wicked Witch of the West in *The Wizard of Oz*, the people who do an abuser's bidding are referred to in the mental health world as "flying monkeys."

Some people are in your circle but not in your corner, and nothing exposes who's who like a divorce does. The flying monkeys in your life will reveal themselves, and the revelation, albeit painful, is God's gift to you. Unfortunately, flying monkeys often turn out to be your own relatives and others you unreservedly trusted before your separation. Their mission is to create confusion and chaos, and also to cause you pain.

Your Former In-Laws: Chiefs of the Flying Monkeys

If you're like most of my clients, you invested in your in-laws with all your heart and love them fiercely. You've spent years with your husband's family, and you love them. You've opened your home to them, celebrated birthdays, holidays and baptisms with them. You've been there for them during times of crisis. You've prayed and worried when they were sick or suffering. You were planning to take care of them in their elder years. You always invite them to the grandchildren's activities and frame the kids' school pictures to give to them as gifts. Perhaps you stayed in that terrible marriage out of a sense of family loyalty; you didn't want to hurt them, so you stuck like glue to prove you cared. And you lost a little more of yourself with each passing day.

Gird your loins and hold onto your hat, girl. Prepare yourself to be rejected and ostracized, no matter how kind you are, how amicably you try to handle the divorce, or how many financial concessions you make in hopes of keeping things peaceful. For some people, nothing you do is enough.

Many families have enabling dynamics. If your in-laws have coddled and placated your ex all his life, they will continue to excuse his bad behavior until the Kingdom comes. There's nothing you can do to change a decades-old, codependent family system. It's much bigger than you. You cannot win. All you can do is step away and leave them in their dysfunction.

Spoiler Alert: YOU will be likely blamed for the divorce.

In the minds of your enabling in-laws, the collapse of your marriage can't possibly be the fault of their Golden Boy (nothing ever is)! Denial is a powerful coping mechanism. Blame has to be assigned somewhere else, somewhere outside the family, in order for them to be able to deal with it. To make the divorce make sense in their minds without shattering their image of your ex, they will regard him as the victim, and you the aggressor. It's a zero-sum game to people who think this way, even if your ex cheated, abused you, or created a toxic home environment with his abusive behavior.

You may be shocked to learn it was your fault he cheated or abused you, for *you* must have done something to instigate or deserve the abuse you received. If you have a job outside the home (and especially if you happen to earn more or have a better professional reputation than your ex), you might be called a workaholic or accused of caring more about work than your children. Your in-laws will disparage you to your children when you're not around. They'll stop waving at you in traffic. They won't allow your kids' cousins on that side to come over to your house to play anymore, no matter how this upsets your children. They will pretend they don't know you when you run into them in public, even when the kids are there, even as they speak to the person sitting right beside you. They'll speak to your children as if you are not even standing there. After praising your parenting abilities since your children were born, they will start acting like you are not even a parent and try to take over your role.

It's always funny to me to see how your once-loving in-laws will turn on you just for standing up for yourself and saying, "no more." They think the world of you as long as you're putting up with Golden Boy's bad behavior and all-out dysfunction. It's not until you decide to stand up for yourself that you suddenly become the enemy.

In an effort to deflect attention from your ex's misconduct or poor choices, in classic flying-monkey form, they create false narratives to attack your good character, and they share those false narratives with their bridge clubs and Bible study friends.

Even after your divorce case is over, your ex's family may even slip up and say nasty things to your face about how you took all *their* money, even if you earned what you took in settlement and paid through the nose for your freedom.

All of this will hurt you. Expect it. Plan to forgive them before it happens. They are hurting and speaking from a raw place in their hearts that they can't process properly. Don't let it make you mad or make you bitter. If you do, they win.

You know who you are, and you know the truth of your story. That's the wonderful thing about the truth—it's true, whether everyone believes it or not.

Amelia's Story

From the first week of our marriage, my husband, Adam, openly flirted with other women. When I would call him out for it privately, he would yell at me and call me crazy, telling me I was imagining things. When I later began hearing from a variety of sources about Adam's girlfriends and would confront him about it, he would always deny anything was going on. I always believed him because I had no real proof of anything, just rumor, hearsay, and conjecture. I wanted to give him the benefit of the doubt.

One night at a charity event, Adam left the party with another married woman, was seen getting into the back seat of a car with her, and then stayed there with her for over an hour. The confrontation over this when we got home that night escalated quickly. He kept calling me possessive and insecure, insisting he and the woman were just talking all that time in the car, for she was having marital problems, and he was just trying to be a friend to her. When I called him a liar and refused to believe him, he began throwing my clothes into the front yard and screaming at me to "get out of his house." I called law enforcement because he was scaring the children (and me) and waking up the neighbors with his tirade, and the officers who arrived on site made him leave for the night. I didn't allow him to come back to the house the next day or any other day after that, except to get his stuff. Humiliated and tired of playing the fool, I filed for divorce the following week.

Adam and his family have always been all about their image, and, while they have serious internal dysfunction, they want people to think they're a perfect family. When his parents learned that I had involved law enforcement in our situation, they were extremely embarrassed and lit into me, saying, "We are a prominent family in this town. We deal with our issues privately. We don't call policemen to the house for all the world to see like a bunch of trashy rednecks." They were horrified that the neighborhood had seen their golden boy's behavior for themselves. They'd kept him in check for years, and the mask was now off. They had heard of his back seat conversation with the other woman, too, but accepted Adam's charming explanation that people were just making up lies about him and none of it was true.

My in-laws had always thanked me for putting up with him when he'd misbehaved before, but this time was different because I'd decided to divorce him. I began hearing from friends that Adam's parents and sisters were saying that I was unloving and cold, mean and unforgiving. That Adam loved me and was desperate to stay married to me. That he hadn't done anything with that other woman in that car, and I was just using the incident as an excuse to take all his family's money. I was the one actually having an affair (a total fabrication out of thin air!). I was an absent mother who worked all the time, and I didn't like sex (another lie), which is why he may have (but no proof that he actually) *struggled with sexual temptation.*

When I would see my mother-in-law out and about, she would ignore me and speak only to the children. It was as if I didn't exist. People told me she was spreading a story that I had just heartlessly stopped loving Adam with no explanation or reason, and that he was just devastated, "so please keep him in your prayers." 🤮

Adam did a masterful job of manipulating those in our circle of friends who I'd call "second-tier"—friends we enjoyed but didn't spend a whole lot of time with when we were together. He got their allegiance by making them feel sorry for him. They came to believe that I was frigid, uncaring, and out for his money. These folks had Adam over for dinner, helped him with his laundry and stopped acknowledging me when I'd see them in public. They'd never heard my side of the story because they'd never reached out to me, not to mention the fact that it was none of their business and I had no reason to spread the details of my divorce all over town.

Periodically, I would hear that some of them were self-declared members of "Team Adam." So stupid. I saw no need for "teams." What was this, middle school?

Some of these people—but not all—have since apologized to me for ghosting me when I needed friends most. They had simply believed Adam's pretty lies. He told them so convincingly.

Adam and his family smack-talked all the people who supported me in the divorce, as well. My friends became their enemies, just as I had become.

The next thing I knew, Adam's dad—not Adam himself, for Golden Boy needed his daddy to take care of his business for him—was reaching out to negotiate the terms of the divorce with me. Adam's dad pulled out a ledger and pointed out the various items he had paid for our family over the years—things like preschool tuition and dental bills which we could have easily afforded ourselves but which he had insisted on paying as part of his estate planning—and then asked me to reimburse him as part of our divorce settlement agreement. That was when I knew they'd never loved me. That they loved their money and their image way more than they'd ever loved me.

When I didn't agree to these terms, I was painted as a money-hungry wench who had come from nothing and had married Adam for his family money. The flying monkeys wasted no time spreading this lie, even though I had always worked full-time and had a higher income and more successful career than Adam's.

I stayed quiet in the face of these false rumors being spread about me, trusting that the truth would come out eventually. I clung to a few close friends and a couple of trusted relatives for support. I did not try to battle all the naysayers. Instead, I retreated into work, childrearing, and solitude until the storm of my divorce had passed. And it did eventually pass, for Adam and his parents knew better than to force the case to a public courtroom.

We settled the case quietly, and it was worth what I gave up in assets to be able to move forward in peace. Before long, my breakup was old news, and the rumor mill had new topics to discuss.

Jesus Faced His Own Smear Campaign

Dear One, if you are the object of a smear campaign, think of it as an opportunity for insight into the trials Jesus endured when he walked the earth. Think of all the false narratives those in power created about Jesus, from the start of his ministry right up until his crucifixion. Their lies were calculated for his ultimate demise and to promote the liars' own agendas. Much like the flying monkeys are promoting your husband's agenda in your divorce case, those who sought to take Jesus out would say anything, no matter how false or how hurtful. If someone is unjustly smearing your name, you are getting a little glimpse of what our Lord went through.

We can find direction in how Jesus handled the smear campaigns that were launched against him. Did Jesus go toe-to-toe with his accusers and naysayers, refuting their arguments point by point? No. If you notice, he usually spoke some undeniable truth in the face of these challenges and immediately walked away, peacefully and quietly avoiding further controversy. Just think of how Jesus was just before his crucifixion. As his accusers leveled their accusations, the Bible tells us Jesus astonished Pilate with his silence. He stayed silent, even as he was facing death.[52]

What extraordinary discipline! There he was, God in the flesh, with all the power that came with that, staying calm and self-controlled instead of taking their bait. The times when he pointed out how the religious leaders were wrong, except for that time at the temple when he turned over the moneychangers' tables in righteous indignation (see my earlier chapter on when it's okay to get mad), he did so with poise and self-control. He didn't get loud or try to convince the religious

---

52   Mark 15:5.

leaders to see things his way. When challenged, he would remain silent, share a parable or generalized analogy, refer to applicable scriptures, quietly depart. All of these responses are likewise appropriate today when we deal with naysayers and those who wish us harm.

Have you ever noticed how hard it is to argue with someone who stays calm and refuses to argue back with you? A kind word turns away wrath and diffuses angry attacks. If you stay silent or just respond with kindness in the face of baseless gossip, several things will happen: (a) the haters and busybodies will stop talking when they see they're not getting to you, (b) your response cannot be used as ammunition to attack your character any further, and (c) you may even convince them, by your calm, unaffected reaction, that none of the stories they've heard about you could possibly be true.

If You're Being Smeared

1. **Do not engage in the PR war**. Jesus didn't respond to every person who criticized him. He didn't have to do that, for he knew who he was and the Truth he came to give the world, and he wasn't going to be distracted from his mission. You only give your abuser power, and his false narrative traction, the more you speak to it.

2. **Let your lawyer handle it**. Tell your lawyer what's being said about you, and follow her advice about how to respond, if at all. If a response is to be given, let your lawyer speak for you as much as possible instead of reacting on your own behalf.

3. **Don't get distracted**. Do not let false narratives distract you from your litigation or larger, post-separation life goals. You're in the fight of your life, and you can't waste time refuting every tall tale your crazy ex may try to spread

about you. You answer to the Lord alone, and no one else. If you can lay your head on your pillow at night and go to sleep with a clear conscience, you are doing everything right. Rest in the comfort of that, remaining focused on the task at hand. It's Operation: Finish Your Divorce!

4. **Prepare your heart and don't feed the beast**. Your ex's power over you lies in your reactions, and your reactions only keep the story going in the community. Responding only minimally will get you out of the community spotlight faster, and everybody will move on to gossip about someone else a whole lot sooner.

5. **Keep your distance and share no information**. You might be tempted to try to win over a flying monkey or two in hopes of rallying more support for your side. Do not try this under any circumstances! The flying monkeys do not want you to live your best life, and you shouldn't let them get close to you. They will undermine you if they can, and you cannot trust them. Give them no information they can twist for your ex to use against you in court.

6. **Cleave to your supporters**. Maybe your supporters are your family who have loved you since you were a kid. Perhaps they are true blue friends, who are the family you have chosen. These are the ones who will be crying at your funeral. These are your people. Identify them, and cling to them with all your might, thankful God showed you the flying monkeys in your past life. You're loved by the people who matter, and it's all good. In your low times, lean on their support. The right people will always be there.

7. **Pray**. Pray for guidance on how to handle the situation. Pray for the flying monkeys, just as you pray for all your enemies. Pray for God to reveal the truth and all things heretofore concealed. Pray that God would guard your heart and give you peace even as you walk through the drama and chaos others may create.

8. **Let the flying monkeys fly far, far away**. Grieve the loss of your relationships with them, compartmentalize the experience and disappointment in a remote section of your brain, and move on. If someone is so easily convinced to turn on you after years of friendship, you don't want them in your life anyway. Cut them loose, learn the lesson, and move on. You're better for it.

9. **Forgive them**. You will hear about the flying monkeys' disparagement of you through the grapevine (from your true friends), and it will undoubtedly hurt your feelings. Brace yourself for that, and plan to forgive them before it happens. You can't allow yourself to become bitter or angry. Let the experience prepare you for future adversity and thank God for using it to make you stronger. The people who matter know you, and they love you. That's what counts. If you can forgive your haters, you can release the burden of what they did to you and carry it no more. There is freedom and holiness in that.

10. **Take heart**! The truth always comes out eventually. I've seen it play out dozens of times with my clients. No matter what the other side says to confuse the facts, the true story has a way of getting out, organically and naturally.

Scripture promises that God Himself will fight for you,[53] that he loves righteousness and justice,[54] and that you need only be still.[55] Nothing is hidden that won't be made known.[56] God is a shield to those who, like you, Dear Friend, live with integrity.[57]

Questions for Reflection

1. Have you ever been the victim of gossip? How did you handle it? If you could go back and handle it differently, what would you change?

2. Think of how Jesus handled the smear campaign of the Pharisees. What can you take away from how he handled that situation and apply it in how you respond to your ex and the flying monkeys?

3. Think of a time in your life where you believed one thing to be true, and then it later turned out to be false. How long did it take for the truth to be revealed?

4. When faced with controversy, is your natural tendency to dive into the drama and try to set the record straight, or do you typically withdraw and become emotional or fearful? What is good about your natural tendency in the context of your divorce? What natural tendencies should you be

---

53 *See* Deuteronomy 3:22, where we are told not to be afraid of our adversaries, for "the Lord your God himself will fight for you."

54 Psalms 11:7.

55 Exodus 14:14.

56 Matthew 10:26.

57 Proverbs 16:7.

careful to keep in check as you maneuver the landmines of divorce?

5. Are you being careful about who you let into your inner circle of trust? Are you trusting your soon-to-be ex-in-laws more than you should? Are you too trusting of the mutual friends you share with your ex? Are you being careful with your words and what you share with others about your situation?

Resources

The Narcissist You Know—Joseph Burgo

Flying Monkeys: The Inner Circle of the Narcissist—audiobook by J.B. Snow

Chapter Soundtrack

"Bad Blood"—Taylor Swift

"When It Rains It Pours"—Luke Combs

"Shake It Off"—Taylor Swift

"Goodbye in Her Eyes"—Zac Brown Band

Questions for Reflection

Consider 1 Peter 2:21, 1 Peter 4:12-13 and 1 Peter 5:10, and their promises that, after you have suffered for a short time, our God, who is full of kindness, will personally come and pick you up, set you firmly in place, and make you stronger than ever! Do you believe it, Sister? If not, what is holding you back?

Resources

Run Like Hell: A Therapist's Guide to Recognizing, Escaping and Healing from Trauma Bonds—Dr. Nadine Macaluso
The Body Keeps the Score—Bessel a. van der Kolk

Chapter Soundtrack

Psalm 23—Bristol House

Part 3

Game Time:
Let's Do This

1

The Big Picture:
Overview of Divorce Litigation

"I just wanna let them know that they didn't break me."
—Andie, *Pretty in Pink*

The previous chapters were all about getting your mind right, preparing your heart and calming your spirit to cope with your transition to divorce more healthily and productively, so that your decisions and behavior will be optimal for examination in court. You're now at the part of the book where you'll learn all the practical ways you can help your lawyer win your case. It's time for a lesson in logistics!

It's time to stand up for yourself and get to work! Your husband hopes you will cave and give him everything he wants in this divorce. You must find it within yourself to assert your rights, stand your ground, and defend your case with grace and courage. Let him know he isn't going to break you!

It's a Marathon, Not a Sprint

I wish I had a dollar for every time I've heard a client in the initial divorce case consultation say, "I just want it over with." They think the pain will end sooner if the legal part can be finished quickly.

But it's generally unwise to rush your divorce case.

Division of property, division of debt, spousal support, and child custody and support matters are complex. You only get one shot at getting the terms right, and those who hurry to the finish line often have great regret when they later realize how much they gave up. Time is needed to expose the full story of your marriage and to ascertain the total value of your assets to ensure a fair division. Scheduling conflicts, inability to get hearing dates due to court docket backlogs, discovery delays, and delays in communication due to attorney workload are all normal and to be expected. It takes time to prepare any kind of lawsuit, and divorce cases, because of the additional layer of emotions to unpack, often take longer to prepare than other kinds of cases. Patience is important. Without complete information, there's no way to make an informed settlement decision, and the result is more likely to be unfair to you. The process can take months—or sometimes years—from start to finish.

Having some idea of what to expect in your case is comforting and helps drive out fear. This chapter is here to educate you on legal terminology and general processes so you can better assist your attorney.

Don't Try to Represent Yourself

Before I go any further, I want to speak to anyone who thinks they can get by without hiring a lawyer. Only in the simplest cases with no assets, debts or children is it even remotely wise to consider handling your own divorce case without an attorney's advice. I will go into all the reasons, and also give tips for how to help your lawyer keep costs down as you prepare your case, in the next chapter.

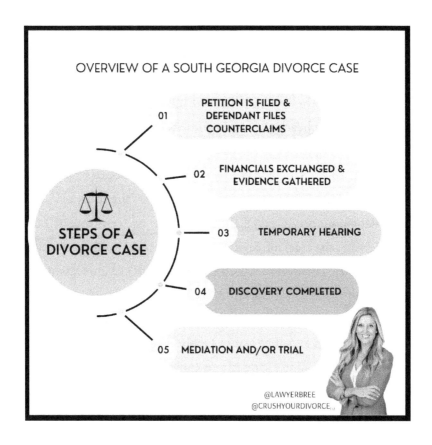

OVERVIEW OF A SOUTH GEORGIA DIVORCE CASE

STEPS OF A DIVORCE CASE

01 PETITION IS FILED & DEFENDANT FILES COUNTERCLAIMS

02 FINANCIALS EXCHANGED & EVIDENCE GATHERED

03 TEMPORARY HEARING

04 DISCOVERY COMPLETED

05 MEDIATION AND/OR TRIAL

@LAWYERBREE
@CRUSHYOURDIVORCE

Steps in the Process

The above graphic gives an overview of how a typical divorce case progresses in my neck of the woods. The divorce litigation process may be different in your state, and there are nuances to the process even within each individual state. I practice law in Georgia, and I can tell you from experience that the way we do things where I live are very different than the way they do things in Atlanta. Different judges have different preferences, sometimes even within the same judicial circuit. For this reason, nothing I'm telling you in this book can be taken as legal advice particular to your case. It's essential that you retain local counsel for guidance on your unique situation.

Step One: Someone Files a Divorce Case

The first step is that one party (commonly called the "plaintiff" or "petitioner") files a petition for divorce at the local courthouse. The petition outlines the legal grounds for divorce that the filing party believes to be applicable, along with general facts about the situation such as the date of marriage, date of separation, why jurisdiction is proper in that particular court, the minor children's names and ages, and what the filing party is generally asking the court to do. The other party (commonly called the defendant" or "respondent") then must file with the clerk of the court, by a certain deadline, a written response to the petition in which the defendant's claims against the plaintiff and requests for the court are likewise outlined.

If you're the plaintiff, you have the benefit of knowing the litigation is coming, and it's nice not to be blindsided. But you may be accused of being the aggressor without cause and labeled the "bad guy" for initiating the case. I generally prefer to be the plaintiff's attorney because of the control it gives you over the timing of the litigation and the initial framing of the issues. Where I practice, the plaintiff gets to go first at the temporary hearing, and I find that to give a certain advantage in most cases. Don't get me wrong, defendants win cases all the time, and it's not an insurmountable obstacle if your husband files before you can. But being on offense from the start of the case is generally preferable.

Being served with a divorce filing can throw you into a tailspin. If this happens to you, take a breath and try to stay calm. It's something that (a) happens every day, (b) can be handled, and (c) will not kill you. You will survive it, with your attorney's help. Immediately secure counsel and get to work defending yourself. Your responsive pleading (the "answer") needs to be a jam-up, comprehensive refutation of your husband's initial allegations and also a coherent and compelling statement of *your* claims. Your lawyer will help you articulate your positions. It's time to find and use your voice!

Step Two: Financial Disclosures are Exchanged & Evidence is Gathered

In every divorce case, each party's financial status—income, assets, debts and expenses—is relevant to the court's inquiry. Georgia has a statutory form every divorce litigant fills out and files with the court. Get familiar with the financial disclosure requirements of your jurisdiction, and make sure you comply with them to the letter.

Evidence for your side of the case also has to be compiled and put in a presentable form for court. You may have to get evidence from third parties if you don't have it in your possession already. Brainstorm with your attorney about all the sources of information, documentation, and other evidence to prove each point you want the judge to understand at the hearing. Ask your lawyer to make a list of the things you can be gathering and get to work gathering what you need!

Your lawyer is likely an extremely busy person who deals with multiple deadlines every single day, and you can save on fees if you do your part to provide evidence of your claims. Evidence must be in a form that is easy to present and admissible in court, so be sure to ask the lawyer or paralegal how they'd like the evidence to be compiled. I generally ask clients to bring me three <u>color</u> copies of photographs, text messages, emails, and everything else they want considered as evidence, already sorted into separate identical sets. I like large video and audio files to be delivered on flash drives for easy download without an internet connection (this comes in handy if the courthouse wi-fi is down the day of your hearing, as you won't need to access files in the cloud server). I can't tell you how frustrating it is to receive one thousand 4x6 prints to sort myself the night before a hearing. No. Fun. At. All.

Do what you can to help your lawyer compile and prepare to present the evidence that is pivotal to your case. Good client support makes all the difference in setting you up for success!

Step Three: The Temporary Hearing

Where I practice, the temporary hearing is the first in-court proceeding with the judge after the case is filed. At this pivotal hearing, the court considers the temporary issues of the case, such as possession of assets, allocation of responsibility for paying the parties' various debts, custody of the children, parenting time breakdowns, child support, spousal support, and temporary attorney's fees, and issues a ruling (I usually call it the "temporary order") to govern the parties "until further order of the court." You don't have to have a hearing to reach a temporary understanding of the terms you'll live by while the case is pending; we often enter into written orders approved by the parties in lieu of airing all the dirty laundry and attacking one another in a hearing. If you and your spouse can agree on the temporary terms, that's usually more comfortable than trusting a judge to get it right after knowing you for two hours or so. The point of the temporary resolution is to put a Band-aid on the situation and make sure both parties' and the children's needs are met while the big issues of the case are sorted out. A temporary order isn't forever, but some of its terms often have a way of carrying the day at the final stage of the case if things have run relatively smoothly while the case was pending. More on this in my "Crush the First Hearing" chapter, later in the section.

Step Four: Completion of Discovery

"Discovery" is what lawyers call the process by which information and documents are exchanged in a lawsuit. Each side requests documents from the other, and the two sides then send one another information that is relevant to the issues of the case. Issues can arise when a party doesn't produce everything they're asked to produce, or when a party refuses to cooperate in depositions or tries to block the other side from obtaining records from third parties. Motions have to be filed if this occurs, and it can expand the proceedings considerably. A case goes much more smoothly if both sides openly share relevant information. Full cooperation in discovery not only promotes a more efficient completion of the matter but also ensures you don't lose credibility with the court. Like with anything else in life, you can't control how your husband handles discovery, but you can control your own compliance, and you should fully comply except as necessary to raise valid objections your lawyer advises you to make. More on how to help your lawyer ensure your full compliance with discovery rules is coming later in the book.

Step Five: Settle the Case or Take It To Trial

Divorce cases are ripe for resolution once all the documents are exchanged, depositions are taken, debts are ascertained, and assets are valued. We can often settle the less contentious cases without the intervention of a mediator or a judge and get people on with life a little faster, but some cases just cannot be settled without mediation or trial. If the lawyers are unable to settle the case at the settlement conference or via the exchange of written proposals, mediation is generally the next option for the settlement-minded to try. Mediation involves the services of a neutral third party (can be an attorney, but sometimes not an attorney) who helps the parties compromise, issue by issue, ideally until every issue in the whole case is resolved. The mediator's only loyalty is to broker a deal. *The mediator has no power to rule in your case or dictate a particular result.* Where I practice, mediation is required in every case after a certain amount of time has passed from the date of filing, and it's usually a very helpful, good thing.

Emotions and tensions run high in divorce settlement negotiations, and the chances of reaching a settlement hinge on everyone staying calm. For this reason, I generally find it's best for the parties to be in separate rooms, with the mediator shuttling diplomacy between them.

Some mediators prefer to conduct at least part of the mediation session with the parties (with their counsel or, in some places, unrepresented) in a single room, around the same table. If you aren't comfortable being in your husband's vicinity, talk to your lawyer about requesting separate rooms, or mediation in "caucus." Wife is in one room (either with or without her attorney—where I am, the attorney is there), and Husband is in another room with his attorney. The mediator goes between the parties' respective rooms, shuttling diplomacy, encouraging compromise, and helping the parties reach consensus, one issue at a time. I'll have more information to share about mediation later in the book, but suffice it to say that mediation is a confidential, optimal way of resolving your case without losing control over the outcome.

In my experience, most cases settle at mediation because people don't want to go to trial. Trial is your last stop if you can't settle beforehand. At trial, depending on your jurisdiction, a judge and/or jury will determine the outcome of your case, dividing your property and debts, determining child custody issues, your parenting time with your children, and setting the amounts of support to be paid by one party to the other.

This is an extremely simplified overview of the litigation process and does not outline all the many kinds of special motions that can be filed for particular kinds of relief or court intervention that may be needed in your particular case. Legal matters are complex, and the court's ruling can drastically impact your daily life. This is why I keep reminding you to find a lawyer in your area who can meet your particular needs.

Questions for Reflection

1. Are you a naturally nonconfrontational person, or are you someone who faces conflict head-on? What are some examples of times you should have been more assertive? How can you use those memories to promote empowerment and dispel timidity as you litigate your divorce?

2. How could your natural aversion to conflict (or boldness) impact how you prosecute your divorce case?

3. How does the thought of a long divorce battle make you feel?

4. What emotions and reactions will you need to keep in check for your case to go smoothly?

5. What can you do to start preparing for your divorce case before your first attorney consultation?

Resources

Marriage Story (2019 film)

www.judgeanthony.com

www.divorcemag.com

Chapter Soundtrack

"We Will Rock You"—Queen

"Eye of the Tiger"—Survivor

2

Get a Lawyer and Tell Them Everything

"He who represents himself has a fool for a client."
—Abraham Lincoln

Your husband may be telling you not to get a lawyer, that you can trust him, that you two can handle your own business and can settle the case without counsel. Rule of Thumb: The moment he says, "you don't need a lawyer," run directly to an attorney's office as fast as your little legs can carry you, my dear.

When people try to represent themselves in divorce, it can end very poorly. You wouldn't try to perform surgery on yourself or try to cure your own cancer, would you? Of course not! You'd trust trained medical professionals with such things. Likewise, you need a skilled lawyer well-versed and experienced in family law to represent you should you find yourself in a divorce case. You're exposing yourself to all kinds of folly if you try to represent yourself. Your husband's lawyer will eat you alive!

Finding the Right Lawyer for You

There are few things as raw and personal as a divorce, and you'll need to share private details of your life with your legal counsel in order to have effective representation. There are many good lawyers out there, and you need to research them before you select the one right for your case. The lawyer needs to be someone with whom you can feel comfortable opening up and telling the whole truth of your situation—the good, the bad and the ugly—without fear of judgment. A good lawyer will make you feel heard and understood.

Asking for personal recommendations of which lawyer to use can be awkward, especially when you're not quite ready to go public with your situation. If this is you, check out online reviews of the lawyers in your area. Strangers who've written lawyer reviews can sometimes be your best advisors on which lawyer is right for you, and hearing from those who've been in your shoes and got through their divorces can be a source of great reassurance. Another good source of lawyer referrals can be the bar association for your state. If you research lawyers on the State Bar's website, look for members of any subgroups of family law specialists. In Georgia, we have an excellent, well-run Family Law Section comprised of legal professionals like me who focus most of their energy in family law. You need a lawyer who specializes in divorce, not someone who dabbles in it.

A good rapport with your counsel is absolutely pivotal. You can't be afraid to speak your mind. A lot of this depends on how your personalities mesh, so be sure communication is easy with your potential attorney before you pay the retainer. You may need to meet with several lawyers before choosing the right one for you.

Look for a lawyer who does the following things during your initial consultation:

- ❖ listens to your concerns and lays out a litigation plan for addressing each one
- ❖ asks thorough questions about how your marriage broke down, your assets, your debts, your children, your story,

- ❖ listens to your concerns and lays out a litigation plan for addressing each one takes good notes and hangs on your every word, from the first meeting,
- ❖ raises thought-provoking questions for you to consider in connection with your case,
- ❖ expresses genuine compassion for the pain you've endured,
- ❖ gives you a homework list to complete, to empower you to take ownership over and contribute meaningfully to the preparation of your case,
- ❖ doesn't "talk down" to you as if you're stupid or inferior,
- ❖ isn't judgmental of you, doesn't condemn you, but rather encourages you that there is a brighter day coming, and
- ❖ has a strong support staff and processes in place to handle your case in an organized, efficient way.

A good divorce lawyer is someone who isn't afraid of a good fight, is assertive and strong, is ethical and knowledgeable about the law and court procedure, but is also kind, empathetic, and compassionate. You need to know your lawyer understands your situation and can articulate your positions coherently and without hesitation. A lawyer whose heart is in her work is unstoppable. Look for that passion when you're interviewing potential counsel.

What if I Can't Afford a Lawyer?

People often fear the costs of legal counsel and say they can't afford the fees. I'm here to tell you that most people can't afford *not* to have a lawyer. The financial ramifications of a poorly prepared divorce decree or a less-than-stellar showing in court can be devastating. If you acquired children, assets and/or debts, during your marriage, you need a lawyer to get the documents right, even if you think you have a full agreement. You don't know what you don't know; there are provisions you will need to include and issues to be addressed which you may not have even thought of, and a lawyer is needed to identify and handle those items. It's money well spent, and should be a high priority in your budget, even if you must borrow from family, forego other (more fun) purchases, or pick up a side hustle.

Ask your lawyer about requesting reimbursement of your legal fees from your husband in your requests to the court. Courts sometimes award fees reimbursement; however, it's a case-by-case inquiry and never guaranteed. It's worth a shot to ask for attorney's fees if your lawyer agrees you have a valid claim for your ex to pay them.

If you want to save on litigation costs:

- ❖ DON'T send daily emails or stream-of-consciousness texts to your lawyer each time you have a question, and,
- ❖ DON'T call your lawyer's office every day.
- ❖ DO save up your questions for your next meeting with your lawyer or send them all in a single email instead of sending individual messages. If your lawyer can address all your questions in one sitting, there's less billable time involved than if you are bombarding your poor lawyer with calls and messages multiple times every day.
- ❖ DON'T have your attorney ask your ex or third parties for financial and other information to which you also have access through another avenue. Financial institutions charge research fees and copy costs, not to mention the cost of your lawyer's time in preparing unnecessary, formal requests. DO gather as much of the information as you can to mitigate your cost exposure.

- ❖ Unless there's just no other way to do it, <u>pretty please DON'T</u> provide evidence in hard-to-digest formats like screen recordings, little giblets of paper, tomes of text messages with handwritten notes on them that will have to be redacted before they can be used in court, poor quality photographs, or uncollated, unsorted stacks of documents which, on their face, have neither rhyme nor reason. Instead, <u>DO</u> print and collate your documents, flag the important things with yellow sticky notes explaining each item's purpose in your case.
- ❖ <u>DON'T</u> take tons of new things to your lawyer's office on the day before the hearing, expecting the lawyer to spend hours reviewing it all that night. <u>DO</u> deliver your evidence to your lawyer's office in digestible chunks, well in advance of a hearing or trial.

Prepare to Do Your Part

The old adage that "a lawyer is only as good as his client" rings true. Even the best attorney cannot achieve the results you desire if you don't give them the information they need. A client once told me, "You're the gun, and I'm going to give you all the bullets you need." That was the right idea! That client gave me all the information I needed, and we crushed that divorce. She was comfortable telling me the things I needed to know to present her case in a compelling way. If you're uncomfortable sharing information with—or even just talking with—your lawyer because of personality conflict or something else, you aren't likely to succeed.

You know your story better than anyone else. Help your lawyer tell it!

You Need an Objective, Unemotional, Cool-Under-Pressure Advocate

Women often come to my divorce consultations nervous, tearful, and almost always uncertain of what to expect. They are gripped by fear—fear of what others will think, fear of the fallout for their children, fear of not making it in life alone, fear of retaliation. But by the end of our process, they are generally more confident and able to face the future with hope. I get a front-row seat to watch their amazing transformation from terrified to self-assured. It never gets old.

You need a lawyer to be your unemotional, objective, strategic, calm voice of reason.

I'm better now, but I've hated flying for most of my life. There is just something so unnatural about being that far off the ground! I grew up going on vacations by automobile, and my first flight wasn't until I was almost nineteen years old. The first ten years of my air-traveling experience, I prayed before takeoff and landing that God would put his angels around the plane and keep us safe. I had to have the air vent directly on my face the whole time I was in the plane and was gripped by anxiety with each bump of turbulence. What helped me conquer my fears of flying more than anything else was looking at the flight attendants. If they were calm in rough air, I knew that I could be calm, as well. I began to find comfort in their calm demeanor, and this helped me overcome fear with logic. All I needed to start enjoying flying was to realize that my anxiety wasn't rational.

The flight attendants were my calming influence, just as your lawyer can be for you as you navigate the fears which inevitably come in every divorce case. If your lawyer isn't panicking, then you shouldn't be, either. There is great solace in that.

In my lawyer role, I can handle almost anything the other side throws at me. I go for the jugular and rarely get rattled. I can see the issues with clarity and put together a game plan in a minute. But when I was the *client*, I learned firsthand in my own divorce how important good legal counsel can be. I was the one gripped with fear at the start of my case. It's such a strange contrast: as a divorce attorney, I'm tough and don't put up with nonsense, but I was a total scaredy cat when I was the Plaintiff Wife. I needed my lawyer to stand in the gap for me and help me be strong. I thank God every day for the support of my lawyer and her staff when I was vulnerable. I couldn't have gotten through it without them.

Divorce is an emotional process, and you won't always be thinking coherently as you anxiously walk through it. I know I wasn't! An attorney takes on your stress and responds unemotionally and logically. Choose a lawyer you feel you can trust to speak for you and protect your interests.

Your Lawyer is Your Buffer

Few experiences are as personal and raw as a divorce. Your parenting ability, your character, and your decisions can all be questioned, and it's important to insulate yourself from the onslaught of allegations from the other side. A lawyer's role is to take those arguments against you on your behalf rather than you having to sustain them as direct hits on your own. It can be unpleasant to go through this process even *with* an attorney, and without one it can be utterly devastating. If you represent yourself and the other side throws barbs at you (i.e., attacking your parenting, your housekeeping, your character, your extended family, your behavior) you *will not* be able to make the arguments you need to make in the moment in response to this onslaught. Instead, it's more likely that you'll be triggered by them the same way you were when you and your ex were together: you'll instinctively *fight* back (with a level of emotion that is inappropriate in a formal court proceeding), want to *run* away or withdraw to avoid the controversy instead of standing your ground and coherently arguing your point (think "shrinking violet" . . . not a good look for the courtroom), or *freeze* and be unable to respond at all. None of these are helpful to your case. A lawyer can be tough and keep their thoughts together to form coherent responses when you're unable to do so because you're so deep in your emotions.

Another thing a lawyer gives you is a little plausible deniability. When divorce litigation gets ugly, you'll be better able to distance yourself from the ugliness if you can "blame the mean old lawyer" and let the lawyer say the things that will upset your husband and point out his shortcomings and misdeeds, instead of *you* having to say them yourself. How freeing to be able to say, "I'm just following my lawyer's lead and advice on this." No one can accuse you of doing anything wrong if you're just following your lawyer's advice and letting her manage your case.

Let Your Lawyer Do Their Job

The whole point of hiring a lawyer is to allow that lawyer to do the work for you. Too often, divorcing parties still try to do the lawyer's job and end up undermining their cases and looking foolish to the court. You should NEVER do any of the following things:

- ❖ email or otherwise contact the judge
- ❖ copy opposing counsel on emails or other communications
- ❖ call opposing counsel's office
- ❖ go to opposing counsel's office

- ❖ tell your husband your lawyer's legal strategies or plans
- ❖ have a friend do any of these things on your behalf

You Need a Lawyer to Get the Documents Right

Even if your case is totally uncontested and a full agreement is reached early in the process, the importance of getting the final documents right cannot be overstated. If the agreement isn't memorialized in writing correctly, significant, life-impacting new issues can emerge. The last thing you want after your divorce case is completed is for some new problem to arise because you tried to draft your own divorce decree and messed something up.

There's a reason law school admission is so competitive, requires excellent grades, and takes seven years of education after high school. To become an attorney takes diligence, thousands of hours studying, and a certain tenacity. The law is complex in every jurisdiction and can ruin your life if not applied correctly. You are almost certain to omit, overlook, misunderstand or misstate something in the final documents without the benefit of an experienced lawyer's knowledge and experience. You should never sign a court order of any kind without having an attorney first review it for you.

You Need an Attorney for Sound Litigation Strategy

Lawyers know how to present the evidence that helps you and also, they know how to object to the harmful, inadmissible evidence presented by the other side. They know the rules of the courtroom, how to present your story in a way that is relatable and understandable, and how to insulate you from the "bad facts" that might undermine your case. Your case is a public relations war of sorts; you're in an internal PR war with your husband in which you're raising defenses to prevent him from turning your children and friends against you, but you're also in a PR war with him with the judge and/or jury as your audience. You're having to present yourself in the best possible light while being attacked—viciously in some cases. A good attorney is needed to get you through that war with as few battle wounds as possible.

Do Not Lie to Your Lawyer

Never lie to your lawyer. Your attorney can't help you unless you tell them the whole story, and the last thing you want is for your lawyer to be blindsided by some terrible fact in open court. A lawyer can't come up with a strategy to help you with your "bad facts" if she doesn't know what she's defending.

I once had a client who was being accused of illicit drug use, and I believed her when she swore up and down that her husband was lying. She was a sweet, attractive woman with lots of energy, but I thought she must just be that way naturally. She certainly didn't look like a drug user. It wasn't until the judge required her to undergo drug testing that we found out she was a regular user of methamphetamines. She had fooled me, and the judge took her kids from her, as he should have. But had I known she would test positive for drugs, I would have suggested a treatment program or some other alternative to the custody hearing. I never would have insisted she was clean if I had known going into that hearing that she was not. DO. NOT. LIE. TO. YOUR. LAWYER.

Don't be Afraid if Your Husband Hires a Good Lawyer

"Jennifer" became distraught when her cheating husband hired an attorney known for being tough after she had filed for divorce. "That lawyer is going to tear me up in court! I'm so scared of what will happen now that they'll be coming after me! Please tell me this will be OK!"

I hear this sort of thing at least once a month.

If this happens to you, take it as a good sign. Isn't it plausible that your husband has hired the best lawyer he can find because he knows he desperately needs one? He knows you have the dirt on him. He's scared you're going to take all his money. He wants to be prepared to deflect your arguments to minimize the impact of your divorce on his financial bottom line. He may have a secret mistress—or even a secret family?! I've seen that before—he's trying to protect. If he weren't concerned about the strength of your case, he may just represent himself. The unrepresented husbands are usually the ones with the least to hide.

We read in Proverbs 15:18 about how a hot-headed man stirs up conflict, but one slow to anger can calm a quarrel. Your irrationally temperamental husband may need someone with some walking-around sense to keep him calm. That smart lawyer he hired can be that cool head speaking reason and wisdom into him. Count it a blessing if he harasses you less as a result of his attorney's influence!

If your husband enjoys creating chaos and keeping you in turmoil, an experienced attorney can be a valuable voice of reason for him. You need a buffer for your husband's emotions. His lawyer is his buffer, just as your lawyer insulates you from having to communicate directly with your husband on difficult topics.

Having legal counsel in the middle fosters an atmosphere conducive to civil, productive communication. If you and your lawyer can convince your husband's lawyer that your husband is the problematic, unreasonable party, his lawyer can sometimes even become an advocate for you and your kids to be treated better, thus bringing peace to the litigation storm. There's nothing better than having *two* lawyers—yours and his—advocating for *you*. ☺

Questions for Reflection

1. Has your husband told you that you don't need a lawyer to represent you? What do you think may be driving his insistence that you not have counsel? Does he have legal counsel? Have you considered representing yourself? Did the warnings of this chapter give you concerns you hadn't considered?

2. Reflect on the following verses: Proverbs 11:14 (there is safety in an abundance of counselors), Proverbs 15:22 (with many advisors, plans succeed, but plans fail without counsel); 1 Timothy 1:8 (the law is good if used properly); Proverbs 12:15 (a wise woman listens to advice). See? Even the Bible says you need a lawyer! ☺

3. Are you comfortable speaking in public? Are you confident that you could present your claims, in the context of the laws of your state, and answer questions from the judge and from your husband's lawyer, without legal counsel? Are you equipped to prepare divorce contracts and other court filings without the help of an experienced lawyer? These questions are rhetorical and designed to make you pause and consider how it will feel if you go to court alone. It just isn't wise, Friend.

4. Think of the claims you will need to prove in court. What kind of evidence do you need in order to prove them? What

can you start doing to gather evidence for your lawyer to use in your case, even before the first consultation?

5. What do you anticipate your husband will do in preparation for divorce litigation? Put yourself in his shoes. You know how he thinks; what is he trying to prove against you, and how can you reveal the truth to refute those claims? How can you stay one step ahead of him?

Resources

It's Not Supposed to Be This Way—Lysa TerKeurst

Chapter Soundtrack

"Fortress Around Your Heart"—Sting

"Who Will You Run To"—Heart

"It Is Well"—Bethel Music

"The Thrill Is Gone"—B.B. King

3

Serve Your Spouse, Set the Tone

"Be brave enough to start a conversation that matters."
—Margaret Wheatley

How the divorce papers are delivered to the defending spouse can set the tone for the entire litigation. In this chapter, we'll explore the dynamics of service of process.

Kevin Gets Served

Kevin and his buddies are golfing on a beautiful, sunny Saturday. Beer is flowing, jokes are flying, and everyone is having a grand time. Just as Kevin prepares to putt on the ninth hole, the group notices a deputy in uniform approaching them, papers in hand. Afraid they're in trouble for public intoxication or something, the men settle down and get quiet. Kevin sinks his putt for eagle, but no one celebrates with him. Puzzled, he looks up and sees the deputy walking toward him. He can feel the vomit rising in his throat.

By this time, local friends sitting in the outdoor dining area near the putting green have taken notice., They watch in horror as the deputy hands Kevin a manilla envelope and says,"Sir, you've been served. Have a nice day." The packet is the divorce petition Kevin's wife, Kayleigh, had filed, in which all of his misdeeds are laid bare in great detail for all the world to see. Also included in the packet is a notice to appear for a hearing in the local courthouse in three weeks.

Kevin is humiliated and enraged. His friends, in true bros' fashion, rally around him, calling Kayleigh every name in the book and saying things like, "Man, I can't believe she did this to you in front of everybody you know."

Of course, Kevin hasn't told his friends how badly he's treated Kayleigh, so it's natural that they would have these defensive reactions. He hasn't told his friends about his online flirtations with other women or about his issues with pain pills. He hasn't told his friends that he asked his wife for a divorce two weeks before and that she's just making the first move.

Kevin had been feeling remorseful and willing to give Kayleigh a large chunk of their assets, along with substantial monthly support, before she embarrassed him in front of his country club friends. But now, all bets are off. Kevin is angry as a hornet over being made the town's laughingstock.

Kevin resolves to get the meanest lawyer he can find to fight Kayleigh every step of the way and he does. He proceeds to drag Kayleigh through months and months of expensive and public court battles, mainly because of how she started the case. She set a tone that poked the bear from the start, when she could have allowed Kevin to save face by serving him privately. Worse, by making a fool of her husband, Kayleigh has increased the amount she'll have to pay a lawyer to navigate her now higher-conflict divorce case, and she has reduced her chances of settling her case in a way that meets her needs.

No One Likes To Be Humiliated

People sometimes don't realize that divorce cases are lawsuits just like any other. The court caption of "Spouse 1 versus Spouse 2" will be listed at the caption at the top of all the court filings. Romeo and Juliet are now Plaintiff and Defendant. You are no longer on the same team, and the lawsuit can't get rolling until (1) the Plaintiff files the petition and (2) the Defendant is served with a copy of the Petition. Effecting good service on the Defendant (i.e., giving Defendant official notice of the lawsuit that's been filed against him, in accordance with local law) is essential for the case to proceed.

We've all heard the in-your-face line, "You've been served," in movies. When my kids were little, they would come home talking about how some kid at school "got served" that day. When I would ask what they meant, the story would go like this:

Child 1: "Your shoes are ugly."

Child 2 to Child 1: "Oh yeah? Well, your mama's ugly."

Child 3 to Child 1: "Ooooh, you just got served!"

Even children understand that if you've been served, someone has taken control over you, humiliated you, or somehow put you on defense. It's implied that the person who's been "served" is not the one in control of the situation. No one likes being humiliated, even when they may deserve it, and no one likes losing control. Remember the Golden Rule: if you wouldn't like for it to happen to you, you shouldn't cause it to happen to him. Divorce litigation is naturally unpleasant but do what you can to keep from unnecessarily publicly tearing down your husband in the process. It's not a good look in court.

Try Not to Serve Him at Work

Whenever I am sending a client's divorce petition for service, I consider the circumstances of each case individually in an effort to serve the petition in a way that will best advance our goals. It is rarely wise to humiliate the opponent by serving them the way Kayleigh served Kevin in the hypothetical above. Whenever possible, I allow opposing parties to accept service of their petitions in my office by signing an acknowledgment of service with one of our paralegals. It's the most discreet way to serve someone, and it sets a classy tone from the very start of what is usually a very difficult conversation for a Defendant to face. The only time I don't offer this option to unrepresented parties is if the person has been violent or has a history of aggressive, irrational behavior, as I can't have an angry opposing party raging in my office lobby.

It is, of course, a case-by-case analysis when determining the best way to serve a Defendant. I don't generally recommend serving someone in front of their co-workers unless it's absolutely necessary for accomplishing service, but if you don't have a home address for your husband after you've separated, you may have no other choice. Moreover, you don't want your husband to lose his job just before a divorce case starts because his employer doesn't like his personal drama coming to the workplace! You need your husband to keep working to earn good money as you start divvying up your respective financial responsibilities. If he loses his job and you still have yours, you could be the one ordered to pay *him* child support or alimony. Don't let your desire to punish him cause you to be foolish. Your lawyer will know the best approach to service for your case; be sure to get advice on this before proceeding!

Service as a Tool to Establish Important Facts

There are, however, times when the method of service can help you establish facts of your case that will be useful for settlement negotiations. For example, if your Husband is cheating on you but denying it, you and your lawyer might consider serving your husband at the home of the girlfriend, in the early morning hours, in his jammies, to prove he's having the affair. Or if you suspect your husband is having an affair while out of town for work, you might consider serving him at the hotel so that the process server can testify that the girlfriend was there with him. The adultery cases I have served in this manner have all settled during the first month of the litigation, in my client's favor. MIC. DROP.

But the most common way to serve a Defendant in a typical case where I practice is via the local sheriff's office where the person resides. We pay a small fee, send the petition and summons over to the deputies, and they take it from there. We usually try to *time* service in a way that protects children and keeps the Defendant from being enraged from the start of the case. You don't want to send a cop to bang on your husband's door at 8:00 p.m. when the children are present and can see Daddy getting served. If you must serve the other party at home, talk to your lawyer about how to schedule the date and time of service when the children are not going to be there. Your children will never forget watching one parent serve the other with divorce papers or the emotional reaction to being served, which can include raging anger taken out on the children. As a parent, it's your job to protect your children from such trauma, and, no matter what you've been through, you should respect your spouse enough on a human level to handle service subtly and with limited fanfare.

What If He Dodges Service?

If a Defendant doesn't want to be served and dodges all other service efforts, the targeted approach employed by a private process server or private investigator, with their added layer of Inspector Gadget sleuthing and staking out the Defendant's location, can be an efficient (though often more expensive) way to serve the Defendant.

If all other efforts are exhausted and you just can't find your service-dodging husband in order to serve him, your lawyer can tell you the other options for trying to perfect service for the record. Sometimes service can be perfected by publication of a notice in local newspaper. Where I practice, I have had to use the publication service option when all other ordinary efforts failed. The drawback I'm seeing with service by publication these days is that fewer and fewer people are reading the newspaper, so the likelihood of the Defendant—or even those close to the Defendant–actually seeing news of the lawsuit is becoming extremely slim. For this reason, service by publication is not ideal where I am, but it could be more ideal or commonly utilized where you are.

Remember: **The tips in this chapter are not legal advice; they are ideas for you to consider as you discuss service options in your unique case. You must ask your attorney for guidance on how best to accomplish service in your jurisdiction, considering the particular challenges of your situation.**

Questions for Reflection

1. Are you planning to file your divorce or be the one to be served? Which do you think is the best strategy for you, in light of the considerations outlined earlier in the book?
2. If you are the one initiating the divorce case, what can you do to set a productive tone from the start of the proceedings, while also preserving safe boundaries for you and your children?
3. What is the best way to serve your husband with the paperwork? You know him better than anyone. What can you do to keep tensions down?

Resources

Reflect on these verses as you consider how to begin your divorce case:

❖ "To sum up, all of you be harmonious, sympathetic, brotherly, kindhearted, and humble in spirit; not returning evil for evil or insult for insult but giving a blessing instead; for you were called for the very purpose that you might inherit a blessing."—1 Peter 3:8-11

❖ "If your brother sins, go and show him his fault in private; if he listens to you, you have won your brother."—Matthew 18:15

❖ Never pay back evil for evil to anyone. Respect what is right in the sight of all men. If possible, so far as it depends on you, be at peace with all men. Never take your own revenge, beloved, but leave room for the wrath of God, for it is written, "Vengeance is Mine, I will repay," says the Lord."—Romans 12:17-21

❖ "Do not merely look out for your own personal interests, but also for the interests of others."—Philippians 2:4

Chapter Soundtrack

"Hit Me With Your Best Shot"—Pat Benatar

4

Establish an Optimal Status Quo Before Court

"I am a marvelous housekeeper. Every time I leave a man,
I keep his house."
—Zsa Zsa Gabor

Setting your case up for success begins long before the first hearing. When the bailiff says, "All rise and come to order" and the judge enters the courtroom, you need to have already established (or be ready to coherently propose) a logical way for your bills to be paid and property be divided while the case is pending. This chapter is designed to help you think through how to put yourself in the best position to achieve a workable set of terms governing your family while you litigate your divorce.

It's absolutely imperative to establish a solid status quo, a/k/a standard way of operating, from the start of the separation period. If you and your husband agree before or early in the separation period how monthly obligations will be paid, property will be used and maintained, and children will go between your homes, the terms of that understanding or the way of operating generally carries the day when it's time to make those plans official in court, as the family has already been operating under those arrangements without issue. I've seen it time and again: it's just easier for a judge to order a continuation of what the parties have already been doing than to reimagine and reinvent how your affairs will be handled after knowing you just a few hours. In my experience, it's harder to convince a judge to place new or increased expectations on one or both parties than to obtain an order requiring them to keep doing what they've been doing what *they themselves chose* to do.

Your Choices Can Disrupt the Status Quo

People in high-conflict marriages often yearn to find a release valve, some sort of relief from the high-pressure home environment they're living in. They are often tempted to run away from the marital home, just for a much-needed break, with every intention of going back soon thereafter. What often happens, however, is that a spouse who leaves the home is regarded as having abandoned any interest in living there, and for this reason is precluded from coming back to the home as planned. Running away like this can spell disaster for your divorce case, your child custody claims, and your financial stability while the matter is pending. That's why I generally advise my clients not to leave the home <u>unless their safety depends on it</u> (always the exception to every other rule), to always take the children with them if they simply must leave, and not to move with the children unless the new residence is safe and would be acceptable to the court.

You can certainly spend time away from home during the day, but it's usually best to lay your head on your pillow at home each night until some formal understanding is reached about division of the home and its bills and custody of the children. Once you leave the marital residence, getting back in again can be more difficult than you expect. It can sometimes be like pulling teeth to get back into the house even to obtain items you need for daily life, let alone get back into the house to stay after you've left for a period of time.

Many women have come to me for their first consultation, already having made the mistake of vacating the house, and leaving the children with their estranged husband just to get some space, fully intending to go back and get the children once a new residence is set up. This approach exposes a mother to arguments that she has "abandoned her children," and at minimum that she believes her husband to be a wonderful father (why else would she have left the children with him for a single day if he's not a great dad?), which makes it nearly impossible to later argue that he's abusive or a less-than-stellar parent. Departing from the home in the early stages of separation like this can also signal to the children that you don't want them and gives their dad a talking point should he choose to alienate the children from you. In general, the judges I know will do their best to make sure their rulings serve the children's best interests, and it's usually more stable for the children to remain in the home they've always known. For this reason, I usually advise women not to move out of the marital home if they want custody of their children, at least not until after the judge has had a chance to weigh in or a formal custody agreement is reached. Consult your lawyer for the best living arrangement for your particular situation.

Unless absolutely necessary for your survival, it's not usually advisable to let your parents or other family members pay your bills, even if they plan to help you later on. To the extent you need financial support, it's not your parents' job to provide it, and it's unwise to establish a post-separation living situation in which your parents relieve your husband of his obligations to you. For example, if you have been a stay-at-home mom or your income is far less than your husband's, you need to establish an early status quo of him continuing to pay your bills or paying you a particular amount of money, just as he's always done in the past, at least for the time being. You may need this support only during the period between separation and divorce or you may need it for a little while after the matter is finalized. In either case, your family should not pick up the slack, and, in my experience, he's less likely to be ordered to pay as much if other people have been doing it for him. Again, the status quo usually persists.

If your husband has always paid your credit card off each month, your car payment and insurance, the mortgage and home utilities, you need to try to make sure he continues paying them (or giving you the cash equivalent so you can pay them) during separation. The whole idea is to keep things afloat for the household and the children while you sort out the terms for your final resolution. If you can get a solid understanding of how your obligations will be managed, inertia just seems to take over the longer you live under those terms. If you can just be still long enough to get a court order meeting your temporary needs, you won't be rushed into a less-than-ideal final settlement. You need a temporary arrangement to live under which will give you a minute to catch your breath and evaluate how your life (and budget) will look as a single woman. You need a little time—and an adequate financial cushion—in order to identify all your needs, as a separated, individual woman with your own budget for perhaps for the first time in your life. Be wise and avoid decisions that will set you up for less-than-optimal results. Don't sell yourself short in your rush to put your pain behind you. It's important that you not rush into a quick settlement that won't meet your long-term needs. Talk to your lawyer before making any big moves.

Mia's Story

Mia arrives at her initial divorce consultation. Here's how the conversation goes:

Lawyer: *Where do you live?*

Mia: *Well, that's complicated at the moment. I found a cute little rental house in town, so I've been staying there to get it situated for the past three weeks. It's not as nice or as big as our marital home on Stonewall Street, but I just wanted to show Mike that I'm able to stand on my own two feet, so I got a loan from my family and went ahead and left. Mike has been at the Stonewall house for three weeks with the kids. I hope he sees now how it feels to take care of all the kids' needs and that big old house without any help. It's been such a nice break since I moved out!*

Lawyer: *You mean you left your children with him?! And you've been staying alone at the rental house?*

Mia: *Yes, but I plan to go get the kids this weekend for them to move into the rental with me. I needed the time to get the house set up for them. I never intended to leave them with him indefinitely.*

Lawyer: *Have you told Mike you're going to get the kids this weekend to move them to the rental? How does he feel about that?*

Mia: *I haven't told him yet, but I'm sure he'll be happy to hand them over to me after three weeks of parenting them without me. He's so overwhelmed that he's moved his mother into the house to do laundry, make the kids' meals, and drive the kids everywhere...basically to do the job I've always done. Can you believe that?! He can't handle anything without his mother.*

Lawyer: *Mia, you never should have left the kids behind. He and his mother may argue now that you just checked out and stopped parenting. And a judge may actually see it that way, too. How are the kids doing since you moved out? Have you been seeing them?*

Mia: *I've been so busy working on the rental house that I haven't had time to see the kids very much, but I've been doing all this work on the house for them, and I'm sure they understand that. Plus, I've talked to them on the phone every day and told them I'm coming back to get them soon.*

Lawyer: *I'm afraid you've made a big mistake leaving the house like that without any formal understanding of custody, parenting time, and financial obligations. Are you sure Mike is going to let the kids go with you?*

Mia: *Mike has never been interested in parenting the children. And I'm sure after these three weeks with him, he will gladly hand them over.*

That weekend when Mia goes to pick up the children and their belongings to move them into the rental house, Mike refuses to let them go. Mike has changed the locks on the house and will not even allow Mia to enter the home. A big argument ensues, and law enforcement officers come to the home. Mia is not allowed to take the children or any property from the house. The police are powerless to help her, as the house and the children belong to both parties, but she has left the kids and been away from the home for weeks. The police instruct her to get an attorney and file something with the court. In the weeks it takes to get the case before a judge, Mike and Mia engage in a daily race to the school to pick up the children, and it turns into an arm-pulling contest, as each party has parental rights to the children. All of this traumatizes the children, on top of the trauma connected with their perception (despite Mia's best intentions) that their mother has left them behind all this time. Their grandmother has stepped into Mia's role in the household.

At the first hearing in the case months later, the judge awards Mike primary custody of the children, citing that the children should remain in their familiar surroundings during this transitional time and finding that Mike is the more stable parent of the two. Mia is allowed visitation with the children during alternating weekends. While the judge doesn't make Mia pay Mike any child support because she isn't working and has no income, Mia is not awarded any child support from Mike, and she had banked on child support when she signed her rental home lease agreement. The judge finds that Mia can continue paying her rent from whatever source of money she has been paying it for the past few months, which means her father will have to continue paying her bills for the time being. Mia eventually finds a job that helps make ends meet, but she struggles financially and misses her children desperately. Inertia takes over, and Mike ends up with primary custody of the children, ownership of the marital home, and an order for Mia to pay him a small monthly amount in child support.

How different the outcome would have likely been had Mia stayed in the home and continued parenting the children daily until the first court date! Driven by an emotional compulsion to get away, to prove she didn't need Mike and could start life independently with no assistance from him, and to teach him a lesson and force him to step up his day-to-day involvement with the children, Mia made some serious missteps that cost her financially and, most importantly, cost her parenting time with her children.

Questions for Reflection

1. In your marital household, how are the household financial obligations divided? Is there enough money to go around to meet all the obligations if you and your husband have separate residences?

2. How will you afford your bills after you separate from your husband? What is your plan?

3. Have you been tempted to move out of your home to keep the peace? How have the warnings of this chapter given you food for thought about why that may not be the best idea?

4. Will you speak with your lawyer before you make any big moves or take on large financial obligations which you aren't sure you can afford? Have you made a budget and figured out your monthly costs?

5. How do you think your husband will handle your separation? Is he a fair-minded fella or the type you'll have to fight for every nickel? What are you doing to put yourself in the best possible position going into your first divorce proceeding?

Resources
The Armor of God—a Bible study by Pricilla Shirer

Chapter Soundtrack
"Time for Me to Fly"—REO Speedwagon
"He Thinks He'll Keep Her"—Mary Chapin Carpenter

5

Crush the First Hearing

"The Lord will stand with you and give you strength."
—2 Timothy 4:17

Where I practice law, the first hearing is typically the one where the court establishes child custody and division of parenting time, awards financial support to be paid by one party to the other, and divides your property and debt on a temporary basis. How you fare at this hearing, often called a "temporary hearing," typically sets the stage for how the rest of the case will unfold. If you make a solid showing at the first hearing, your husband might very well fold up his tent and give you a quick settlement. By contrast, if you crash and burn at the temporary hearing, you will only embolden your husband to think he can continue to push you around for the rest of the litigation.

I say it all the time: **divorce cases are won or lost at the first hearing**. It's crucial to present the strongest case you can early in the proceedings, as the terms set in place early in the case have a tendency to live on for a long while.

My hope is that this chapter will take the fear out of going to court by giving you an idea of what to expect, along with some practical tips for staying poised and put together as you learn your way around the courtroom.

Have Your Stuff Together

Find out what your lawyer needs from you well ahead of the first hearing and provide it on time and with nothing left undone. By providing what the court requires, in the form the court requires it, you are demonstrating your respect for the court and its procedures. Moreover, being organized goes a long way toward establishing the veracity of your claims when you get in front of the judge.

How to Handle Yourself in Court

If you've never been in court before, the prospect can be daunting. The following are some general rules of thumb I give my clients before any court appearance:

1. **Don't be late.** The judges where I practice have the power to hold you in contempt, fine you, or even put you in jail if you show up late to your hearing. Even if you're not put in jail or fined, being late shows a lack of reverence for the court's authority. Be on time.

2. **Leave your phone in the car.** Check the rules of your local courthouse before you arrive and don't bring any devices with you that are not permitted by the court's rules. You don't want to have to return to your car to put your cell phone away when you're already nervous about making it to your hearing on time.

3. **Dress appropriately.** Don't wear anything too sexy or too casual. Do not, under any circumstances, wear shorts or noisy, rubber flip flops. Nicer jeans are okay if there are no holes in them, but dressy pants are better. Wear what you would wear to a job interview: understated and classy. If you have prescription glasses or use readers, bring them with you

to court. Understated jewelry is best; small, stud earrings and necklaces are always good selections for court. The official employee handbook for a firm I worked for early in my career expressly instructed its female employees that earrings should be "business-like" and not "party-like." I always loved that description. Everyone knows what kind of earrings you can wear to a party (mine are oversized, made of feathers and brightly colored) but would never wear for a business meeting (small, not too flashy, not too bright). When in doubt, go small and neutral instead of large and distracting.

4. **Remove piercings and cover tattoos**. I don't have any tattoos myself, but I think they're cool on other people because of the symbolism and meaning they carry. But they can also be seen as a sign of rebellion, and rebellion isn't cool in court. If you happen to draw a judge who views tattoos this way, it could be a detriment to your case. If you can, just to be safe, cover your tattoos with clothing or body makeup for court appearances. The same can be true of larger ear piercings and piercings of the nose, eyebrows, tongue, and lips. Some judges just don't agree with piercings like these, so it's best not to take a chance. Remove those piercings before you come to court. Also, remove your hat or other head covering as a show of humility, unless, of course, the head covering is part of your normal religious practice.

5. **Spit out your chewing gum**. At our local court, the deputy will make you spit out your gum before addressing the judge. It just smacks of disrespect. Pun intended.

6. **Be appropriately groomed**. Style your hair conservatively, and if at all possible, only color your hair a color that occurs

naturally in humans. While your friends, family and even your lawyer (I once had a client with blue hair, and it was absolutely stunning on her!) may think your fuchsia hair is lovely, the judge may not. Court is not the forum for fashion statements.

7. **Take your medications and bring snacks and comfort items**. Be sure you take all your medications as prescribed before court, and if you will require another dose during the day, bring them with you to take in case the proceedings are long. Consider bringing a few snacks in your purse in case you don't get a break for lunch; you don't want to run out of energy on this very important day! Bring a soft cardigan in case the courtroom is chilly. In South Georgia, the air conditioning in some courthouses freezes us half to death. You don't want chattering teeth on top of being nervous when you're trying to testify.

8. **Bring supporters**. If your attorney agrees it's a good idea, bring all the supporters you can muster to sit behind you during the hearing. A strong showing of support on your side of the courtroom can demonstrate to the judge that you're loved and, most likely, to be believed if all these folks in the courtroom also believe you.

9. **Make sure your supporters stay composed**. The last thing you want is your peanut gallery becoming unruly, angering the judge, and undermining your case. If you bring supporters to court with you, make sure they know how to behave.

10. **Try not to lock eyes with your ex**. Ignoring him and his posse like they're air will help you get through the day without being intimidated. He can't rattle you if you refuse to look at him.

Tips for Testifying

Most people dislike public speaking in general. But testifying in an open courtroom in front of a bunch of strangers, in front of a judge who will make major decisions for your life, is a whole other level of stress. Following are some tips to help you crush your testimony:

1. **Speak clearly and understandably.** The court reporter and judge must be able to understand what you're saying in order for you to prevail in court. Address the judge as "Your Honor" and try to make eye contact with the lawyer or judge with whom you are interacting while on the witness stand. If you misspeak, just say so and ask for a chance to correct your answer. Never raise your voice. Keep your tone of voice level and controlled. Keep your voice even and, for the love of Pete, try not to burst into tears or ugly cry on the stand. Countless times, I've seen judges roll their eyes and even say, "Ma'am, you're gonna have to stop crying. I can't understand what you're saying." Composure is key. If tears enter your eyes and you need a moment, politely request a pause, and collect yourself before continuing. If permitted by security personnel and the judge, take a bottle of water with you to the witness stand so you can take a sip when you need a moment to think about your next answer. Never direct your testimony to your husband directly; speak of him in the third person rather than turning toward him and addressing him as "you." It's bad form. And use verbal responses instead of nodding or shaking your head, "yes" or "no" instead of "uh-huh" mumblings the court reporter can't easily transcribe.

2. **Don't lose your cool**. Your husband's lawyer's purpose in life is to try to get a rise out of you. He's doing everything possible to make you lose your cool in front of the judge. Do not fall for it! Rise above it, and you will look like the credible voice of reason. Be polite to opposing counsel, even when under attack, and even if you're being insulted. Address the attorney as "Mr. [surname]" or "Ms. [surname] or whatever formal prefix that person prefers. NEVER call your husband's lawyer by his/her first name, even if you know the lawyer personally outside of the litigation. You are not on a first-name basis with that lawyer for purposes of this proceeding. And never bring up the attorney's personal life in court. Conduct yourself as if it's a business interview. Do not ask your spouse's lawyer questions when being cross-examined, except as necessary to politely request clarification of a question. If you try to turn the conversation around on the lawyer, you will appear disrespectful and hostile, and you will run the risk of ticking off the judge.

3. **Stay focused on your story, and do not let opposing counsel rattle you**. You can expect your husband's lawyer to bring up trivial matters while ignoring the issues you deem most important to the case. He will naturally focus on the points he views most helpful to his case. Expect it, don't let it frustrate you, and don't let it divert your focus from the points you're there to make. Focus on YOUR version of how this thing went down. Polite people naturally get rattled and defensive when opposing counsel is loud, accusatory and aggressive. If this happens to you, remind yourself that:

   • Louder and meaner does not mean smarter.

296 | Crush Your Divorce & Keep Your Faith

- Louder and meaner does not equal more believable; in fact, the louder the lawyer gets, it's an indication that they're overcompensating for weaknesses in the facts of the case. Let not your heart be troubled.
- The attorney is just trying to scare you into submission so you'll crack on the witness stand. It's a trap to make you emotional so you'll show the worst part of yourself to the judge. Do not be tricked!

4. **Take notes with you if you need them.** If you need to refer to notes for your testimony to be accurate and complete, take them to the witness stand with you if your lawyer agrees it's appropriate. In some places, opposing counsel is allowed to read anything you take up to the stand with you, so ask your lawyer if this is the case in your court. At a temporary hearing I handled one time, I tripped up a testifying father by asking him the names of the children's schoolteachers. He didn't have a clue who they were, and this was my point—that the mother, my client, had always managed the children's educational needs. By the time of the final trial in that case, he'd gotten smart though. This time, he secretly brought notes with him up to the stand with the all the teachers' names written on them. He testified like a champ when I questioned him about teachers this time. If only I'd seen the notes before he headed up there; I didn't find them on the witness table until after the trial was over.

5. **Don't answer questions you aren't asked.** Some people just get what my mama always called "diarrhea of the mouth" and lay traps for themselves while testifying. They ramble on and on until everyone has forgotten what the question

even was, and they often testify themselves right into some damning admissions without meaning to. For example, I once got a guy to admit on the witness stand that "everyone has tried meth at one time or another," when the original question was just whether he had ever used meth before in his life. His broader statement demonstrated an abnormally casual attitude toward illegal drug use. My client got custody of the child! Another time, in response to my question about how property should be divided, a husband said, "I made all the money, so it's my money, and she shouldn't get anything." His attitude was contrary to Georgia's laws on division of marital property, and the judge knew it. The man's testimony demonstrated a lack of respect for his wife of thirty years and undermined his case considerably.

6. **Know when to stop speaking**. If your attorney stands up or objects to a question you're asked, stop speaking to allow the judge an opportunity to rule on the objection. When the judge is speaking for any reason, you shut your mouth immediately and let him finish. It's the judge's courtroom; you're just a guest.

7. **Tell the truth and watch your body language**. You owe the court honesty. I always tell my client that they must either tell the truth or plead the privilege against self-incrimination when testifying; lying is not an option and deceiving the court can get you into really hot water. Similarly, your body language should demonstrate that you are approachable. Relatable. Believable. Credible. Body language experts say you should avoid doing things that can indicate dishonesty, such as touching your face, leaning away, crossing your

arms, or fidgeting with your fingers while speaking. Don't be afraid to ask for a bathroom break if you need one. Don't roll your eyes or give snarky, rude or sarcastic replies to embarrass the attorney.

8. **Do not clinically diagnose your husband from the witness stand**. Unless you are his mental health or medical provider, do not diagnose your husband with narcissism, bipolar disorder, or any other mental health issue or addiction. It's not your place to do that. You can describe his behavior, but you do not label him unless you have the credentials and licenses to back that up.

9. **Don't be holier than thou, but do not be meek**. Without being too self-deprecating, be willing to own your part in the breakup. Do not blame every single problem in your life or in your marriage on your husband. Remember that the judge is much less interested in your broken heart than he is in resolving the financial and practical issues of your children's well-being, where you're live and how you'll pay your bills. No one likes a person with an attitude of superiority over others. You don't want the judge to hate you. And while we all know "blessed are the meek," your divorce proceedings are not the place for meekness. No one knows this story quite like you do. Only you can enlighten the court on all the details required for a fair decision to be rendered. Be bold, Dear Friend! There's nothing unladylike about standing up for yourself and telling the truth, even if it will be hard for you to say it and for your ex to hear it.

10. **Pray ahead of time**. Put on your armor, and pray for your attorney, the judge, the witnesses and even your husband

and his attorney, no matter how mean they may have been to you. Pray that your words will bring God glory. Pray that your children will be shielded during this season. Pray that God would remove your anxiety and throw up a hedge of protection to surround you. There's inexplicable power in prayer, Dear One. If you're my client reading this, I ask that you pray for me, even now.

Have Your Evidence Locked and Loaded

Winston Churchill once said to "speak softly and carry a big stick." Your evidence is your big stick, your powerful weapon in the argument before the court. Compelling evidence will do most of the talking for you.

Your lawyer will be ever so thankful if you, well in advance of the hearing date, provide evidence to back up each point you need the court to understand. Without evidence, your claims are simply your word against your husband's. I generally like to have something (i.e., a text message, email, photograph, etc.) to illustrate each point of my client's case. When presenting your case, I've found it's most powerful first to STATE your position, then to SHOW the court with evidence why your position is true, and then EXPLAIN each point and why it matters to the court's analysis of that particular issue. Doing this for each point brings significant clarity and makes it hard to deny that you're right.

For example, if your husband ripped your sweater when you were fighting or broke the heel off your favorite shoes in a drunken rage, put those babies in Ziploc® bags and slap an exhibit sticker on them. They're evidence.

If your husband was fired or written up at work because of an insubordinate attitude like the one he shows you at home, obtain his personnel files and have them ready to show the judge that you're not the only one he has trouble getting along with. If he's an illegal drug user but denies it, maybe you can find some text messages where he discusses buying or using drugs or actual drug paraphernalia he's left lying around the house. If he has abused you physically, have photos of your injuries ready to show the court as you testify about his assaults.

Identify Witnesses to Help You Make Your Case

If you're fighting for custody of your children, you may need a school counselor, teacher or child psychologist to testify that you should have custody of the kids. You probably also have family members and close friends who can bear witness to much of what you're alleging. Talk to your lawyer about which one(s) should testify on your behalf.

Perhaps you've heard the old adage that "the enemy of my enemy is my friend." Try to think of all the people from whom your husband is estranged and ask them how that came to be. You may just find out things about him you didn't know, things that are relevant to your proceedings, things that the witness may testify about in your hearing to help your case.

How to Assist Your Lawyer During the Hearing

While your husband and other witnesses are testifying, you will probably hear things in their testimony that agitate you or make you downright angry. Do not let the judge see the anger in you and do not utter a word. Your talking will preclude your attorney from listening to the testimony to raise the necessary objections, and the other side could actually hear what you're saying. Instead, have a notepad and a pen ready to jot down counterpoints to everything they're saying on the witness stand and hand these notes to your lawyer for their cross-examination of the witness. Stay calm.

Hearsay

If you've watched legal dramas on TV, you've likely seen a lawyer raise a "hearsay" objection. Hearsay testimony is testimony about what a *third* party who isn't in court has *said*, and it's generally inadmissible, and you can save yourself some consternation at the hearing if you learn what hearsay is and train yourself to leave it out of your testimony altogether. Anything your ex said is generally not hearsay, as he is both in court and a party to the case. Ask your lawyer to explain the hearsay rules of your jurisdiction, well ahead of your hearing.

If the Hearing Goes Well, Don't Gloat

After your great day in court, you may be tempted to go online and tell the world all about it, but you must not do so, especially if the hearing isn't the final proceeding in your case, and especially if you have children with your husband. If you take to social media to gloat about what an idiot/abuser/jerk/bad dad your husband (and/or his attorney) is, it will likely come back to bite you in later proceedings. Always be a gracious winner.

Questions for Reflection

1. Are you a naturally gifted public speaker? If so, great! If not, what are some things you can do to help compose yourself as you prepare to testify in your case?

2. Would it make you more comfortable to have notes to take with you to the witness stand? What things do you want to have written down for reference while you testify?

3. Have you and your attorney discussed what to expect at the hearing? Have you made a list of questions to ask your attorney about the coming proceedings?

4. Who in your life is an eyewitness to events relevant to your divorce? Which of these people would make the best witnesses in court?

5. Try to put yourself in your husband's shoes. What do you expect the crux of his testimony to be? How can you prepare your lawyer to respond to it? What evidence can you provide your attorney not only to prove your allegations, but also to disprove your husband's? What can you do to gather this evidence for your lawyer?

Resources

Spy the Lie: Former CIA Officers Teach You How to Detect Deception—Philip Houston

Speak With No Fear—Mike Acker

How Highly Effective People Speak—Peter Andrei

The 4-7-8 Breathing Technique—*The Mel Robbins Podcast* ("How to Handle Negative People: 6 Strategies to Protect Your Peace")

Chapter Soundtrack

"Roar"—Katy Perry

"By Your Side"—Tenth Avenue North

"Lion and the Lamb"—Leeland

"Love is a Battlefield"—Pat Benatar

"Heartbreak Warfare"—John Mayer

6

Crush the Discovery Phase

"Tell me and I will forget, show me and I may remember; involve me and I will understand."
—Confucius

To Win Your Case, You Must Be Understood and Believed

In this day and age, we're digesting loads of information—in small doses on social media and other electronic formats—on a daily basis. Judges are human beings like everyone else, and you have to be mindful of limited attention spans when presenting your divorce case. You will *not* prevail in your case unless you are able to present your side of the issues *clearly and succinctly* and support your allegations with evidence of their truth.

The key to presenting a compelling case in court is for your attorney to boil down your positions to easily digestible "fact nuggets," illustrate each nugget with some kind of proof, and explain to the court why it matters in the grand scheme. As Albert Einstein said, "If you can't explain it simply, you don't understand it well enough." I don't know any judge who has patience for rambling, redundant testimony. Good preparation and organization of evidence is key in being the party most favored by the court, and discovery is the first step in your attorney's preparation. You can say very little if the evidence you present alongside your testimony illustrates your points for you. You *tell* the court your position, then you *show* the court why you're right using evidence. After you've *told* and *shown* the court all of this, the judge is much more likely to *understand*, and, ideally, agree with you.

Discovery is the process by which you gather documents and other evidence to *show* the court why you're right. In this chapter, you'll learn about the various tools your lawyer might use in the discovery phase of your case. why your full cooperation in discovery is important even if you're not thrilled about it, and how you can help your lawyer optimize results during the discovery period of your divorce.

The Importance of Financial Disclosures

Where I practice family law, every party to every divorce case is required to provide a financial disclosure of their income, assets, debts, monthly payments to creditors, and expenses. This disclosure form can be a wealth of useful information about the opposing party and can efficiently illuminate the financial situation if you've been kept in the dark about the family finances. The disclosure form is a helpful tool for thinking through how to structure your post-divorce budget, especially if you've never had to create or follow a budget before. When/if you are asked to fill out a financial disclosure form, it's important to follow your lawyer's instructions, as various jurisdictions (and sometimes even different judges) have divergent standards and expectations.

I always tell my clients to be honest when completing their financial disclosures. When litigants submit incomplete or false financial disclosures, a complete discovery investigation and analysis becomes all the more important.

Discovery Tools

There are various discovery tools in your lawyer's toolbox, and each one has a specific purpose and value. This section will outline the different mechanisms used in discovery:

- ❖ <u>Written Discovery</u>: Written discovery can take the form of lists of questions for your opposing party or a third party to answer, lists of "gotcha" accusations to be admitted or denied, and written lists of documents to be produced within a particular amount of time, at the hearing, or at some other time and location. The written responses to these written questions and requests can be used later to impeach (or undermine the credibility of) the person who gave the answer, or to hold the opposing party accountable or keep them honest on a particular topic. If someone lies in written discovery given under oath, perjury allegations can arise, or, even worse, all credibility with the court can be lost. If not all requested items and information are disclosed, and it's later discovered that the information and documentation existed and would have revealed the existence of a concealed asset or obligation, the non-disclosing party can be in hot water with the judge and can be compelled to pay the other party's litigation costs.

- ❖ <u>Depositions</u>: Depositions involve a lawyer questioning someone in a formal setting, under oath, with a court reporter present to take down everything that is said. Depositions are sometimes video recorded. Depositions are often not conducted until after all the documentary discovery has been exchanged, so that the lawyers have more fodder for questions. Don't get wigged out if you are required to sit for a deposition. Just think of it as a conversation. Your lawyer can tell you what to expect and how to prepare.

❖ <u>Third-Party Requests for Records and Subpoenas to Appear</u>. Your lawyer can send formal requests to third parties with information relevant to your case, asking them to produce that information for review. Subpoenas are sometimes necessary to require production of the items you need or to require someone to appear in person to produce the items so that your lawyer can ask questions, either in a deposition setting or in court. Evidence from third parties can sometimes be even more compelling than evidence provided by a party to the lawsuit, as third parties "have no dog in the fight" in your divorce and, therefore, no reason to lie or fabricate evidence. Brainstorm with your attorney about which third parties in your world should be requested to provide answers or information. Does your husband have business partners, associates, or even enemies who could shed light on the issues of your case? Do you have questions for any other women in his life about the nature of their relationships? Give your lawyer a list of these people you suspect may have information, and let your lawyer determine the propriety of taking their depositions or otherwise involving them in your case. There may be strategies for and against doing so.

❖ <u>Witness Affidavits</u>. Check with your lawyer about the procedure, if any, for submitting witness statements in your case in your jurisdiction. Where I practice, we gather affidavits from witnesses so that testimony can be nailed down early in the case. They're great to have on hand to keep witnesses honest throughout the litigation should they be inclined to change their minds, and they're also helpful guides for your lawyer to use when questioning the affidavit writer in open court should they come to court to testify on your behalf. Affidavits from nonrelatives are helpful because they are perceived as more objective than a family member's statement. While you may be concerned about the perceived bias that comes from family connections, it's still a good idea to have your family and close friends write affidavits for you. They've likely witnessed most of the things that will prove your case. Just make sure they include details and examples of events that support your positions, rather than vague, sweeping opinions that are unsupported in fact. The judge will separate the wheat from the chaff. I always tell my clients to make sure the affidavits are printed on one-sided rather than double-sided paper, and that typewritten statements are best but handwritten are fine so long as they're legible. Ask your lawyer for tips on whether affidavits or witness statements are allowed/encouraged in your case, and, if so, how you should prepare them. Every judge and every lawyer have preferred ways of doing things. Follow the proper procedure for your area.

Why Depositions are Golden Tools

Of all the discovery tools at your lawyer's disposal, I believe depositions are the most useful in divorces because they afford you the element of surprise. Because depositions are, more or less, just a conversation around the table, it's easy for an inexperienced deponent (i.e., the person giving testimony at a deposition) to give more information than they should, lose their filter, and get caught in inconsistent statements. In written discovery, the party answering questions has time to craft a response that is less likely to incriminate them, but depositions do not allow much time for thought, as there's no way to predict all the questions the lawyer will ask, and responses are required instantly. The deponent's slightest pause before answering or change in facial expression can reveal the deponent's dishonesty or effort to hide something, and this can lead to more and more pointed questions as the lawyer tries to get to the heart of the matter. A deponent's own words are powerful weapons to expose their dishonesty, should they give different testimony in later proceedings in front of the judge or jury. In short, depositions set liars up either to tell on themselves or to be exposed later, using *their own words* against them.

Some of the most dramatic moments in divorce litigation take place during depositions. Because of the on-the-spot nature of the proceedings, depositions are a place where bombs get dropped, hidden truths come out, tears are shed, voices are raised, fingers are pointed, and tempers flare. Depositions are where a guy's secret business dealings, sources of income, debts, concealed assets, secret purchases, perceptions, drug habits, double lives, demons, extramarital affairs and even "love children" are often revealed. And a deposition gives you your best chance to get something you've always wanted: your husband's *truthful* responses to your questions.

Sometimes the mere *threat* of a deposition is enough to prompt a settlement on terms favorable to you, and this is especially true when your ex has something he doesn't want to be asked questions about with you sitting there listening. Sometimes it's more valuable to you in the final resolution of the case to allow your ex to keep his secrets to himself, to give him a pass and not make him reveal his misdeeds.

Telling the truth in his deposition would set him free, and if you make him tell all the gory details of his bad behavior, he has nothing more to lose from saying it again. The mere fear of revelation can drive a quick settlement. And even after the deposition is completed, the deposed party may decide they do *not* want to answer questions under oath ever again, so they settle the case without a trial. Either way, the pressure applied by a deposition can push the case away from further drama and toward peace. And reaching a place of resolution and peace should be your ultimate goal in divorce litigation.

The Importance of Cooperating in Discovery

Where I practice, discovery rules are lenient in divorce cases, and information is expected to be freely exchanged, at least for the most part. Courts frown on folks who withhold relevant, discoverable information in divorce cases, and you can be penalized for abusing discovery procedures or withholding information. It's best in most cases to cooperate honestly and completely rather than stonewalling and over-objecting, unless of course your objections are grounded in valid legal principles.

How to Help Your Lawyer Conduct Successful Discovery

❖ **Don't miss deadlines**. You are an adult. Your lawyer shouldn't have to remind you more than once to provide necessary information for your discovery responses, and you could be disadvantaged in the case if the judge finds you're being uncooperative.

❖ **Produce what you're supposed to produce**. No one wants to gather documents and answer long lists of questions, but it's necessary for your divorce case to proceed. I'll never forget one client saying, "I mean, we're not the Trumps. Why do I have to do all of this?" Her point was well taken, but of course we had to cooperate in discovery if we expected the same from her husband. There's an old adage in the law: "In order to demand equity, one must do equity." You can't sit on your fanny and refuse to cooperate while demanding the other party's cooperation. If you fully comply, you're more likely to convince a judge to compel the other party's compliance.

❖ **Answer the questions to the best of your ability**. Just answer the questions with honesty and integrity. Object to the questions to which your lawyer will allow you to raise a valid objection but answer fully—and honestly—otherwise. If you don't, you could be precluded from elaborating on your points when you get in front of the judge.

❖ **DO NOT LIE**. I've said it before, and it bears mentioning again. You mustn't lie to your lawyer about anything. Your lawyer can only help you if you tell them the full truth. You don't want to set up your attorney to be caught flat-footed (and you certainly don't want to be exposed as a liar) in open court. You are certain to get less-than-optimal results if the other side catches you in a big lie. Always be honest, unless your attorney agrees you have a valid objection which permits you to say nothing. And when you testify, don't say "to be honest..." or "honestly" when you start a sentence, or else everyone will wonder if everything *else* you've said that day was a lie.

❖ **There's an app for that**. Look for applications that will help you organize and produce evidence in a form that is clearly understandable. Applications like Decipher Text Message and Legal Text Collector are great for sorting text messages (rather than screenshotting them individually as photos... what drudgery that is!), and organizes texts onto easy-to-read, 8.5" x 11" pages for easy copying, saving your lawyer time and, therefore, saving you money. Other applications like MixCaptions and Kaptioned transcribe and add captions to video and audio recordings (a real timesaver which makes recordings easier to understand in open court). There are myriad other apps out there that can save you time; ask your lawyer which ones they recommend. Don't work harder when you can just work smarter!

❖ **Tell your lawyer where to look.** You know your husband better than anyone, and even if you don't have full financial or other information for your case, you likely have at least some insight into where his assets are located and/or who would have the information if you can't put your hands on it.

A few examples:

- If your husband is self-employed and uses credit from banks, he has likely submitted loan applications for financing his enterprises. If you have an idea of where he banks, who invests with him, or who helps him with financing arrangements, give your lawyer their names so that loan applications and other financials your husband submitted to those folks can be requested.

- If your husband deals in cryptocurrency, tell your lawyer so that requests can be sent to the major crypto trading platforms.

- Accountants usually have financial information relevant to divorce cases. If you know the name of your husband's accountant, consider asking them for income- and asset-related documents if your husband refuses to hand them over. While you won't be allowed to get the privileged communications between accountant and client, you may be able to get something useful. Moreover, going to the third party may be the impetus your husband needs to get moving a little faster and produce the requested items himself, so that valued members of his financial network won't be inconvenienced.

- We live in a highly digital world. If you husband uses digital wallets like Venmo, CashApp or PayPal, tell your lawyer to request those records.

- If your husband has a criminal past or has had run-ins with law enforcement, tell your lawyer which law enforcement agency was involved so that the applicable incident reports, police bodycam footage, court filings, and E-911 call transcripts can be obtained. There's nothing better in court than to have your ex caught *on recording* behaving badly, with the intervention of an objective, respected law enforcement officer. It's even better when the victim of your ex's behavior calls 911 and is recorded saying, in real time, how scared they are because of how your ex was behaving in that very moment. I've played many a recording in court, and they are always golden evidence. Your lawyer will know how to obtain such evidence pursuant to the rules of your jurisdiction.

- If there's cash stashed in a safe somewhere, tell your lawyer so that appropriate requests to inventory and count the cash can be arranged. If the cash is in a bank's safe deposit box, the bank's record of sign-ins to open the box, complete with dates, can likely be requested. If you can show your husband accessed the box after your case was underway and the money is now missing, it may be worth showing the court.

- If you suspect there is a treasure trove of information on a computer or other device's hard drive, tell your lawyer to see if such devices can be requested for inspection.

People lie in court all the time, thinking they won't get caught. But it's awfully hard to get away with lying in the face of admissible proof to refute one's claims. Evidence is pivotal to break the tie whenever it's your word against his.

Ruth's Story

Ruth has always trusted her husband, Max, with all financial matters throughout their eleven-year marriage. Except for the occasional item of mail that would come to the house from a bank or investment firm, Ruth has never seen much of anything on paper to explain Max's income or financial activities. A successful real estate developer who's always on the go negotiating the next big deal for his investor group, Max has always done a great job making sure the family is well supported, and Ruth has appreciated that he took care of that part of their life together so that she could focus on nurturing the children and meeting their needs. Their marriage is now ending, and Ruth is terrified that she will not get a fair division of assets, and that she will not be able to nail down Max's true income for purposes of establishing child support and alimony. Max swears he has told Ruth everything she needs to know about his income assets and development deals, and he is pressing her to sign a divorce decree his lawyer has prepared at Max's direction. "Don't spend all our money on lawyers, Ruth. Be reasonable! You're smarter than that. You can trust me to be fair to you. Just sign the papers, and let's both move on."

Ruth wisely seeks the advice of a well-respected lawyer in another town (all the local lawyers know Max from various business dealings and, therefore, have conflicts of interest that preclude them from helping Ruth), and this lawyer convinces Ruth to request documents to confirm the fairness of Max's final settlement proposal.

Three months later at the first hearing of their case, Max, the Plaintiff, with his perfect hair and Armani suit complete with cuff links and tie, is a compelling witness as he insists that he has not diverted or hidden any assets of any kind. Max's lawyer sits down, and Ruth's lawyer stands up to cross-examine Max. The proceedings then go downhill in a hurry for poor old Max:

> *Ruth's lawyer*: So, you say you're being honest with us all about your finances, assets and income, right?
>
> *Max*: Yes, absolutely. I am not diverting assets or hiding anything.
>
> *Ruth's lawyer*: I'm going to show you what I've marked Defendant's Exhibit 1. May I approach the witness with this document, Your Honor?"

The judge: Yes, you may.

Ruth's lawyer: What is this stack of pages, sir?

Max (thumbing through a nine-inch-thick stack of documents): Well, this appears to be a collection of bank statements from several different bank accounts.

Ruth's lawyer: And whose name is on the accounts which relate to these statements?

Max: My name.

Ruth's lawyer: Is Ruth's name anywhere on any of these accounts, some of which having several hundred thousand dollars in them?

Max: No. All the bank accounts are in my name. I always gave Ruth all the cash she needed to run the household, and she used the credit card, but I always paid everything out of the bank accounts in my name only. Ruth's name isn't on any of the bank accounts.

Ruth's lawyer: So, Ruth never had a way to access these accounts or the funds they contained?

Max: No, I'm the only person with access to these accounts.

Ruth's lawyer: Thank you. Please look with me on the first page of each statement for the past year. Can you explain these entries for wire transfers from your account on the 15th day of every month, in the amount of $20,000, to an account ending in -5489 at a bank located in St. Thomas, Virgin Islands?

Max (sweating, face turning red): It's highly complicated. You see, I'm involved in some very complex real estate deals, and I use banks everywhere. But I don't remember exactly why I set up this automatic draft from my account to the St. Thomas account. I'd have to look into it further and circle back. Maybe my partner will know. I will ask him.

Ruth's lawyer: But, sir, with all due respect, you just told us you're the only one with access to the accounts in your name only. So how is your partner going to be able to explain these wire transfers?

Max: I don't know what to say except that I'll look into it and get back to you later.

Judge: Answer the question, sir.

Max is speechless and knows he's been caught.

Ruth's lawyer: I've gone through these records thoroughly, and it appears you've diverted some $280,000.00 into this off-shore account in recent years. You really have no explanation for these transfers?"

Max: I'd like to assert my 5th Amendment privilege against self-incrimination. I cannot answer further questions concerning this matter.

Ruth's lawyer: Nothing further, Your Honor.

It was later revealed that Max had been putting money in the St. Thomas account of a trusted business associate because he'd been planning his divorce for some time and didn't want to have to divide the funds with Ruth. The plan was for the associate to hold the funds just long enough for Max to get divorced, and then Max would get the money back and repay the associate by allowing him to buy into a Caribbean real estate development at a discounted price. Without Ruth's lawyer's diligent pursuit of financial details, Ruth would have missed out on nearly $150,000 in financial recovery in her divorce.

Beware of Rushed Settlements

Listen close, girl. If your ex is pushing for a quick settlement of all issues without first providing you a full opportunity to ask all the questions you want to ask in discovery, this is a giant RED FLAG. If there's nothing to hide, he should be more than willing to show you whatever information you want to review. Do not settle without a satisfactory understanding of what you're giving up in the property and debt division Mr. Used-To-Be-Wonderful is offering you. It's tempting, especially when you're in emotional turmoil and just want the pain to end, to sign whatever contract is put in front of you. Do not be deceived into thinking that signing a document will bring automatic peace; you could be selling yourself way short or, worse, creating new problems for yourself. You and your husband are love birds no more. Your new names are "Plaintiff" and "Defendant," and you can bet that your husband is prioritizing his own future over yours. Be smart and get all the information you need before entertaining any particular settlement terms, and always trust your lawyer's advice.

Questions for Reflection

1. What do you know about your financial situation and what do you *not* know? Make a list of items you can provide your attorney to give clues of where to begin in your discovery process. Also make a list of those items you don't know anything about that you'll need your lawyer help you discover.

2. Who are the best witnesses for your case? What does each witness know, and how likely is each witness to share that information publicly?

3. Will subpoenas be needed to force witnesses to come forward with information and testimony to help prove your case? What are the pros and cons to involving these third parties in your divorce case?

4. How do you think your husband would respond to being required to answer your lawyer's tough questions in a deposition? What are the pros and cons you see, knowing your husband as you do, to making him sit for a deposition? Do you have burning questions you'd like him to answer under oath?

5. Is your husband pressuring you to settle your case without first allowing you a chance to ask questions or review all the financial documents for yourself? Is he telling you just to "trust him," that you don't need lawyers, or that you should just agree to his terms and be done with it?

Resources

How to Survive a Deposition—Stuart B. Shapiro

Chapter Soundtrack

"I Won't Back Down"—Tom Petty & the Heartbreakers
"Tell Me Lies"—Fleetwood Mac

7

Is He Cheating on Me? Why It Matters and How to Prove It

"One lie is enough to question all the truth."
—Samaira Ansari

"Sally" and "David" have been married 26 years and have four beautiful children. Their life looks perfect to everyone else. No one knows that Sally caught David talking with sex workers years ago, but Sally forgave him and now believes the marriage is in a good place. They have enough money for nice vacations and cars and college for the children. Their businesses are doing well, and they are beloved in their church. Their friends envy their good marriage and perfect life.

While doing laundry one day, Sally finds a crumpled note in her husband's pants. It's a woman's name, address and phone number—*in his handwriting*—along with the words "call upon arrival."

Perplexed, Sally searches the name and address in Google and discovers the woman bills herself as a "model," and all her public social media posts are quite suggestive. Panicked, Sally then checks the credit card and bank records and sees proof of David's Uber rides to the address on the note, along with large cash withdrawals around that time while he was supposedly in that area for a "networking conference."

Remembering that David had not answered her texts while he was away, Sally looks back at her messages again and confirms her efforts to reach David during that trip were largely ignored. It's now clear: David has had sex with a prostitute.

Sally's world is shattered. Sally confronts David and he denies it all—repeatedly—not knowing Sally already has all the evidence she needs to prove his affair.

Lying is what cheaters do best. They believe their own lies and tell them convincingly. We believe them because the truth is so painful to accept. Ladies, they think we're stupid.

Maybe you can relate to Sally's experience and your husband's betrayal is undeniable. You just can't go on in this marriage, and you're blessed to have all the proof you need to support a claim for divorce on adultery grounds. It hurts, but you have clarity about what to do.

More often, however, cheating husbands downplay their cheating or even shamelessly deny it to the end, hoping you'll never prove it or find out the whole truth. Many women never know the full story. Cheaters deny it or make excuses until they know with certainty they won't get away with it.

When caught, some men show remorse and pledge to change, but this remorse is often because they're sorry they got caught and fear the life changes that will result, not because they regret having hurt you. It is often difficult to discern the difference, and this leaves so many women feeling confused.

If you have a feeling your husband is having an affair, but you have no proof of it, his denials can make you feel crazy for having suspected it in the first place. Dear One, let me tell you, if you feel in your gut something is awry, it probably is. If your body is telling you something isn't right, believe it. God built that intuition into you.

It's in your DNA. Trust it. And don't let that lying turkey talk you out of what you know in your heart (and a good amount of evidence also tells you) is true. Be wise, my friend.

Adultery: Know the Signs

Women often come to my office seeking divorce advice on an informational basis only, hoping never to need it, hoping to keep their marriages together. I always ask them whether they suspect infidelity. "I don't think so, but I'm not sure" is a common response. When I probe a little further, they tell me all the things that make them think he could be cheating. There are behaviors and themes common to all adultery cases, clear signs that he's a cheater.

If you're thinking your husband may be straying but aren't sure, review the following list of signs to help you analyze the situation logically, putting all emotion aside for the moment:

I. **Sudden changes in behavior**. He's easily agitated in a way that is out of character. He's antsy or paranoid without good reason. He won't make eye contact. He won't give straight answers about basic things. He always seems annoyed with you lately, especially when you show him kindness. All of these are indications of a guilty conscience. He suddenly has no interest in physical contact with you (because, in his twisted mind, he doesn't want to cheat on his girlfriend with his wife). He rejects your affections. Perhaps he has removed or keeps "losing" his wedding ring and gave an illogical excuse like "it's too restrictive" or "it makes my hand sweaty" when you asked him why. Some men are so bold as to joke that they need a flesh-tone wedding band that will blend with their skin so as not to broadcast their marital status. Remember—there's truth behind every joke.

It's almost like he's trying to run you off. After all, if he can make you so miserable that ending the marriage will be your idea, he can say you abandoned *him*, thereby making him the victim in the story. The cheater knows he can avoid embarrassment if the headline of your story is "It Just Didn't Work Out" or "They Just Grew Apart" rather than "Cheater Gets Caught, Marriage Ends in Divorce." Do not be fooled.

2. **He's got new bedroom moves.** Once you've been married awhile, there's usually a certain rhythm to the intimate things. A sudden introduction of new bedroom experiences can be a red flag that some other "lady" (word used loosely) has been teaching your husband new tricks.

3. **He's super secretive with his phone.** He used to leave his phone unlocked on the counter all the time, but lately he's keeping it close and may have even added a passcode. He becomes irrationally angry if you look on or even touch his phone. I can't tell you how many smashed phones are evidence in my cases; a cheating husband will often smash his phone to bits to keep you from seeing what's on it. Sometimes men will obtain additional, untraceable phones commonly referred to as "burner phones" dedicated to their extracurricular activities and communications. If you find a new phone in his vehicle or hidden somewhere, be suspicious.

4. **He's unreachable and hiding his location, yet uber paranoid about *your* activities.** You've always been able to see one another on location-sharing phone applications, but he has suddenly started concealing where he is for hours at a

time or frequently allows his phone to "go dead" when he's always kept it charged before. What's worse, he won't tell you where he's going or where he's been during those "dark periods." If he's not coming home right after work as usual, taking more out-of-town trips "for work" or "with the guys," especially while refusing to share his location with you, something's up, my friend.

Cheating men are Uber paranoid about your activities, often keeping close tabs on your location out of the insecurity their own cheating creates in them. After all, if it was so easy for him to trick you, that you could be doing it to him, too, right? So, they watch your every move using location tracking apps and then irrationally and baselessly accuse you of wrongdoing. This is a telltale sign of a guilty conscience.

5. **Changes in diet, fitness and grooming habits**. He has taken a new interest in physical fitness and his appearance. He's started trimming down, eating better and working out. He's dressing like a younger man, when looking good was never a priority before.

New grooming habits are another big indicator. If your husband is suddenly shaving body parts that have never seen a razor or bleaching his teeth when they've always been contentedly mother-of-pearl before, something fishy is going on.

"Looking back on it, I should have known my husband was cheating on me," said one anonymous online friend, a recent divorcee whose ex-husband was an accomplished investment manager. "He started whitening his teeth, which I thought was strange but overlooked. But then he was suddenly covering his gray hair, leaving dark stains everywhere. I naively offered to find him a professional hairdresser to save our porcelain bathtub from imminent-death-by-Just-for-Men, thinking he was just insecure about getting older. I should have clued in when he began manscaping his body like never before and working out daily, but I didn't. Soon thereafter, he left me for a much younger woman."

6. **His new friends are single**. He has a new friend group, and they're all single men. He has started spending more and more time with these men, in bars or on other outings that never interested him before. He either stays over at their houses or comes home very late at night for the first time in your marriage.

7. **He's "single" on social media**. His Facebook and Instagram profiles used to be filled with your date night and anniversary photos, but he has deleted all of those. His new posts do not include any mention of you or give any impression that he's married. He has new female followers and friends, and you don't know any of them. He posts photos of himself looking his fit and successful, lifting weights, being Super Dad, with your kids or your dogs as props.

8. **He constantly accuses YOU of cheating**. You have neither the time nor inclination to cheat on him, but he's suddenly obsessed with the idea that you're stepping out. There's no evidence to support his accusations, and it's the furthest thing from your mind. A cheater has paranoia like no other; he knows how easy it's been to live his double life, so he may have convinced himself that you're doing the same to him. If you're cheating on him, his behavior would somehow be

justified, right? "Accuse the other side of that which you are guilty" was the mantra of Joseph Goebbels, chief propagandist for German Nazis during World War II. Your husband is trying to throw you off the scent with his wild accusations. Do not fall prey to these mind games.

9. **Cash withdrawals**. He's always used a debit or credit card for purchases, but he's suddenly taking frequent cash withdrawals—sometimes large ones—at the ATM and operating in cash. Where is that money going? #redflag

Mark 4:22 tells us that everything hidden will eventually be brought into the open, every secret brought into the light. The truth just has a way of coming out.

If this chapter is making the nausea rise into your throat, please stick with me.

Take heart! What's tragic for your life is usually good for your divorce case.

Why Adultery Matters

First and foremost, your husband's adultery matters because it has hurt you. You need the evidence to prove to yourself that it happened, especially if your husband is lying about it and trying to make you feel crazy for accusing him. Plus, his pattern of systematic deception, once exposed, calls every other thing he says into question. Can anything he said be trusted as true? His credibility on all matters—not only with you, but also with your friends and perhaps even with the judge—is now in question. Telling the truth is central to courtroom litigation, and lies are usually exposed with evidence. Duplicity gets litigants nowhere with the judges I know.

Depending on the laws of your state, there may be legal implications from your husband's affair. Every state's laws are different, and no two clients' stories are the same. It's important that you consult a competent family lawyer in your jurisdiction for guidance for your particular case. In some jurisdictions, a party's conduct has bearing on the court's analysis when dividing your property. Where this is true, you can sometimes be regarded as having condoned or forgiven an affair if you have intercourse after you discover the affair. If your lawyer tells you this is true where you live, listen to your lawyer's advice and stay strong, sister. Sleeping with him after you've found out he's cheated could impact your case.

Another legal concept which applies in some jurisdictions: If a party's adultery was the cause of the couple's separation, the cheating spouse may be barred from receiving any award of alimony from the other.

Consult with your attorney about the laws in your jurisdiction with respect to adultery.

No One Has to Know: Give Him the Grace of Saving Face and Help Yourself, Too

No matter where you live or what the law says about it, perhaps the most powerful litigation advantage you gain from your husband's affair lies in the basic human desire not to have one's dirty laundry on display for all to see. No man wants his transgressions examined in court.

John 8:32 reminds us that "the truth shall set you free," and I've seen it play out just like that time and again. Knowing the truth about his infidelity sets you free to feel okay about ending your marriage. But publicizing all the gory details of his affair will only set *him* free, giving him *nothing to lose* in fighting you for more of the marital pie. After all, if all his sins are already public, the threat of them coming out will no longer be present, and he will have no incentive to be fair to you in settlement negotiations. If you're smart, you will allow his humiliating indiscretions to remain private and use it to your advantage in settlement negotiations. Handling it this way will also allow your children and his extended family to avoid unnecessary embarrassment.

Solomon cautions us in Proverbs 5:1-2 to "pay attention to wisdom . . . so that you may maintain discretion and your lips safeguard knowledge." With knowledge of your husband's bad behavior comes the power to transform the outcome of your divorce case. But so many women squander the advantage by sharing details with others, and in doing so lose the much-needed litigation leverage it could have brought them.

I'm always reminding clients to be careful what they share, and with whom.

While you are gathering your evidence, you must use great discretion and trust few with your suspicions. You especially do not want to confront your spouse on his infidelity, at least not until you're reasonably able to prove it. If you need a safe place to spill the details you've uncovered, tell your lawyer or find a counselor where you can download and process all your thoughts in a healthy, coherent way. These professionals are trained to walk you through it, and they are duty-bound to keep your secrets confidential.

Time to Get After It! Gathering Your Proof

I. **Legally obtain the phone records**. Your husband's cell phone call and text message records should be examined carefully for clues. If the records show tons of lengthy calls and texts to the same number or handful of numbers you don't recognize, especially at late hours, you most likely have your smoking gun. If you need help obtaining the records, ask your attorney for help to ensure they are obtained without breaking any privacy laws.

2. **Get the bank and credit card records, and don't forget the digital wallets**. Have your attorney obtain the bank and credit card records for the accounts your husband uses, carefully review them for strange purchases at places like restaurants, bars, jewelry stores, florists, Victoria's Secret, and the like. If those purchases were made and you weren't a part of them, you can prove he's been spending on someone else. If large ATM withdrawals were made, that likewise raises questions. With Zelle, CashApp, PayPal, Venmo and similar apps now allow them to purchase goods and services and send money to women ... under the radar, right from their cell phones. Ask your lawyer to dig for these digital sources of evidence during the discovery process.

3. **Screenshot his social media**. Check his social media pages and make a screenshot *showing the date* of each post you find relevant to your situation. Has he slipped up and made a practice of "liking" everything a certain woman posts online? Is that woman "liking" everything he posts? Is he posting things that indicate a sudden affinity for partying and sources of entertainment he's never shown interest in before? Is he posting vague quotes about new love or fresh starts? Is he showing off his newly-trimmed physique, athletic prowess, bleached teeth or no-longer-gray hair? Save it all, sister. It's evidence.

4. **Hire a private eye**. In my state, private investigators have access to information attorneys and regular people can't get their hands on. You should consider hiring a private investigator if your husband is gone for periods of time without explanation or if you have other reason to suspect he's cheating. Be strategic about when you send the investigator to check on things; weekends are usually the best times to catch a man who's up to no good. Your attorney can help you find a qualified investigator in your area.

5. **Record Conversations**. If and only if permitted by the laws of your state (check with your attorney), start recording all conversations with your spouse. There are many apps for this purpose. You might just get a recorded admission of guilt which will promptly resolve your case. Or perhaps he will tell you what a wonderful wife and mother you are, which would undermine his position later if he chooses to fight you for custody of the kids. He could also tell you where key assets are hidden or give a glimpse into the financial picture after having previously kept you in the dark.

6. **Receipts and payment records**. It's very helpful when you can find receipts from purchases he's made at florists, restaurants, jewelry stores, lingerie shops, etc., while courting the other woman. Give them to your lawyer. More than once, I've discovered evidence of the husband's utility accounts in another city, and each time he was forced to admit that he was supporting another woman's household. If this is happening, he's paying for it somehow, and there's a paper trail with an address to lead you

right to the woman's identity. In all the cases where I've seen this, the other "lady" didn't even know the guy was married. Busted!

Online pornography sites like OnlyFans.com offer a gateway for men interested in cheating. These sites allow men to subscribe to the pornographic sites exhibiting women's real-life pornographic videos and images, often with chatting and meet-up options. The only good thing about these sites is that all payments are digital, and there's a paper trail if your husband is a subscriber or paying for videos or meetups a la carte. I suggest you investigate any unusual charges you see on his statements, digital wallet records and figure out who is really being paid, as sometimes the names of the payment processing entities for these sites can be unusual or seem innocuous at first glance. For instance, "Only Fans" seems like it could be an online sports merchandise shop; I've had clients who overlooked the charges, assuming their husbands were buying stuff to take to ballgames.

7. **Personal Notes**. If your husband writes you an apology email or letter to say he's sorry for cheating on you or confessing any other fact helpful to your position, save it in case he later denies it happened. You should also save any love notes and greeting cards he exchanged with his paramour, along with any evidence of his rendezvous with her.

8. **Old Computers and Smashed Phones**. If you have old computers, cell phones or tablets around the house to which you have legal access (check with your lawyer to be sure), you might consider having their hard drives forensically examined in search of evidence. Old emails and other digital

communications and photographs may lie within these old devices. Nothing is ever really gone, even if it was deleted. I'm telling you, friend, these computer experts are geniuses and can sometimes unlock all the proof you need if it's there. Your attorney will know the right ones to call for your jurisdiction. The same is often true for broken devices. If you husband smashed a phone or iPad to keep you from seeing its contents, put it in a Ziploc bag and give it to your lawyer. It's evidence. The forensic folks can often access information you don't expect them to can find, but your attorney needs to oversee that process to ensure all legalities are followed.

9. **Undergarments & Lipstick**. It's awkward to discuss it out loud, but there are times when my lady clients find other women's undergarments in a bed, vehicle or their husband's office. Remember Monica Lewinsky's blue dress? If you find undergarments that are not your own, go All-CSI: pick them up with tongs and place them in a Ziplock. Same with his clothing if it's stained with rogue lipstick or smells of a perfume that isn't yours. I've also heard of forensic analysts who can test your husband's boxer shorts for the presence of female DNA to prove it isn't yours. All of this, while admittedly disgusting, is evidence and can be analyzed, or at least used in open court to confront the lying shmuck. Your lawyer can take it from there.

10. **Get Yourself Tested for STDs and STIs**. My dear, if you suspect he's stepped out of the marriage, the first thing you need to do is head over to your OB/GYN and get yourself tested for

sexually transmitted diseases and infections. If you're ill, it's better to know it and get the medical intervention you need than to live in denial, not get checked, and compromise your health.

If you know you've only been with your husband, and yet you test positive for something Ajax won't wash off, that positive test is evidence for your case and can sometimes be used to get to the bottom of what he's been doing, and with whom. Get. The. Test.

To Sum Up

Adultery makes more difference in your case if your husband has spent money on the woman, conceived a child with her, brought home an STD, involved your children with the woman during your marriage, or exposed your family to stalking or other dangers from a crazy mistress.

As you obtain electronic, documentary and photographic proof, save it fourteen ways to keep your spouse from finding and destroying it. Email it to yourself and to your mama. Save it on a jump drive, print it, and put it all in a safe deposit box at the bank. Hide the key and tell no one you have it. You must check with your lawyer for advice on the best way to preserve your evidence as you gather it. *And above all, tell only those in your most trusted inner circle what you've discovered. Do not confront your husband with it until your lawyer says it's time.*

It's always best to approach divorce settlement negotiations from a position of strength. You must stay strong, get focused and gather the evidence you need to fortify the positions of your case, even as your heart is hurting.

Questions for Reflection

1. Do you have a sick suspicion that your husband may be cheating on you?

2. What have you seen that makes you suspect he's been unfaithful? Are any of them similar to the signs outlined in this chapter?

3. Talk to a close friend, counselor, or divorce coach. Do they think he's probably cheating based on the evidence you have?

4. What can you start doing to gather the evidence you need?

5. How can you help equip your lawyer to prove your case?

6. Are you taking care of your emotional health as you process this devastating information? Is there a counselor, pastor, or divorce coach you can trust to help you?

Resources

The State of Affairs: Rethinking Infidelity—Esther Perel

Chapter Soundtrack

"Take It On the Run"—REO Speedwagon

"Leave the Pieces"—the Wreckers

"Does He Love You"—Reba McEntire, Linda Davis

"Whose Bed Have Your Boots Been Under"—Shania Twain

"Hands Clean"—Alanis Morissette

"Promises, Promises"—Naked Eyes

"Burn"—Phillipa Soo, from *Hamilton*

8

Crush Your Property & Debt Division

"I am not throwing away my shot."
—Alexander Hamilton, *Hamilton*

You get one shot at dividing your assets and property in your divorce case. Don't throw away your one shot at getting it right. You must 1) locate all the assets to be divided, 2) put a value on each asset, and 3) divide them fairly. One shot. Get it right.

Step 1: Leave No Stones Unturned— How to Identify All Your Assets and Debts

Before you can divide your assets, you first must identify and locate them all. You *will* sell yourself short if you don't do the work necessary to locate all your assets.

The following is a list of the asset categories I always look for in every case:

❖ *real estate: houses, land, mobile homes, rental homes*

❖ *automobiles*

❖ *all-terrain vehicles, lawn mowers, tractors and implements, trailers*

❖ *bank accounts (yours, his, joint, and the children's)*

❖ *stocks, bonds and brokerage accounts*

❖ *stock options in a business*

- cryptocurrency
- retirement, defined benefit and pension plans
- military retirement and defined benefits
- vocational retirement funds specific to a union or trade (electricians, law enforcement officials, plumbers, railroad workers, and others sometimes benefit from these)
- cash on hand (currency, bills and coins, wherever located . . . under a mattress, in a safe, buried in the backyard)
- precious metals
- accounts receivable (i.e., someone owes money to you or your spouse)
- income tax refunds (whether already collected or still expected to arrive)
- hotel and credit card rewards points
- frequent flyer miles
- club memberships
- gun collections and ammunition
- art, antiques and other collectibles
- livestock
- crops
- cash value of life insurance
- annuities
- business ownership interests, sellable inventory, and business-related assets
- tractors and heavy machinery
- pending claims for personal injuries, worker's compensation or other claims for damages that arose during the marriage
- personal property, furniture, housewares, stuff in attics and storage spaces

It will be an immeasurable help to your lawyer if you come to your first consultation armed with some idea of the assets you've accumulated during your marriage in each of the categories listed above. You must *identify* all assets so that you can *divide* them all and separate all your present entanglements so you're free of him—at least financially—for good. Cases are completed much more efficiently when all the assets are on the table to be valued and divided.

Things like your husband's loan applications (where he states all his assets in the most favorable light in hopes of getting approved for a loan), tax returns (with lists of property(ies) being taxed, the county deed and tax assessor's records, personal financial statements, proof of purchase documents, certificates of title, and even your husband's own handwritten notes can be good sources of information for identifying the property at issue in your case. Put on your Nancy Drew hat and start sleuthing! Anything you can give your lawyer to kickstart the analysis is going to be helpful.

<u>Don't Be a Trickster, and Do Not Be Tricked</u>. It's human nature to try to find the gray areas and stretch the rules as far as you can. But if you cross ethical lines by concealing assets or creating new debt unnecessarily to skew your financial picture to gain unfair advantage in the divorce, I don't want to be your lawyer. Trying to pull a fast one over on the court by hiding or transferring assets or creating senseless new debt just to make yourself look poor for your divorce generally won't work, will keep you married longer, and could subject you to sanctions.

<u>Bottom line</u>: do not try to deceive the court or your spouse in your divorce case. Even if you're able to trick the lawyers and the judge, God sees it all. It's better to live with a clear conscience, even if it means you lose some material thing you might have kept, than

to know you lied. Your spiritual health is much more important than physical wealth.

But what if *your ex* is the one hiding assets, lying about his wealth and income, and being altogether shady? You can't let him get away with it. It's one of those righteous-indignation, turn-over-the-money-changer-table moments. Find your backbone, stand your ground, and go for his jugular.

It's imperative that you hold that lying man to account. You have no choice but to expose all the assets so they can be fairly divided in settlement or at trial. And if he's lying about his income, it's pivotal to nail down the truth there, too. Otherwise, your child support and alimony analysis will be off-kilter.

If you're worried your husband is going to transfer real estate out of his name, pocket the cash and keep it from you in the ultimate division of your marital property, ask your lawyer about whether something can be filed in your jurisdiction to put the world on notice that the property at issue is subject to pending divorce proceedings and not to be sold at this time without your consent.

Don't transfer property without your lawyer's okay. You should check with your lawyer on the advisability of giving away or selling property while a divorce case is pending. It's not fair to take property out of the equation for dividing with a spouse, and you could find yourself in very hot water if you're caught hiding or cashing in assets to keep them from your husband's reach. And he may be in trouble if he does this to you, too. I'll sometimes expose someone for giving assets to a family member to hold until the divorce is over, with full intention of giving it back to the divorcing party after the divorce dust settles. Liars and cheats usually get caught, my friend. Don't do it.

Don't create new debts or deliberately increase your debts for advantage in your divorce. Clients sometimes ask me if they should deliberately incur new debt before filing for divorce to make their financial circumstances appear more dismal than they actually are. The train of thought is that the other party can't get money from you if the creditor is first in line to get it, or that the appearance of financial instability will result in you being able to keep more of the marital asset pie when it's divided.

The short answer I give is generally *no*, you should *not* incur new debt unless it is what you have ordinarily done in the usual handling of your affairs when you were *not* going through a divorce. For example, farmers, real estate developers, small business owners and other self-employed people often use lines of credit and secured financing arrangements for borrowing money in the ordinary course of their regular business. If debt is a necessary part of your operating budget and you have always had to borrow regularly for your business to function, then it *could* be okay to continue doing so while your divorce case is pending. If you haven't ever (or rarely have) borrowed large sums of money or opened new lines of credit in the past, then it's probably not a good idea to start right before you file a divorce case. *Bottom line: You need to ask a lawyer in your jurisdiction* for advice before making any big financial moves like these.

The truth generally has a way of coming out, and you shouldn't insult the Court's intelligence by thinking you'll get away with any funny business. If you go finagling the family finances to skew the division of property or debt in your favor, your husband's lawyer could spot what you've done from a mile away and expose it all. It's always best to be honest and play fair. Once you've lost credibility with the Court, it's awfully hard to get it back.

Step 2: What's It Worth? Put a Value on Your Assets

Once all the property has been identified, the next step is to figure out what it's all worth. Statements from bank accounts, retirement accounts, and brokerage accounts make it easy to figure out what they're worth. But things like real estate, campers, RVs, automobiles, boats, annuities, stock in closely-held businesses, cryptocurrency, gold, silver, crops, livestock, mobile homes and personal property at your house are much more difficult to put a value on. Here are some tools that may help you and your lawyer figure out the value of the assets in your case:

❖ **Appraisals** involve a certified, professional real estate or other property-specific appraiser who examines the property's condition and age in the context of the local market for the asset and comparable, recent sales of similar assets. Appraisals are great tools for finding the value of real estate, vehicles, personal property, business inventory and other business assets, large machinery, and similar items. The testimony of a respected, credible expert is wonderful to have in a divorce trial if you can afford it. In my part of the country, many people own firearms, firearm accessories, ammunition, and fire-proof safes to hold all of the above. You'd be amazed how much those things can be worth! I've worked with clients whose husbands' gun collections turned out to be worth upwards of $100,000.00. Get the guns appraised, girl. And take lots of photos of them in case they go missing later. I've seen appraisers give solid assessments of values without ever seeing the assets in person, all because my client provided detailed photographs of the items at issue.

- ❖ **Online valuation resources**. In the South, we have lots of motorized toys. From boats (with motors, which are often the most important component) to motorcycles to all-terrain vehicles (ATVs) to golf carts to tractors to dune buggies, and sometimes even airplanes, divorcing couples have often put lots of marital money into buying toys like these, and they are hot commodities in the divorces I handle. Folks have sentimental attachments to their motorized toys, and they tend to hold their value much better now than they did before COVID-19. To establish the values of your toys, photograph their condition, serial numbers, and odometers to show the number of miles or "hours" each one has traveled or been operated, as that information can then be used by appraisers and/or put into online calculators like www.boattrader.com, www.kelleyblue-book.com and other platforms to nail down valuation figures.

- ❖ **Insurance policies** and related documents typically include a complete list of all the assets you have insured, with its assigned replacement value for each one. The insurance policy can be a holy grail of reliable valuation figures, as the stated insured values are your husband's admissions of what he thinks it will cost him to replace each asset in the event of loss. For example, if your husband has insurance coverage on an asset for $200,000.00, but he's now saying it's only worth $150,000.00, you can argue for that insured value to be accepted as true.

- ❖ **Tax returns and depreciation schedules** contain lists of assets you may not have known about. Check them out, and don't be afraid to ask a CPA to help you understand what they mean.

❖ **Loan applications** are wonderful because they contain your husband's own lists of assets and what he thinks their values are, with a dated signature in his handwriting. Folks try to look as rich as possible when applying for loans, for they want the bank to take the risk and loan them the money, and the loan is more likely to be repaid if the person has a higher net worth. If your husband erred at all on his loan application, you can bet he erred by *inflating* his assets' values rather than understating them.

Step 3: Use a Marital Balance Sheet to Craft Your Proposal

Accountants use something called a balance sheet to give a one-stop snapshot of one's personal or business assets and debts in one place. In divorces, it's common for a Marital Balance Sheet to be prepared for use in settlement negotiations and at trial. The Marital Balance Sheet contains all the assets and debts of the parties, along with a column for the share of each property item each party is to receive in the final division. It's a handy tool for allocating ownership of assets and allocation of responsibility for paying marital debts in one document for easy analysis of all the different settlement scenarios.

You may have heard someone refer to division of property in terms of dividing "equity." The equity a couple holds in an asset is just the value of an asset, less the debt that asset secures. For example, if your home is worth $200,000.00 but you still owe $100,000.00 on your mortgage, the equity in the property you're actually dividing is just $100,000.00. If dividing that equity in half, each party would receive $50,000.00 in equity, or value, in the final division of the assets.

In a divorce, except in rare circumstances, it doesn't really matter how much you paid for the property or what you owed for the asset's related debt when you bought it. Courts can only divide actual assets and debts that exist at the time of division, so what's most relevant is the here and now—what's owed now, and what the asset's value is now.

We discussed assets at length in the paragraphs above, but it's also important how debts get logged on the Martial Balance Sheet. Locating secured debts (debts with assets held as collateral) is usually easier than locating unsecured debts. Running a credit report will help you identify the unsecured debts (like credit card debts, store card debts, medical debts, student loan debt) in your name, and your ex will do the same if he wants his debt load considered in the final division for your case.

DISCLAIMER: The Marital Balance Sheet is just a tool for collecting your thoughts and visualizing the various scenarios for resolving the asset and debt division issues of your case. There are serious tax considerations to take into account before deciding on a particular course of action, which is why you should run any possible settlement scheme by an experienced CPA or licensed tax attorney before finalizing any particular set of terms.

For a sample Marital Balance Sheet, scan this code:

Scan Me for Book Resources

Crush Your Divorce Resources

Encumbrances that reduce the value of your real estate.

Things like liens, leases, and other encumbrances can reduce the value of your property, so it's important that you and your lawyer do your best to locate and consider them all before finalizing your divorce. Common types of liens include tax liens for unpaid property, payroll or income taxes, materialman's liens against real estate and mechanic's liens against automobiles.

A leasehold interest is another kind of encumbrance. Consider this hypothetical: The parties separate. Then, without Wife's consent or involvement, Husband leases out the marital residence to a third party and starts collecting all the rent without sharing any of the rental income with Wife. If that wasn't enough, Husband then tries to take custody of the children on the argument that Wife (a stay-at-home mother) can't afford housing on her own, all while refusing to kick out the tenant and let Wife use the home. Wife has a good argument in this example that Husband has violated the rules against encumbering marital property while a divorce case is pending, as he has conveyed an interest in real estate to someone who is not a party to the case, thereby complicating Wife's ability to regain possession and perhaps even hindering the parties' ability to transfer the property in the future as part of a divorce settlement.

Liens attaching to the property likewise fall into the encumbrance category. The goal in every divorce is to get all the property and debt separated so that each party can proceed individually with no financial tie to the other party. Liens make property harder to divide and transfer, and they can complicate the division of debt when one party is to pay the debt secured by the lien while the other party is to receive the property to which the lien attached. If it is in your power to prevent a lien from attaching to your property while your divorce case is pending, you should do your level best to prevent it or ask the judge to intervene. Liens can make property much harder to divide and transfer, and they can cause your case to drag out and take longer to finalize.

Separate Property and Mixed/Commingled Property.

Each party's separate assets (i.e., assets that are not subject to division in the case because they were one party's inheritance or given to one party by a relative or friend) sometimes appear on the Marital Balance Sheet just for reference, for they can sometimes have relevance in the analysis of alimony or child support, but they don't typically get divided in the divorce except in the rare case where giving up a separate asset somehow gets the deal done. If you have property you do not believe should be subject to division in your divorce, be sure to ask your lawyer how best to prove it's your separate property. Your lawyer may tell you to gather purchase records, gift receipts, old wills or estate documents showing inheritance, bank records showing funds directly paid to you without involving your spouse, records showing you never commingled the gift or inheritance with your ex. Please note: the rules about separate property are different in every jurisdiction, so be sure to ask a local lawyer for advice.

Separate property you obtained from your family or had before you married can lose its character as separate, and thus be thrown into the pot of assets to be divided, if you put your husband's name on the asset, borrowed against the asset and paid on that debt during the marriage, if your husband improved the asset by his efforts, and other ways. The same is true for your ex's separate property. Have you improved his property during the marriage, either by your physical or mental efforts or with marital (or your separate) funds? Have you paid down a mortgage on his property during the marriage? Did he place the asset in your name? Classifying assets as separate, marital or mixed can be a complex exercise. Be ready to bring all the documents related to this analysis to your lawyer for guidance.

Retirement Account Transfers.

Federal law created a way to transfer retirement assets from one spouse to another, by rolling the assets from one account directly into the other party's account, without either party receiving an immediate tax ramification. A special, qualified domestic relations order ("QDRO") is required for accomplishing this tax-free result, and they are tricky and often expensive to prepare. Try to get your ex to fund the preparation of the QDRO if you can, and if you absolutely have to fund the preparation costs, be sure you factor those into your settlement terms.

The Two "Os" of Property Division: Ownership and Obligation

A lot of folks get in such a rush to finish their divorce and move on with life, that they'll sign any old contract that looks halfway fair to them, often without having a lawyer look it over first. It's of utmost importance to recognize that there are two (2) components in dividing property: Ownership and Obligation. The Ownership piece is easy . . . one of the parties will *own* the property after the divorce, and the other party will no longer own any part of it. Problems primarily arise when one fails to recognize that the Obligation to pay the remaining debt secured by the property will remain long after the divorce is over. When one party signs over their ownership interest in an asset without addressing the related debt (or only partially or insufficiently addresses the debt), problems indefinitely arise. For each asset, it's extremely important to address not only which party will *own* it going forward but also which party will be responsible for paying any debt secured by the asset, along with all other costs associated with owing it.

Pitfalls in Property and Debt Division

Clients often come to me after they've finalized their own divorces without an attorney's input, freaking out because the property division language is either incomplete or incorrect. Issues most commonly arise when:

❖ *There are assets not addressed in the documents at all, and uncertainty exists as to how they are to be divided and who is to finish paying for them;*

❖ *They divided their property, but they didn't also divide or assign responsibility for paying the associated debt. This is the case when, for instance, Husband receives ownership of a car, but the papers don't address the debt, and Wife's name is still tied to it, thus making her unable to get approved when she needs to buy a new car with credit, and keeping her responsible for paying for the Husband's vehicle;*

❖ *Each party agreed in the decree to pay all debts in their own respective names, but one or both of them were unaware of all the debts held in their own names, and the client has legally assumed debt they never even knew about, let alone intended to assume;*

❖ *Wife agrees for Husband to pay certain debts but doesn't require him to pay them in full by a certain deadline, thus leaving him free to increase the debt related to that obligation or to defer or postpone payment of the debt indefinitely, thereby leaving the Wife's credit score subject to damage should Husband fail to make timely payments;*

❖ *Wife agrees in the decree for Husband to keep the marital home and to pay the debt related to it but doesn't also require him to refinance the debt into his own name, thus keeping her credit worth tied to the Husband's obligation indefinitely and potentially making it impossible for her to ever get approved for another home mortgage when she finds a house to buy. In such a case, the Wife becomes a perpetual renter.*

It's a common mistake to think the party who's receiving the property is somehow automatically responsible for paying the debt related to it, and that the party giving up the property is somehow automatically relieved of the obligation to pay the associated debt. When a piece of land or a home has a mortgage in your name, merely signing a quitclaim deed conveying your ownership interest in the property does *not* relieve you of your obligation to repay the lender under the terms of the mortgage documents you signed. Banks don't care if you're getting divorced. If your name is tied to a debt obligation secured by a property, the bank can come after you to collect that debt, and it doesn't matter that you don't own any equity in the property anymore, or that you moved out of the house a long time ago.

The lesson: if you're going to give your husband your real estate, a mobile home, a vehicle or anything else that is collateral for a loan, you need to try your best to get him to *refinance* that debt to remove your name from it entirely. Otherwise, your name is still tied to that debt, your credit worth is tied up and can preclude you from getting a new house or vehicle, and you could be exposed to having your credit score plummet should your ex fail to pay the debt.

Don't be in such a hurry to get out of a terrible marriage that you make these mistakes. They could follow you for years.

How Forensic Accountants Find Hidden Personal Assets and Establish True Incomes

I've worked with forensic accountants over the years in cases where assets are hard to value or income is complex and hard to establish. Forensic analysis is usually most necessary when families live out of a family business and commingle their personal and business affairs, funding personal purchases or pay personal debts with business funds. In such a case, a forensic accountant and valuation expert will examine bank deposits, currency transactions, accounts for cash payments, un-deposited receipts, gifts, insurance proceeds and the like to reconstruct the parties' true income, expenditures and assets. It's an in-depth analysis of the family's use of cash during a given period of time—if more is spent than was taken in, there is usually unreported income there. To estimate a family's net worth, the expert looks at things like bank and brokerage statements, credit card applications, loan applications, and real estate records searching for mismatches between the finan-cial situation reflected in the accounting data and the parties' real-life lifestyle and actual spending practices. This kind of lifestyle analysis provides a useful, accurate, easy-to-understand financial profile that is powerful leverage in settlement negotiations. Forensic experts can be expensive, but they more than pay for themselves by giving you a high-level summary, from the mouth of a credible expert, which is hard for the other side to overcome in court. If your expert is the only voice in the night, you can be fairly confident that the court will adopt the expert's income figure and asset valuation as fact.

Considerations When Dividing a Business

If you think (but aren't sure if) your husband owns interest in one or more closely held (as opposed to publicly traded) businesses, check for his name on your state's entity registration website to see if his name shows up as a registered agent, officer or organizer of any businesses. You can also look on the Better Business Bureau and Dun & Bradstreet sites to see if any businesses are tied to his name. Private investigators also have resources for locating business assets and related connections.

Once you find information about his undisclosed business ties, you can search public records like tax assessors' and local court files to see if any property has been purchased in the business name(s). Your lawyer may also want to send requests to your husband's favorite banks, insurance companies, vehicle dealerships, and lending institutions for documents of accounts, purchases and loans tied to the business(es). Follow each trail to the end, and you could be amazed at what you find out about your husband's secret (and lucrative) dealings that he's never mentioned to you. It happens more than you might think.

But the most common scenario in which we use forensic analysis involves a family business both parties know about. Usually when a couple owns a business, one party does the day-to-day management and knows how the business operates. All too often, the other party knows very little about it, and this makes the parties' bargaining power unequal, as one party holds all the financial information, and the other party is left scrambling—not just to get the necessary information, but also having to hire experts to explain the data. Knowledge of the inner workings of the business is invaluable. The one with the knowledge has all the power in the negotiation, and there is no way the discussion will be fair without a full analysis of the financials. A good lawyer will conduct thorough discovery and assemble the experts necessary to level that bargaining table.

An appraisal of the business enterprise itself is pivotal for obtaining reliable valuation numbers, for there are unlimited opportunities to hide income and assets when a business is owned and controlled by one spouse. Forensic accountants use special techniques for tracing and valuing the assets and finding all the ways the owner is paid, all to arrive at a solid, provable income figure for use in your divorce. To ascertain the value of the business, the forensic folks review bank account records, purchase orders, invoices, accounts receivable and accounts payable records, QuickBooks or other electronic bookkeeping records, and customer invoices and payment records to make sure all value is included and that nobody's been "cooking the books." Business owners can downplay the health of the business, among other things, by misusing business funds (often in violation of IRS rules and regulations) to buy personal assets or to pay large personal expenses using business funds, by taking loans from the business or from banks in the business name, pocketing or concealing the cash in some way, or by showing an ominous liability on the books that either isn't real or is only there temporarily because the deceptive business owner (let's call him "Shady Spouse") fully intends to repay the loan in full after the case is over, using the borrowed funds he's concealed instead of used.

Shady Spouse can also conceal his wealth with the assistance of third parties, both real and invented, as follows:

❖ Use of fake vendors and overpayments to real vendors—
Sometimes you'll see Shady Spouse creating a dummy vendor account under auspices of "paying" that fake vendor for goods and services for the business. A vendor account is set up in the accounting software and checks to the fake vendor are logged as business expenses, but there are no goods

or services actually being provided by the vendor, and the checks are either never cashed or Shady Spouse is cashing the checks and stashing the money somewhere else for later retrieval, after the divorce is done. I've also had cases where Shady Spouse deliberately overpaid his buddies in the business for legitimate, business-related goods or services, and then the buddy gave Shady Spouse his change back in cash to be concealed from division in the divorce.

❖ Creation of "consultants" is another way Shady Spouse can cheat you out of your property. The books will show Shady Spouse is paying "commissions" to "consultants," but he can't show what he got for his money. Most often, the funds paid find their way back to Shady Spouse, either by the "consultant" funneling it back to Shady Spouse in cash or another hard-to-trace form.

❖ Creation of "dummy employees"—Shady Spouse will sometimes issue checks to fictitious employees, cash the checks himself and conceal the cash in a hidden bank account or elsewhere. This fraudulent activity is often best exposed by cross-checking payroll lists of past and present employees, personnel files, and employment applications the business has received and processed.

Forensic experts are masters at conducting business appraisals (including appraisals of inventory, machinery and complicated infrastructure used inside the business). They are skilled at using collateral documents (like business loan applications, financial statements, disclosures to shareholders, business property insurance information, business tax returns, depreciation schedules and the like) to bolster confidence in their valuation analysis and final estimates of business value.

A comprehensive forensic analysis takes time, but you can move things along faster if you can locate information they need for the investigation. It's best to expedite the forensic accountant's process as much as possible, as you don't want to give your husband any extra time to alter his accounting records or stop being productive to look like the business is struggling. There's an old saying that a farmer never makes a crop in the year of his divorce, and a merchant never shows a profit. This is why you need the help of an efficient and fast-moving forensic analyst to help you.

Once you have a good idea of the value of the business, there are several ways to approach dividing the business in the divorce:

1. **Let him buy you out with cash**. If one spouse is a partner/stakeholder in a medical practice, accounting firm, law firm, real estate brokerage, or other business with partners, there will often be internal agreements among the partners that a partner's spouse isn't allowed to own any part of the company in the event of a partner's divorce. Sometimes these internal partnership agreements even establish the per-share value of the business' stock, which makes it easy to figure out the value of the partner's spouse's share of the value. In such a case, the spouse of the business partner is simply paid in cash for her portion of the partner's ownership interest in the business. The same analysis applies where the divorcing couple are the only owners; once the business is officially valued by an expert, one spouse can request half or some other equitable share of said value, in the form of a cash payment and/or ongoing, periodic future payments

from the business's income stream, and the paying spouse remains owner of the business.

2. **Step into his shoes and run the business yourself**. A family business can be like a goose laying golden eggs. You probably built the business into what it is today as a couple, with joint effort, and you may have extensive knowledge about its inner workings. Why not keep the business and run it yourself? If you are so inclined, don't be afraid to take on the new challenge. If you think you can do it without Mr. Used-to-be-Wonderful, consider buying him out.

3. **Don't divide it at all**. Every divorce petition I ever filed asked the court to divide the couple's marital property. I've never seen a case where a judge required parties to continue owning property together, as the whole point of a divorce is to extricate the parties from one another entirely. But in the rare case where both parties want to keep the business and cannot agree to divide its value, the parties may consider remaining in business together so that both can continue reaping the future rewards of the business' success. It's shocking, I know, but believe it or not, some people can get along well enough to do that after they divorce. It's certainly not the norm, and it's rarely ideal in practice, but it is what some people do.

If this is your choice, you must carefully craft the final divorce contract and court orders to address all the contingencies you can think of to circumvent the issues that will inevitably arise, and the company's internal governing documents may require revision to reflect these agreements. Such issues may include how net profits will be spent, allocated, or drawn out by the owners, and how disputes (over such things as how to run the business or terms upon which the business could eventually be sold) will be resolved, as you can almost guarantee that you and your ex will argue over something, someday. You will likely need skilled corporate counsel to assist your divorce lawyer with the final decree language if you choose this route.

Words of Wisdom from a Forensic Accountant

IAG Forensics in Marietta, Georgia, is one of the best forensic accounting and valuation firms in the business. IAG Managing Partner Laurie Dyke, CPA/CFF, CFE, offered the following words of wisdom to parties in divorces that involve forensic work:

❖ *Valuing and dividing a business is one of the most complicated issues in a divorce. It's important for business owners to recognize that a business is an asset of the family that needs to be shared with their soon-to-be-ex-spouse. It's important for the "out spouse" to understand that, while the business is an asset of the family, any valuation is only an estimate with risk involved in realizing the value. Business assets are illiquid and the "out spouse" may need to accept less than half of the estimated gross value and with payment over time.*

❖ *One of the most important things that divorcing people can do to help yourselves and your team is to provide everything that is asked of you in an organized way and don't fight the process.*

❖ *Trust the people you hire to help you and listen to their advice.*

❖ *Contrary to what people often expect, this is not a justice system, it's a legal system and you cannot count on the courts to make everything right. Judges, juries, attorneys, and experts are required to play by certain rules that you may not understand if you have never played before.*

❖ *Psychologically, prepare for a marathon, not a sprint. Discovery takes time and this is your one bite at the apple so it's important to get it right.*

❖ *Be willing to compromise. It's better to pay your soon-to-be-ex-spouse and preserve your assets for your family, rather than spend it on lawyers and accountants.*

Don't Get Hung Up On the Stuff

Never let an unhealthy attachment to personal property (or your desire to hurt your ex's feelings) keep you from settling your divorce. Read that again.

I see it all the time. We fight long and hard to get the big assets of the case divided, and then we tie up and throw down over things like rugs and end tables.

When people argue over personal property, it's sometimes because both parties truly *treasure* the item for whatever reason. Maybe it's a special antique or heirloom, or maybe it's tied somehow to a special memory or connected to the children. Often, people will fight over the family dog or cat, usually because they both truly adore the animal, but sometimes just because they think that if the dog is with them, the children will also want to be with them more.

But more often than not, the fight over the stuff isn't about the stuff at all. Rather, it's about hurting the other person. It doesn't make one lick of sense to pay your lawyer's hourly rate to divide the stuff in your house in hopes of hurting your ex. You're only hurting yourself if you waste money on attorney's fees in pursuit of the things that have the least monetary value in your marital portfolio. Don't let your need for revenge drive you to this type of foolishness.

Consider the following scenarios:

1. **Antique Antagonism**. You and your soon-to-be-ex-mother-in-law share a love of antique furniture, and she has purchased you many lovely pieces that you selected at various times during your marriage. Now that you're divorcing, she claims all that furniture is *hers*, and she has Golden Boy fighting you for every armoire, Heriz rug, and four-poster bed in your house. Your lawyer tells you these items are your separate property, as she gifted them directly to you, that they're yours to keep, as they aren't legally subject to division in the divorce. These things fit your home perfectly, and you hate to part with them because you don't want to alter the look of the children's home, but you know Golden Boy will fight you for them to make his mama happy. What do you do? Do you let her have them, or do you fight like the Dickens for them?

   My two cents: Let her have it all, even though it may legally be yours. You will go through much turmoil fighting the family over it, and it could cost you a fortune in legal fees to make your arguments. It just isn't worth it, Dear One! I always tell my kids that "people are more important than things." Consider yourself blessed to see that Golden Boy's mother treasures her *things* over her *relationships*. Just give her that junk, and do it with a smile. The sweet memories associated with picking it out with her are no longer sweet, and you don't want to look at that stuff every day now that you know the truth. Besides, it's the best excuse to give your home a whole new, modern look!

2. **Cleave from thy collections**. Did your parents, like mine, have collections of things that they added to each year? My mom loved the Department 56 Christmas village figurines. She would set up tables full of those little houses, shops, a post office, churches, and villagers milling around, surrounded by poly-fill "snow" and twinkle lights every year starting around Thanksgiving. As a child, I thought it was magical. And if any husband of hers had ever tried to take the Department 56 village in a divorce, you can bet she would have fought tooth and nail to keep it. And she would have been making a huge mistake. At my conference table, I've divided collections of: Precious Moments figurines, NASCAR driver bobblehead dolls, pottery, stamps, coins, artwork, firearms, crystal, fine china, baseball cards, Pokemon cards, electric train sets, and even live plants from the couple's backyard. The great thing about collections is that there are multiple items to go around, and both sides leave with something they want. One easy way to divide a collection is for each side to take turns picking items until everything is claimed.

3. **Identify your deal-breakers**. Is there any junky clutter-ish thing like that in your house that you're super sentimental about? My thing is my children's handmade Christmas ornaments from preschool, and all their art from when they were little. You can bet your fanny I would still be married to my kids' dad if he had fought me for those. Is there something you collect or treasure that you would never agree to part with? Go ahead and identify your deal-breakers early in the case.

4. **Ask yourself: Will you still want that thing in five years?**
    People often fight for the sake of fighting. You might be
    tempted to say "no" when your husband asks for some par-
    ticular thing, just because he wants it, and just because he's
    hurt you, and don't want to help him furnish a home for
    some new woman to enjoy. But ask yourself: do you really
    even like this thing you're fighting about? Is it timeless, or is
    it some trendy item that won't be in style in five years? Ask
    yourself this question before you dig in your heels—at your
    lawyer's hourly rate and at the risk of losing your husband's
    agreement on other more crucial settlement terms—and
    before you play tug-of-war over something that will end up
    in a yard sale. Don't die on that hill.

We are cautioned in Luke 12:15 to be on guard against all kinds
of greed, for "life does not consist in an abundance of possessions."
Your life is not measured by the amount of clutter you've collected,
and this is not your grandmother's divorce. Gone are the days of bric-
a-brac, elaborate window draperies, and decorations on every surface
and wall. Less is more. Think of your divorce as a great opportunity
to clean out your house and make a fresh start!

Questions for Reflection

1. Are you tempted to hide assets or create unnecessary new
    debt to gain advantage in your divorce case? Have friends
    suggested you do this? How does this suggestion sit with
    your conscience?

2. Do you suspect your husband has concealed assets, hoping you'll settle before you discover them? What can you do to help your lawyer expose his deceit?

3. Did you notice your husband moving assets around or spending time with new business partners in recent months? Are there stones you should be turning over to investigate the full extent of his business operations?

4. Did your husband creating new debt obligations or allow liens to attach to your property in the period just before your divorce case began? Is he still doing it?

5. What can you do to help your lawyer streamline the division of your personal property?

Resources

Never Split the Difference: Negotiating As If Your Life Depended On It—Chris Voss || Tahl Raz

The Forensic Accounting Deskbook, 2nd Edition—Miles Mason

Chapter Soundtrack

"Picture to Burn"—Taylor Swift

"Give It Away"—George Strait

"I Can See Clearly Now"—Johnny Nash

"Honey in the Rock"—Brooke Ligertwood

9

Child Support and Alimony

But if anyone does not provide for his relatives, and especially for members of his household, he has denied the faith and is worse than an unbeliever.

—1 Timothy 5:8

If you have children or have been dependent on your husband for financial support during your marriage, child support and alimony are pivotal considerations for your case. Child support and alimony rules vary from jurisdiction to jurisdiction, so it's important to consult local counsel for guidance on how it works where you are, but this chapter will outline the basics and maybe bring questions to mind for you to ask your attorney.

What is child support? Child support is the payment of funds, usually monthly but sometimes on another payment schedule, by one parent to the other parent as financial support to ensure the child's needs are met in the receiving parent's household.

How much child support can I get? The amount of a child support award depends on the financial status of each party and is jurisdiction-dependent. In Georgia where I am, child support is calculated based on the incomes of both parties and various other factors. Be prepared to give your lawyer all the financial information requested of you (things like proof of both parties' incomes, day care costs, health insurance premiums for the children's portion only, your child(ren)'s extracurricular activities costs) when you meet to go over the child support analysis for your case.

What are some factors that affect the child support amount? Where I am, a party's child support obligation may be reduced by things like (1) the noncustodial parent's payment of the mortgage or rent where the child and custodial parent reside, (2) the noncustodial parent's visitation-related travel costs where the parties reside some distance apart, (3) the extraordinary educational, medical or extra-curricular activities costs of the child(ren), (4) the extensive amount of parenting time the child-support-paying party has with the child, (5) other children living in the respective homes of the parties, and (6) the day care costs being paid by each party, respectively. Child support calculations are not as simple as you might expect, so be sure to consult a local child support attorney before agreeing to any financial obligations for your children.

Will I still get child support if we share parenting time equally? The award of child support is a case-by-case inquiry. Where I practice, equal parenting time doesn't mean child support automatically becomes zero. The party with more income typically still pays alimony of some amount to the lesser-earning spouse even with equal parenting time where I practice. Because child support is the right of the child to be supported, it's not usually a right a parent can easily waive with the court's approval. The judge is duty-bound to make sure the child's needs are met. If you're trying to agree to a zero-child-support order, the judge will probably have some questions for you before it is approved. Consult a great, local lawyer for insight into how to approach this question in your area.

Will I have to give an accounting of how I spend the child support? The child support receiving party will often ask me whether the child support has to be put in a separate account or otherwise accounted for after it's received. Check with your local lawyer to see if the rule is different where you are, but where I practice, the receiving party is *not* obligated to give an accounting of how the child support is spent, as it is designed to meet not only ascertainable, child-specific needs, but also basic needs of the entire household such as utilities, rent/mortgage payments, groceries and other costs the child enjoys along with everyone else who lives there.

May I claim my child for income tax purposes? The ability to claim your children for the purpose of obtaining income-tax-related benefits, stimulus, and other credits depends on the policy of the courts in your state. This is a tricky question, so it's important to consult a local attorney and CPA where you live before you claim a child for tax purposes without your ex's knowledge or consent. It's important to establish an understanding of which parent will claim the child before tax season arrives, as you don't want to be racing to beat each other to file each year, and you need to know how you will file well in advance so that you can adjust your employer's withholding from your paychecks throughout the tax year in question so that you don't get hit with an unexpected tax burden when you file your return.

What is alimony? Alimony is support paid by one spouse to the other spouse to ensure the dependent spouse's needs are met for a period of time. Factors considered in alimony awards can include one party's need, the other party's ability to pay, the parties' ages, the length of the marriage, disparity in the parties' incomes, and the parties' relative education levels and employability. Alimony can be paid as a lump sum or in periodic payments over time. Rehabilitative alimony is designed to give the historically-financially-dependent spouse a shot in the arm for getting on their feet after a divorce, and usually ends after a period of months or a few years, at most. Think of it like an airplane taking flight; alimony makes your runway long enough for a productive liftoff as you enter your new life. The longer the runway, the safer you are taking off. Once you're airborne, Dear Sister, you won't need it anymore. There's no feeling in the world quite like financial independence. Get ready to soar!

Enforcement of Child Support and Alimony Awards

What if he gets "in the rears"? Oh, for the love. Please, oh please, if this book doesn't teach you anything else, please let it teach you to call money owed to you "arrears." While you certainly may feel like you're being sodomized when he doesn't pay you what he owes you, he's not "in the rears." If your ex fails to pay child support or alimony and owes you a child support or alimony arrearage, ask your lawyer about your options, both public (whereby you'd explore local government resources to collect what is due) and private (involving an attorney's help and a filing in court).

Private Actions. Courts generally have authority to enforce their own orders, and enforcement actions vary among jurisdictions. I file what we call "contempt of court" actions for my clients, asking the court to find the non-paying party in willful contempt of the court's order to pay. If someone is held in contempt, he can be made to pay the support recipient's attorney's fees or even put in jail as the court deems appropriate. It's serious business. If you're ordered to pay child support or alimony, you better pay it.

Public Agency Collections. Another option for enforcing an order and collecting arrears is to go through a state-run collection agency, if one exists where you are. The biggest benefit to a public collection effort is that it's typically very cheap or even free of charge.

A state-run agency can work with agencies of other states in a collaborative effort to collect child support across state lines. In Georgia, the child support services office can suspend the driver's license or passport of a delinquent child support payor, intercept his income tax refunds and stimulus payments to pay you, and garnish his wages. They can compel compliance in ways private lawyers often can't. You may have to wait longer for results with an agency action, but, again, it's typically a much more cost-effective approach.

Self-Employed Payors

Where the support-paying party is self-employed, the analysis of what is owed and the process of trying to collect can be more complicated than with a W-2 wage-earning payor. If your ex is self-employed, it may take some digging to identify all his income sources so that child support and alimony are fair to you and your kids. you absolutely need highly competent counsel to maximize your award.

High-Income Families

The law (at least where I am) generally favors keeping a divorcing woman and the children in their same pre-divorce lifestyle, and alimony is supposed to accomplish this, at least for a period of time, after the divorce. But in my experience, it's often hard for a woman in a high-net-worth, high-income divorce to get the full alimony and child support she should have if the case goes to court. Judges and juries sometimes have trouble understanding why you should be permitted to continue getting your facials and Botox, buying designer clothes and handbags, sending kids to private school, driving that Escalade, going on vacations, and similar luxuries most people don't have. It's generally better to try to nail down an agreement on alimony and child support you can live with, even if it's not quite as much as you really want, rather than taking your chances in court on these matters. Even with the purest intentions, it's very hard to avoid looking like diva when talking about your luxurious lifestyle from the witness stand, and no one likes a diva. Envy is a real human struggle, and judges and juries are only human. The numbers are sometimes just too high to be relatable, so it's often best to control your outcome with a solid settlement if this is your scenario. Ask your local lawyer for guidance on what to do.

Questions for Reflection

1. Have you analyzed your post-divorce budget? How much money will you need to continue running your household after you and your husband are separated?

2. What are some expenses you can cut out of your budget to be able to afford necessities more comfortably? How long will you need your ex's financial support before you can get on your feet?

3. Do you have a good idea of your husband's income? How will his budget change when you're living in separate households?

4. If your husband is self-employed, be thinking about how you can prove his income. What do you need to tell your lawyer in order to make sure the child support calculation and alimony obligation are correctly calculated?

5. If you're in need of spousal support, what is the ideal way for you to receive it under your particular circumstances? Would one or more lump sum payments or monthly/biweekly payments be better? What is your plan to be self-supporting when the child support or alimony ends?

Resources

www.supportpay.com

Institute for Divorce Financial Analysts (www.institutedfa.com)

Chapter Soundtrack

"Child Support"—Barbara Mandrell

"Alimony"—"Weird Al" Yankovick

10

Crush Your Parenting Plan

Children are a heritage from the Lord, offspring a reward from Him.
—Psalm 127:3-5

If you have children, the parenting plan—that part of your court order outlining how you will share time with and make decisions for your children—is the most important agreement of your divorce. The parenting plan addresses custody placements, parenting time and visitation schedules, each party's rights concerning the children's care, and coparenting guidelines related to contact, communication and mutual respect. It's also the place in the documents where special concerns *particular to your scenario* are addressed with special safeguards. The parenting plan is not a one-size-fits-all thing, but it's often kept simple too. You must be ready to educate your attorney on your particular coparenting concerns from your first meeting so that evidence can be gathered to get your points across, coherently presented in court, and thoroughly addressed in your final settlement documents.

Custody Terminology: Sole, Primary, Joint, Legal and Physical

"Custody" involves each party's rights of access to and information concerning the children, along with each parent's responsibilities and decision-making roles. The terminology varies from state to state, so it's important to consult a local legal professional for guidance so you understand the issues to be addressed in your case, where you are. Hollywood has normalized the use of the term "sole custody" to mean that the children remain with one parent more of the time than the other, but where I practice, custody usually isn't "sole" custody unless one parent is out of the picture due to things like incarceration, drug/alcohol abuse, or past incidents of child abuse or domestic violence.

Where I practice in South Georgia, most families agree to "joint legal custody" (meaning both parties have legal rights to the children, parenting time with the children, and the ability to give input on decisions for the children), with one party or the other being named the "primary physical custodian," meaning the children are in that parent's care most of the time and have visitation or scheduled parenting time with the other parent on a regular basis. One party is the ultimate decision-maker as to those decisions which have to be made for the children in various categories which can include things such as religious upbringing, medical care, extracurricular activities and education.

There's also "joint physical custody," which is usually what we call it when the parties share parenting time equally or almost equally. When a family chooses this kind of arrangement, we usually assign decision-making roles (i.e., medical, religious upbringing extracurricular activities and education) equally, as well.

With coparents who get along fairly well for the children's sake and can coparent productively, the assignment of these decision-making roles makes little to no difference in the grand scheme, as such folks usually agree on the major decisions to be made for the children. Problems arise, however, when coparents disagree on a particular decision to be made. Giving your ex final medical decision-making authority cause you to incur health care costs you may not approve, such as rhinoplasty or what is widely known as gender-affirming care for children confused about gender. Giving your ex final decision-making authority on activities can disrupt your parenting schedule by imposing commitments on your time that you may not want. Giving your ex final decision-making authority on educational matters can result in him having a leg up as to the child's residence, for if he can pick the school, he can dictate how far you have to drive the child every morning and afternoon on your parenting days.

Following are a few examples to illustrate the issues that can arise:

1. Bob and Josephine are divorced parents to little seven-year-old Bobby. Bobby is a lights-out left-handed pitcher, much to his father's delight, and travel baseball coaches are recruiting him to play tournaments every weekend. Bobby is also an outstanding math student, with a penchant for piano performance. Josephine has had Bobby involved with church choir, and he takes organ lessons with the church organist every Saturday she has Bobby with her. Travel baseball would require Bobby to travel most weekends and miss not only his organ lessons but also church much of the year every year. Josephine opposes travel ball, but Bob has ultimate decision-making authority over Bobby's extracurricular activities in their court-ordered parenting plan. Bob threatens to use his legal authority to pull rank on this issue, require Bobby to quit piano (or, at least, miss it most of the year), and thwart Josephine's ability to take the child to church on her weekends. Josephine has ultimate decision-making authority on issues related to the child's religious upbringing, and she does not agree

that Bob can use travel ball to interfere with her choice to have the child in church, especially not on her weekends of designated parenting time. Bobby loves baseball and music, and he just wishes his parents wouldn't fight so much. Guess who's going back to court to sort this out? Bob and Josephine.

2. Donnie and Deidre have joint legal custody of their eleven-year-old twins, Polly and Paul, with Deidre having them in her care about seventy percent of the time and Donnie having them thirty percent of the time. Deidre has ultimate decision-making authority over all decisions (including medical care) for Polly, and Donnie has the same concerning Paul. Polly begins having issues with gender dysphoria and thinks she may want to change her gender. Donnie believes she should be permitted to transition with hormone therapies and puberty blockers toward becoming a male, but Deidre disagrees, opting instead to put Polly in counseling. Deidre wins this issue because she has the power to overrule Donnie's view. If it were Paul with the desire to become female, Donnie would be able to make the final call, per the parties' agreement in this hypothetical.

3. Caleb and Cindy have equal parenting time and joint legal, joint physical custody of their twelve-year-old son, Christian. Christian is a skilled soccer forward, and Caleb and Cindy have always had Christian playing with the local rec teams. Christian has been invited to join a prestigious soccer club in a town 30 miles from the parties' town, and the practices are two weekday evenings each week, with additional practices and tournaments every weekend. Cindy is a

busy professional with her own business, and she can't make the drive for weeknight practices on her weeks of custody. Caleb insists Christian join this club, and because Caleb has ultimate decision-making power over Christian's participation in sports, he can dictate whether Christian commits to the team and, therefore, impose a travel obligation on Cindy against her will. Caleb signs the contract with the team, and Cindy has to figure out how to get Christian to practices during her parenting weeks. The parties ultimately resolve the issue with Caleb benevolently agreeing to drive Christian to all the practices, but not all couples are able to do that, and thus end up back in court.

Visitation and Parenting Time

Visitation and parenting time schedules are important to spell out with specificity so that both parents can plan around them. You must always remember that an agreement to agree later is no agreement at all, and while you should endeavor to reach consensus with your ex in all coparenting matters, it isn't always possible, which is why you need a solid, carefully worded parenting plan.

When crafting your parenting time schedule, it's important to consider the following:

- *Your family's holiday traditions.* Try to craft your holiday parenting time schedule to ensure your child's ongoing ability celebrate holidays and birthdays with your family.
- *Your work schedule.* If you work 12-hour shifts and rotate day to night shift on a period basis, you may want to consider building some adjustments into your parenting time schedule to ensure you'll be available when you have your

children. It's best not to trust your ex to accommodate you in this regard. If it's not in the written order, he has no enforceable obligation to work with you.

- *Your priorities.* Is your birthday particularly special to you? Do you want your child with you every year to celebrate? Do you want to be given the first right to care for your child if your ex is working during his designated parenting time? Do you want to control your child's exposure to other women in your ex's life, at least for a little while? These are all things to address in the parenting plan. Are you concerned about your husband's drinking or other life choices? Consider those concerns and be ready to address them with your lawyer in the parenting plan. If they're not addressed there, you won't have any power to hold your ex to particular behavioral obligations as issues arise in the figure.

The court will issue a parenting plan and parenting schedule if you and your ex are unable to agree to a unique parenting plan of your own. Most judges are amazing and do their best to address the issues you present, but with court time always being limited, court-issued parenting plans are often one-size-fits-all generic and cannot address all the issues you'd like to include. One of the biggest perks for settling your case is to control the parenting plan's terms to ensure they include all the details you need in there.

Here are a few practical considerations to contemplate including in your parenting plan:

- School preference, especially if your ex will have ultimate decision-making authority over educational decisions

- Restrictions on overnight guests of the opposite sex being in the home with your child before your ex has remarried
- Restrictions on alcohol consumption during parenting time
- Helmet use when the children ride on all-terrain vehicles, golf carts and other motorized machines
- Age- and weight-appropriate child safety seat and booster seat use during parenting time
- Duty to keep one another informed of the child's location, along with any injury or illness
- Obligation to do all you can to foster and promote a positive relationship between the children and the other parent
- Duty to follow the pediatrician's instructions as to the child's diet, feeding (especially important with young babies and toddlers), nap and bedtime schedules (nothing worse than a toddler off his schedule and cranky for days), medicines, treatment regimens, and other medical care
- Obligation to share school papers, report cards, parent-teacher conference schedules and other information from the school with the other parent as received
- Communication guidelines (and, where needed, strict schedules) to govern communication with the child during the other parent's parenting time
- Communication guidelines for coparent communication, including mandatory use of coparenting apps (like Our Family Wizard and Talking Parents) and other restrictions where needed to keep abusive communication to a minimum
- Obligations to shield children from adult matters like limiting talk of the parties' litigation when the children are present

- Prohibitions on disparaging one another in front of the children or allowing any third parties to do so
- Rules about who can transport the children to and from visitation exchanges and in general
- Lists of those people to keep the children away from due to criminal history or history of substance abuse
- Restraining provisions keeping the other parent a particular distance from you when you're in the same spaces for the child's activities, which is especially important in cases with histories of emotional and physical domestic abuse
- Limitations on the child's caregivers
- Right of first refusal to allow you to have the first option of keeping the child if your ex is working during his parenting time
- Prohibitions on smoking or vaping around the children
- Limitations on corporal punishment—whether it's allowed and who can administer it
- Time limits on introducing the children to your new significant others

It's not easy to release your precious babies into the care of your ex, especially if he hasn't had them alone a whole lot before your separation. There are umpteen million things you can let yourself worry about—and, therefore, countless provisions your heart may want to include in the parenting plan to document to try to cover every danger out there. In the end, at least with a normal coparent living a fairly low-risk lifestyle, you must allow yourself to trust him with the children, to have their best interest in mind, to love them and provide the care they need from their father.

Perhaps you're releasing control of your child for the first time and riddled with fear of what's going to happen during your ex's parenting time when you're not there to ensure good parenting choices are made. This is the stuff that keeps abused women married to horrible men for way too long—those concerns that the child won't be safe without the mother there to run interference and insulate him. In these scenarios, you must always remind yourself that God loves your children even more than you do, that your divorce is not a surprise to Him, and He has a plan for every child's life.

Sample Parenting Plan

Here's some sample parenting plan language for your perusal. If you see anything here that appeals to you, talk to your lawyer about how you might incorporate some of these principles into the parenting plan or court order for your case:

Scan Me for Book Resources

Crush Your Divorce Resources

Some of these provisions may be unnecessary for your child, and are thus more restrictive than you'd want to include in a written parenting plan. The point of this section is to educate on all the kinds of things you might be thinking about—and suggesting to your lawyer—as you enter negotiations on coparenting matters.

Equal Parenting Time Isn't Right for Every Family

All too often, people in divorce decide that, in the interest of altruistic fairness, that the children should live with each parent on an equal parenting time schedule. It can be 2 days on, 2 days off, 3 days on so that the weekends naturally rotate, it can be a weekly rotations of parenting time such that the children are with each parent for seven days at a stretch, or it can be anything in-between. While fairness is a nice goal, it isn't always right for each child to split time equally among two homes. I hear that 50/50 parenting time orders are the courts' new status quo/standard approach in some places, and if this is true where you are, your lawyer may tell you you're just stuck with it. But if you have a choice, it's important to give careful consideration before blindly agreeing to give up half your child's childhood years to a coparent who may not appreciate it or, worse, cannot handle it.

What adults consider fair to them is often unfair to the children. Can you imagine having to pack a bag every week to move your residence? How you may not feel like you're settled in any particular place? While some children do fine with this back-and-forth arrangement and feel it's the fairest approach for both of their parents, many children (and I may even go so far as to say *most* children) function better with one home base where they spend most of their time. In their effort to be fair to both parents, judges and divorcing parties unintentionally implement equal parenting time schedules which are hardest on the children. Not every child functions well in equal parenting time, and it's especially difficult where the parties are unable to communicate.

It's also imperative that you consider the life circumstances in each home. If your ex has a career that now requires or could in the future require overnight travel away from home, you need to be good with your ex's choice of caregiver for your child while he's away. Search your soul and decide if you can handle watching your darling baby, flesh of your flesh, being raised half the time by some random lady who's now sleeping with your ex-husband. It can be enough to drive a lot of women bonkers, so know yourself. If you aren't over the breakup yet, nothing will make you crazier than seeing some other woman fill the mom role at the other house. You also need to identify whether *your* individual child(ren), with their particular needs, is adaptable enough to cope with a back-and-forth schedule. Are your kids the kind who adapt well to change, or do they function better with the stability of one home base? This is something to consider carefully before making any permanent deal on custodial timesharing. Consider consulting a competent and experienced child counselor for insight into what is best for your family. Each child is different.

My two cents on the matter: don't enter into a knee-jerk 50/50 parenting time arrangement just to get your divorce behind you, and if you're seriously considering it, please consult a competent attorney and a child psychologist for guidance before you sign any kind of agreement.

Bird Nest Custody

Some folks try what's called "bird nest custody" on a temporary basis while the divorce case is pending but not final, and the parties are living apart and adjusting to a new normal. Bird nest custody involves the children remaining in the primary home and the parties rotating in and out of the home during each party's parenting time. It's a nice idea in theory, for the children get to keep their home, are not up-rooted or made to adjust to changing environments, and still get to enjoy the company of both parents.

I have to say, though, that I've never seen bird nest custody work seamlessly.

The first difficulty to overcome is the sheer cost of maintaining three households—the marital household for the children and an-other location for each parent to occupy during times they're not in the home with the kids. Only the richest people can afford such an arrangement, and arguments will invariably ensue over perceived cost-sharing imbalances.

Second, it is awfully difficult to share space with your ex, even if you're not there at the same time. Deliveries to the home are in-spected and questioned by your ex. It can be problematic to retrieve belongings inadvertently left behind when you vacate for your ex to come in for his parenting time, and, worse, what if your ex leaves belongings behind indicating he's got a new love interest? What if he's ordering gifts for a new love that arrive when you're there with the children? Not to mention the practical difficulty of living out of a suitcase. I don't recommend it.

If He's an Addict

There are, of course, special considerations to be taken into account if your ex is addicted to something harmful. Addiction changes people and creates an environment in which you're coparenting with what-ever the addiction is more than coparenting with a rational human. That's the trouble with addictions; they take hold of a person and en-tirely alter his judgment. If he's addicted to a drug, then you're co-parenting with a drug. If he's addicted to alcohol, you're coparenting with a bottle. If he's addicted to pornography, you're coparenting with a person who views people as objects for gratification rather than as beings to be honored, respected and cared for. It's all illness akin to cancer, and the addict often hates it about himself as much as you do, so a certain measure of grace and understanding is warranted. While they need your prayers and well wishes, safeguards are also necessary to protect the practical safety of your little ones if your ex is an addict.

The most difficult thing about protecting children from addict parents is *convincing a judge that a safety concern even exists*. It's generally assumed everyone is a decent parent unless you show otherwise with evidence.

<u>How To Prove It</u>. If your husband is an addict, it's really important to document your daily life with him so that you're equipped to give dates and details about what you're enduring on a daily basis. The details are necessary to flesh out your story so that it's believable. Anyone can say, "my husband drinks too much and it's really hard for the children and me to live with him." It's much more powerful to be able to say something like this in court:

Last Tuesday, Bill got drunk and drove his truck into a ditch while the kids were in there with him. Little Gavin got a concussion from the crash. Here are the photos of the damage to the truck, the medical records from Gavin's cranial CT scan, and the police report from Bill's arrest for DUI and child endangerment. When I tried to stop him from leaving the house with the kids, he slapped me across my right cheek, at which time I fell to the floor. Here are my medical records showing the contusion to my right cheek and photo of the resulting black eye. I also have photos here of him passed out on the floor, still holding a beer on June 18, with fresh urine on the front of his pants. This is how he gets at least three nights every week. I have his credit card records here to show the hundreds of dollars he spends at the liquor store every week, along with the affidavit of my friend who sees him enter the liquor store every day after work. Please give me a restraining order and custody of my children and require my husband's visitation to be supervised by his mother.

The power is in the details of your story. Judges are human, and stories resonate with humans.

I once helped some grandparents get custody of their toddler grandson because they had the good sense to test the baby for the presence of drugs in his little system. They suspected he may have gotten the powder on his hands from the home's coffee table where the parents were rumored to have snorted the drug. And sure enough, when the test came back positive for cocaine, that custody battle was a cake walk. There was no judge around who would send that baby back to parents who'd allow the child to ingest cocaine.

You can also prove drug addiction a lot of times using evidence of large ATM cash withdrawals, cryptocurrency transfer records, and digital wallet records for someone's transactions on Venmo, CashApp, Zelle, and other electronic funds transfer applications.

<u>Pornography Addiction</u>. Many people will tell you pornography is not a big deal. I'm here to tell you, sister, it IS a big deal. I've seen countless marriages break down over porn addictions. Why is that? It's because pornography makes a stranger an object of a man's pleasure. The stranger is made in the image of God, with a soul, should not be diminished to be made a mere means of pleasure for man. The more a married man views pornography, the less he regards the souls of women or their value as individuals, and the more likely he is to mistreat his wife. It's a betrayal not only of the marital intimate relationship but also of the woman's very sense of individual personhood

in the marriage. Allowing pornography in your house is to give that man a discount on your worth.

Dads who are porn addicts pose a risk to your children's moral development and sometimes, in this time of child trafficking, can even expose them to grave physical danger from outside forces. More and more news reports are coming out these days about men selling inappropriate images of their own daughters on the internet. If your ex is a man with this sort of sickness, you have a whole other set of issues to safeguard your children against. Physical evidence of the porn addiction (computer and other records analyzed by a forensic expert) is often needed to prove to a judge that the addiction exists, and testimony from a qualified, credentialed psychologist with psychosexual therapy credentials, training and experience is often essential to educating the court on your concerns.

To address this concern, you can request that your ex be prohibited by court order from allowing the child access to his cell phone or other electronic devices, from photographing your child in a bathing suit, from placing your child under video surveillance at his home, and from placing images of your child online or otherwise disseminating them. A court order is just a piece of paper, of course, and he can do whatever he wants behind closed doors, but bringing the issue to the forefront of discussion in court can be a powerful deterrent. People just behave better if they know others are watching, especially when that "other" is a judge.

Safeguards to Consider

It's not enough just to present the problem to the judge; you must also be ready to propose rational solutions that allow safe, positive contact opportunities for the children to see their father. I always tell my clients that visitation should be permitted so long as it can be safe and positive for the children, for every child needs to know they are loved by both parents, even if the parent has some issues. Coming into court with solutions to propose rather than just complaints about your ex's failures is key in building credibility with the Court, and those proposed solutions, if reasonable, make the Court's job a lot easier.

Following is a list of safeguards to consider if you're coparenting with an addict:

1. Request supervised visitation. Having a neutral, trustworthy third party present during your ex's visits with the children can relieve a lot of stress and ensure the children's safety. This third party can be a relative of the children or a close friend of the family, some benevolent soul who's willing to give up time on their weekends to help you. The key is finding a third party who isn't an enabler of the addict, someone who can hold the line and put a stop to any nonsense that should take place during the visit. Mothers of addicts are usually and appealing supervisor options, but they're not always the most reliable because they can tend to enable the addict and lack the ability to stand up to him or call out his bad behavior. An enabling mother can be a contributor to why the addict is an addict in the first place because she fails to see her darling boy as anything less than perfect and overlooks his issues. Paid supervisor services also exist and are staffed with individuals trained in child protection and psychology, with skills at the ready to intervene to shield your child from harm should the supervised parent show up to the visit high or pull some other stunt when the children

are present. Because they are objective and unbiased, paid supervisors can also make excellent court witnesses if you need them to educate or inform the judge of visitation issues as they arise.

2. Control the custody exchange. If the visits aren't supervised, keeping the exchange of the children as seamless as possible can reduce your children's stress. I usually recommend exchanges at the local law enforcement precinct where there are surveillance cameras and deputies nearby to size up your ex to see if he's high or drunk before he leaves with the kids. If you ever suspect he's on something, all you'd have to do is suggest you're getting a deputy to check him out, and he'll surely high-tail it out of there (leaving the children safely with you) faster than you can say "DUI." Police officers can offer credible testimony should your ex become combative toward you or show up inebriated at the exchange. And police station parking lot footage and officer bodycam videos are slam-dunk evidence in custody cases.

3. Drug and Alcohol Testing. If your ex is an alcoholic, ask your lawyer about Soberlink and other blow-to-crank-the-car technologies that would prevent your ex from starting his engine without first blowing alcohol-free carbon dioxide into a machine attached to his steering column. My understanding is that it will even take his photo and report to your phone every time he drives the car during visitation to tell you his blood alcohol content. Worth looking into! And if your ex is a drug abuser, ask your lawyer about including a drug test provision your final court order to empower you to spring random drug tests (of his urine, blood and hair

follicles) on him whenever you're afraid he's relapsed or actively abusing substances. The mere *threat* of a drug test can sometimes be enough to keep someone on the straight and narrow.

The important thing is to tailor your parenting plan to your children's particular needs. Start talking to your lawyer early in the process about all the things you'd like to address, so that either the parenting plan can include all the safeguards you need or, in the event you can't settle your case, so that your lawyer will know how to demonstrate your concerns in court.

Questions for Reflection

1. What are your child(ren)'s particular needs? Identify the things that give you the most anxiety when trusting your child to your coparent's care. What are some provisions you could propose to include in your parenting plan to address those?

2. Is your ex addicted to something? How will you articulate your concerns about this addiction to your legal counsel? How can you prove the problem exists, and how can you use your parenting plan to safeguard your children?

3. Consider your children's individual needs. How do they generally adapt to new things and life transitions? What parenting time schedule would be best for *your* individual child(ren)? What safeguards should you consider including in your parenting plan, for the good of your children?

4. Do you trust your ex's ability to make good decisions for the children? Do you trust him with some decisions more than

others? Are there parameters you need to include in your parenting plan to limit your child's exposure to unhealthy lifestyle choices and/or unsavory third parties?

Resources

Parenting Plan Idea Workbook—Gretchen Baskerville & Lisa Wilson
Soberlink—www.soberlink.com
Help! My Family's Messed Up—Emily Parke Chase
Helping Children Survive Divorce—Dr. Archibald D. Hart
Hope No Matter What: Helping Your Children Heal After Divorce—
Kim Hill and Lisa Harper
What Children Need to Know When Parents Get Divorced—
William Coleman

Chapter Soundtrack

Waymaker—Passion 2020
Her Town Too—James Taylor
When You Love Someone—James TW

11

Crush Your Mediation

*"Settle matters quickly with your adversary who is taking you
to court. Do it while you are still with him on the way,
or he may hand you over to the judge."*
—Proverbs 5:25

I get it. You want this divorce over and behind you, like YESTER-
DAY, but don't be a fool and rush into an unwise settlement. As
Tom Petty said, the waiting is the hardest part. But there are some
things that you only get one chance to get right in the final terms
of your divorce, and you don't want to botch it up because you were
in too big a hurry to move on. Plus, keep in mind that all things
happen in God's timing. It takes *time* to sort out the issues, reveal
all the secrets, identify the property values, and sufficiently calm
the emotions in order for settlement talks to be productive. When
you feel like God is keeping you in the limbo longer than you'd like,
remember there may be a good reason for it, a hidden blessing you
can't see right now.

This chapter offers food for thought as you and your lawyer negotiate with your ex and his counsel.

More Logic, Less Emotion

Humans are thirty-one percent more productive and mentally sharper when in a positive mental state.[58] The whole first section of this book was about getting your mind right, and for good reason. It's absolutely crucial that you do the mental health work necessary—with your therapist, your pastor, or by whatever means necessary—to get yourself into a positive frame of mind before you start negotiating the terms of your final divorce. It's all about shifting your lens to believing the future can be happy, that each day has potential for changing your circumstances for the better, that your future is going to be good. It's best to postpone settlement talks until you're in this kind of positive, coherent, focused, unemotional frame of mind, even if you're desperate to move on with your life.

You will know when the time is right for settlement discussions to commence.

Divorce Litigation is a Game of Chess

In chess, the player has to think forward multiple moves to analyze all the possible countermoves from the opponent, *before* making that initial move. You can set yourself up for checkmate if you're not constantly thinking ahead.

Divorce negotiations are like a game of chess. An offer is made, and a piece on the board is moved. Before making an offer, you have to consider how the opponent will respond to that offer (i.e., move), how that response could keep you from winning the game, how you'll respond to that offer, how they'll respond to your latest offer, and so

---

58   Achor, Shawn. "TedX Bloomington: The Happiness Advantage: Linking Positive Brains to Performance." (May 2011).

it goes until you reach a settlement or an impasse. It's all strategy and no emotion.

One common question I get is whether it's best to make the first offer or let your ex go first. I generally prefer to let the other side make the first settlement proposal because it gives us an early glimpse into their thoughts before we have to share ours with them, and sometimes I'm pleasantly surprised that my client won't have to give up nearly as much as we initially predicted. Sometimes, however, it's impossible to get the other side to jump first, and my client is so eager to settle that we don't wait. Whenever I'm representing the party making the first offer, we always try to leave plenty of room for negotiation on each item in the deal. You never reveal your bottom line, i.e., the least attractive settlement amount or option you're willing to accept. If it's a day-long mediation or settlement conference, for example, it's most wise to hold back your most generous proposals until late in the day. The goal is never to reach that bottom line position, but rather to settle for more than that whenever possible. If you impatiently go straight to the lowest amounts you'll accept early in the discussion, you'll most likely end up either settling for far less than you'd hoped for or not settling at all because you will have boxed yourself into a negative position way too early. This kind of impatient negotiating makes you lose credibility and appear irrational to the opponent, and discussions almost always break down as a result.

When you make your first offer or counteroffer, you shoot for the moon. Pie in the sky. Ask for the best-case scenario you could ever hope for on all points, knowing your ex will come back with a lower offer. You're surely heard the old adage of "ask and you shall receive." It doesn't hurt to ask, does it? You may just get most of what you're hoping for, especially if your ex prioritizes different things than you do.

Like in chess, incremental movements are key in settlement negotiations. You don't ever want to jump too far, too fast toward your ex's side of the equation. Doing so exposes you to a greater risk of loss. Know where your line is, stay focused. Don't make some giant move out of emotion and blow your chance at a fair settlement.

You can't win in chess if you don't know the rules. Have your lawyer educate you on the laws of your state before you try to negotiate a settlement of your case. Some states are community property states, while other states call for an equitable division approach to dividing property. Custody, child support and alimony rules also vary from state to state. You can't make realistic proposals unless you know the minimums and maximums the law will allow you to get. Ask your lawyer for guidance on this.

The Mason Jar Approach to Property Division

Visualize a large, glass Mason jar like your grandmother may use for putting up vegetables. Now, imagine that you have a pile of large rocks, smaller pebbles of various sizes and a pile of sand you must put into the jar. There's no way the big rocks will fit in the jar if you put sand in the jar first. You have to start with the big rocks, then fill in empty spaces with pebbles, and *then* pour in the sand for all items to fit.

Settling your case is like filling that Mason jar. The big rocks are the biggest items to be placed in the jar first—then next smallest rocks, then pebbles, then sand goes last. Define the big rocks of property division and resolve those first, followed by the pebbles and the sand, in that order.

The big rocks: the marital residence, any other real estate, big bank and retirement accounts, stock and other investment accounts, aircraft, and a division of the debts attached to each item.

The pebbles: automobiles, boats (with motors—don't forget the motors), motorcycles, campers, trailers, zero-turn lawn mowers, tractors/heavy machines, ATVs, firearm and tool collections, gold/silver, Bitcoin/cryptocurrency, and a division of the debts that may go with each item.

The sand: furniture, home décor, housewares like pots and pans and bed/bath linens, credit card rewards, hotel chain rewards, frequent flyer miles, club memberships, the school supplies, the water hoses, rakes and shovels, and the spices in your spice drawer, should your ex be that tacky.

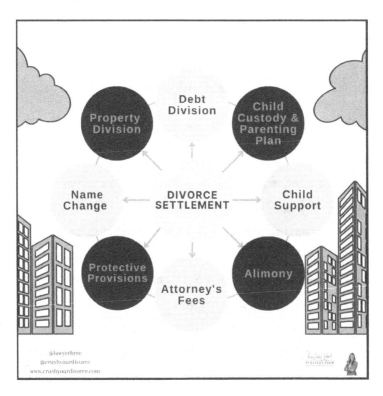

Settlement Categories

Envision each item in a negotiation as a bucket of issues to be resolved, one bucket at a time: property division, debt division, child custody/parenting plan, child support, alimony, attorney's fees, name change, and protective provisions.

Tax Returns

Are there outstanding income tax returns you and your ex never filed? How will you file going forward? Which party will claim the children for income tax benefits purposes? Do you owe marital back taxes to be addressed as marital debts in your case? Did your ex take off with part of your marital tax refund? What is necessary to address these issues?

Attorney's Fees

Are you entitled to have your ex pay your lawyer's fees or reimburse you for fees you've already paid? Ask your lawyer if you have a valid fees claim.

Name Change

Do you want to change your name as part of your divorce? If so, ask your lawyer how to go about that as part of your divorce case. It can save you from having to file a name change petition later.

Provisions to Safeguard your Settlement

There are various provisions lawyers like to put in the final settlement documents of a divorce case to safeguard collectability of the deal, ensure the parties follow through to effectuate the terms of the deal, and to encourage good faith dealing between the parties going forward. Ask your lawyer about whether you should include the following provisions in your documents: It's usually wise to include a catch-all provision requiring the parties to sign documents like deeds and brokerage and bank forms as needed to carry out the terms of the final divorce agreement. You might also consider including a life insurance provision which would require the party obligated to pay support to keep life insurance in place to pay the obligation, or to make the obligation the first obligation to be paid from the party's estate, should the party untimely pass away before the order's obligations have been fulfilled. Another way to ensure enforceability of those obligations set forth in the final order is to allow for the attachment of liens to the obligor's assets so that the obligations are backed by real collateral.

In a case where it's not entirely clear whether the other party has been entirely transparent about assets, I've seen nondisclosure penalty provisions which provide financial relief to the party who later discovers assets that were hidden during the litigation. If the other party won't agree to include such a provision, that may be a sign that they're not being entirely honest. If they will agree to include such a provision, it's a nice safeguard to have. Ask your lawyers if any other provisions like these are advisable for your scenario.

Winning Negotiation Strategies
Identify a Common Enemy to Fend Off Together
I call this the Common Enemy Approach to settlement. For all your disagreements, you and your ex have common fears and goals in this litigation. By identifying an enemy common to both of you, you'll shift the focus away from what you disagree on and bring a fresh perspective. When the focus shifts in this way, a positive dynam-

ic emerges, one in which issues get resolved with greater common sense and less emotion. When we stop focusing on how much we want the other party to suffer or "lose" and fixate instead on how to reach consensus so everyone involved comes through it with hope for the future (which is what every one of us should want for everyone else in the world, even our enemies), we're all better for it.

The easiest common enemy to identify in divorce is The Unknown. Neither side should want to lose control of the outcome and have to trust a judge they don't know to resolve the issues fairly and thoroughly. Court is a real wild card, unpredictable and capable of imposing restrictions and limitations on your life that you won't like one bit. Attorney's fees and litigation expenses are another common enemy. A wise divorcing couple will do their best to reach agreement on all issues to stop the bleeding on lawyers and court costs.

A mediator friend of mine keeps this image (painted on an old piece of wood) in his office and pulls it out at almost every mediation:

What is depicted is a tug of war over a cow. The Plaintiff is pulling the horns of the cow, and the Defendant is pulling the tail of the cow. Both of them *want this cow*. And while they're fighting and struggling over who's gonna get this cow, the lawyer is down there *milking*

the cow. You definitely need to fight the good fight over issues that matter to you, especially if they impact your children's safety and well-being. But there will come a point when it's time to stop paying lawyers to fight over the cows in your life, Dear One. You'll know when the time comes.

Tactical Empathy[59]

If you're getting divorced, it's highly probable you and your ex view your situation-and perhaps even the world—quite differently. It's often difficult to see your enemy's point of view even for a moment. But you are wise—at least for purposes of settlement discussions—to put yourself in your ex's shoes and try to identify those issues that are most important to him in this divorce, and how he would most likely want to resolve them. For example, is he emotionally tied to the house or a particular item of property? Consider giving him something he's particularly fixated on receiving but use that concession to get something else *you* care about more. Is he hung up on a particular parenting decision-making role or nailing down particular parenting time with the kids? Consider giving him that thing he's asking for, in exchange for some other parenting-related concession important to you. Is there a joint debt he's concerned he can't pay? If you offer to pay part of it over time, that may help grease the wheels toward getting an asset in your hands right now; an asset now is often worth incurring an obligation to be paid over time. Every case is different, and every party's priorities are, too. Talk to your lawyer about how to

---

59   Chris Voss, best-selling author and former FBI negotiator, offers tremendous resources on this tactical entity negotiation concept. Check out the resources listed below to read more about it.

identify and empathize with your ex to the extent necessary to identify his trigger points and come up with ways to address each item.

Another way to use tactical empathy as a divorce settlement strategy is to accept a *framework* for settlement to give your opponent a moral victory, without accepting the particular terms being proposed. For example, a guy may be willing to pay $12,000.00 per year in alimony for a maximum period of five years, and not a minute longer. From the way the proposal was made, it's evident he may be more worried about the length of time he'll have to pay, perhaps due to an upcoming retirement or other expensive life change he expects in five years, or maybe for some other reason you, as his wife, will easily be able to diagnose. The bottom line is that if you are able to identify whether the *amount* or the *duration* of the alimony term is what's got him concerned, you can accept his framework of *either* duration or amount, and then shift your counteroffer on the opposite element. In the example above, you might come back with a counterproposal accepting his five-year term but increasing the amount you receive every month, or perhaps you demand part of it in a lump sum. Lump-sum, upfront money is usually much preferred over payments to come in over time. By coming back with a counterproposal which accepts the duration *framework* he proposed, you're more likely to maximize the amount of alimony received (a win for you), while also giving him a small moral victory in the discussion.

I can almost hear you screaming, "But why should I have to baby him and assuage his fears? I've don't that my whole marriage, and I'm done with that now!" Believe me when I tell you I get it. This is one of those hard moments when it's imperative to set aside emotion and think logically. Isn't it better to show empathy for where his heart is, and recognize and assuage his fears, no matter how much he's hurt you, if it means you can create a cooperative environment conducive to a settlement that 1) benefits you and 2) stops the fighting?

You may think empathy equals weakness. But I'm here to tell you—empathy is your superpower, girl! You can stay strong in your discussions and show no weakness while also having a rational decency about you to recognize and manage your husband's emotions during settlement talks. It can be done all day long without giving up any ground.

I advise my clients to be as kind as can be in settlement without undermining future financial stability or the children's well-being, expecting good things will come back to you as a result. I've just seen it happen too many times to ignore it—the healthier clients are reasonable, fair and not out for blood, and they heal from their divorce wounds more quickly and with greater personal and emotional success than the ones who, in their sadness, bitterness and anger, try to mete out punishment and get their pound of flesh. Your peace is worth more.

My Top Ten Negotiation Tips

1. **Identify your dealbreakers, hold your line, and don't be afraid to walk the heck out.** Identify and hold fast to your non-negotiable terms, those items or positions you absolutely will not give up, under any circumstances, to settle your case. Everyone has them. It's usually custody of children or a particular dollar amount in asset division. There's nothing wrong with having things you just won't budge on, and there's no obligation to explain why you feel that way or apologize for it. Even Jesus instructed us in Matthew 5:37 (NLT) to "just say a simple, 'Yes, I will,' or 'No, I won't.'

Anything beyond this is from the evil one." And don't be afraid to end negotiations if your ex insists on breaking a dealbreaker.

I once attended a divorce mediation out of town where the opposing party/husband flatly refused to pay child support or even discuss sharing the marital home's equity with her. We did two rounds of stalemate over these issues before my client and I decided to call it a day. I was 30 minutes down the highway headed back to my office when the mediator called my cell phone and asked me to return, saying the husband had changed his mind. We returned, and the case was settled that day in a way that satisfied both parties. Walking out is a risk, so only do it if you're absolutely sure the opposing party won't budge, but it sure can be effective to show your ex you're not playing his games.

2. **Never bid against yourself, and never invite a counteroffer**. A good lawyer will smell weakness if you make an offer and then immediately qualify it with something like, "…but please send a counteroffer for us to consider." Your ex and his lawyer know they can always counter any proposal you make, so there's no need or purpose in concluding your settlement proposal begging them to counter. Just state your proposal with confidence and await his reply. He might surprise you and agree with some terms you never thought he'd accept! Negotiate with confidence, and if you are insecure in any part of your proposal, never let him see it! It's a good rule of thumb never to bid against yourself in negotiation. For example, if you offer to accept $50,000.00 for your equity in the house and your ex then counters that he'll give

you *zero* dollars for it, you don't need to come down from the $50,000.00 figure until he shows some movement first.

3. **Never split the difference**. In most negotiations, one party starts low (far on one extreme), and the other party starts high (or far to the other extreme) on each issue to be resolved. You may find yourself becoming impatient as you negotiate, especially if you're at a scheduled sit-down conference or mediation. You may be tempted to "go to the middle" each round just to get out of there faster. Do not do it! You want to negotiate in good faith and show incremental movement each time, but it's almost always better to make small, unpredictable, incremental movements instead of splitting the difference between your positions each time. You will most certainly sell yourself short if you negotiate that way. Instead, try to come up with creative solutions to mutual problems that you know will be palatable to your husband and make him more likely to accomplish your settlement goals, as well.

4. **Use your tools and rely on your experts**. Remember the marital balance sheet discussed in an earlier chapter? Make sure you bring your electronic marital balance sheet with you to mediation; it can be adjusted throughout the day to double-check whether the proposal on the table is fair. Time is often short during negotiations, so use of tools like these can be crucial to quick analysis and on-the-spot decisions. You should also consider bringing your financial planners, CPA, valuation expert to mediation, if appropriate and affordable to have them there. Their guidance in real-time as you consider each proposal can be a game changer.

5. **Throw in some extra demands to take back later**. Identify a few things you can request in the negotiation which you could really live without, planning to withdraw those demands later in the negotiation. You need things to release in order to show movement at each round of the discussion. For example, you can request more money in attorney's fees, cash settlement or an extra list of furniture items just to have something to give up later in the negotiation for something you *really* want, like increased parenting time or a higher alimony award.

6. **Do not agree to a piecemeal settlement without sound legal advice**. All parts of a divorce case interrelate; it's a complete package. Division of debt and assets, combined with support provisions is sort of like a large pie. You can't take one piece out and have the rest of it look the same. In only narrow circumstances is it wise to settle one issue/term in isolation, as doing so changes the whole psychology of the case and inevitably benefits one side over the other. For example, dividing the bank accounts at the start of the case gives the higher wage-earner the ability to argue that funds earned after that early division are each party's funds to keep. In such a case, you might maximize your recovery by waiting to divide the funds later so that the account balances are higher by the time you divide them. Always consult your lawyer and carefully analyze your situation and advice given you before making any big moves, and never make a binding commitment on any one issue before you know the entire picture.

7. **Keep Your Expectations Realistic**. Keep in mind that lawyers are limited in what they can do by only the law, the court's rules and schedule, and their own schedules, but also to the extent your own choices have limited your prospects for success. Delays are inevitable, and attorneys aren't miracle workers. You can't bring your lawyer scrambled eggs expecting her to give you back an uncracked dozen. We lawyers do what we can do with the hands we are dealt, but family law situations are messy, and it's usually difficult for even the most skilled attorney to get you everything you want in your case. Keep your expectations realistic and reasonable, and don't make unattainable demands.

8. **In your pain, don't be shortsighted**. So many clients are non-confrontational by nature, and this often leads them to accept terms they later regret. One example of this I often see is giving the other parent 50/50 time with the children, even though they've never been the best parent, instead of fighting the fight they should for the long-term benefit of the children. The first time the kids are exposed to something unhealthy at the other home, the client is back in my office looking into modification of the decree. Other examples include one party giving up too much of the marital estate, not insisting on appraisals of property or valuations of business assets, or settling before all assets have been disclosed in discovery. These folks are so desperate for personal peace that they sell themselves far short of where the settlement should have landed. And their exes laugh all the way to the bank. Be wise.

9. **Don't trust an "agreement to agree" or an unofficial side deal**. It can be tempting to punt some of the harder issues down the road by agreeing in the document to agree later on a particular term. Beware! An agreement to agree is no agreement at all, and you will likely find yourself back at Square One dealing with the same issues sometime in the future. Try to address all the issues you can when you finalize the divorce. It can also be tempting to trust your ex's promises to do more, pay more, give more after the case is over, but also saying to you, "let's just not put it in the court order." For example, say your ex promised to pay more for the children in practice, if only you'll agree to keep child support lower in the actual court order. What happens if you rely on his promise, the promise turns out to be false, and you can't afford to buy your children school clothes the August after your divorce? Be wise and think ahead.

10. **Do Not Wheel and Deal Behind Your Lawyer's Back**. You have an attorney for a reason. Let them communicate your positions to the other side formally to avoid confusion. Take their advice when negotiating. A wise woman takes the advice of her counsel before negotiating or binding herself to any set of contractual terms, and never forwards her lawyer's communications to her ex-husband, as doing so *destroys the attorney-client privilege* concerning their content. *Do not sign anything* without first getting legal advice from a competent lawyer who specializes in divorce. Anything you sign could be evidence in your case and used against you later. I once saw a case where a high-asset couple scratched out some settlement terms on notebook paper at the kitchen

table, signed it, and filed it with the court. The terms were one-sided and unfair to one party, but the deal stuck as the order of the court. You can really mess yourself up signing something all willy-nilly. <u>Let your lawyer help you</u> so you can be sure what you're signing is fair, legitimate and not going to bite your fanny later.

There's a common misconception about friendships among lawyers, that we're all an "old boys' club" of comrades who settle cases on the golf course and prioritize our friendships with one another over our clients' best interests. There's no truth to it. Lawyers are co-workers and colleagues, but we're all too competitively wired to allow friendship to overshadow our drive to win for our clients. If the lawyers in your case are cordial with one another during settlement communications, do not see that as your lawyer showing weakness. Rapport and mutual respect among counsel is important to have if any progress is going to be made.

Big Issues to Consider Before You Settle

What might seem like a fair agreement can actually be a disaster if tax ramifications are ignored. Some accounts can be transferred from one party to the other via tax-free transactions, but others cannot. Will you have to liquidate assets after your divorce? If so, consult a CPA or tax attorney to determine the extent to which you will owe capital gains taxes when you sell. You also need an idea of how your tax refunds (or tax obligations over and above the withholding you're paying into the system, pre-divorce) will be impacted by your changing filing status after you're single. You don't want to be hit with a tax burden you didn't expect, just as you're trying to rebuild your life.

Another thing I suggest some clients do is to check their Social Security accounts to find out how much they can expect to receive in Social Security benefits, and at what age they can start drawing such benefits. This is especially important if yours is a later-in-life divorce or a divorce after more than ten years of marriage.

Health insurance premiums are a moving target and vary greatly from person to person, state to state. State marketplace exchanges can be difficult to maneuver, and you need to confirm you qualify before assuming cheap benefits are available to you. COBRA coverage is an option for some people which makes your existing coverage available to you for a period of months following your divorce, but COBRA premiums can be much higher than what you paid when you were married. Make sure you know what you're getting into before you finalize the terms of your divorce.

This is, of course, not an exhaustive list of the things you need to consider, and every case is unique. Be sure to ask your lawyer if there's anything else you in particular should be considering as you weigh your settlement options.

Peace Has a Price

At the end of negotiations, it's often wise to settle and cut your losses even if you're not getting every single thing you wanted. I've often heard mediators say you know a settlement is fair if both sides leave a little sore about how it ended, if both parties lost something they wanted to keep. If you're holding on for court, believing the judge will tell him off and punish him for the way he's behaved, you may be throwing good money at a pipe dream that will never come to fruition. Unless the behavior is extremely egregious, it could be difficult to convince a judge to give you a one-sided award. There is a price or a value on getting to a peaceful result, one that allows you to move forward with certainty and saves you from the agony of having to rehash your marriage story in front of a room full of strangers.

I once knew a woman whose dealbreakers were to keep the home and primary custody of the parties' children. She gave her ex *all* their savings and financial account holdings, and she even took out a large mortgage to finish buying the husband out of their home and business, just to ensure her child custody and home ownership goals were met. She often commented that her monthly mortgage checks were the best checks she wrote each month. With each payment on that mortgage, she reclaimed her life and felt the freedom. It was hard to start over with no savings, but she trusted God had her best interest in mind, and she rested on that promise. And do you know that she ended up paying that mortgage off early? She never regretted buying her peace, not one single minute.

Also keep in mind that some people just *need* to have the last word in an argument. It could be something as simple as a last-minute adjustment worth ten dollars to him that gets your deal done and behind you. This final-word nonsense can be ever so ego-driven and stupid, but if your husband ticks this way, give him his little victory and move on, knowing he might have gotten that last ten dollars out of you, but you're still the real winner because you rose above the nonsense and made the mature decision to settle your case.

And if for some reason, try as you might, you just aren't able to settle the case at end of the day, do not feel shame over it. You haven't lost; you have learned! You've gained valuable insight into your ex's talking points for trial, and you will be better prepared for the coming battle as a result.

Once Your Case Is Settled, Act Fast to Get the Deal Signed

Time kills deals.[60] Once a deal is reached, act fast to get the deal on paper and signed ASAP. If your ex has too much time to think about the downsides of the agreement he's reached, he's more likely to renege on the terms. For this reason, whenever feasible, I try to go into mediation or settlement conferences with skeletal documents already drafted so that final tweaks can be made, and they can be signed as soon as the deal is reached. Talk to your lawyer about how to expedite the finalization of the matter by having final documents ready in advance of settlement discussions.

It's tempting to let the other lawyer prepare the final documents in order to save on fees, but please consider letting your attorney do the work. If your lawyer controls the framing and language of the documents, it's more likely that (a) nothing you prioritize will be left out and (b) that all of your biggest concerns will be thoroughly addressed. If the other side prepares the final documents and doesn't capture the true spirit of the deal as you understood it, your lawyer will have to request revisions anyway, so it's often easier to have it done by your lawyer, on your terms and with your oversight, to start with. And some things, if omitted, cannot be revisited later. You get one shot at getting the paperwork right.

When it's time to sign the documents, read them carefully, all the way through, before you sign them. Lawyers are only human, and clerical errors are possible. Sometimes, a client will say, "I trust you" and start to sign the documents without even glancing at the content, and

---

60   I've heard businesspeople say this all my adult life, but the quote has most recently been attributed to Erik Huberman, author of *The Hawke Method: The Three Principles of Marketing that Made Over 3,000 Brands Soar* (2022).

I stop them every time and *make* them read the papers first. You are the final reviewer of the terms. They are terms *you* will have to live with, and it can be difficult to modify them later, if they are modifiable at all.

It's very common to have multiple revisions of the documents floating around before the final draft is approved by both parties, so it's important to be clear about which version you approve. Initial every page of the final version you approve, to make sure it's clear that you approve *this particular draft*. Putting your first, middle and last initials at the bottom right corner of each page makes it clear to anyone who later reads the document.

Questions for Reflection

1. Consider your husband's point of view with tactical empathy. What are the things that trigger his fears? What assets is he determined to walk away from this marriage with? What does he want more than anything else out of this settlement, and what do you want the most? Do these things align, or are they at odds? What can you concede to him to get something you want more than that thing you'd be giving him? Can you accept his framework in the discussion while maximizing your recovery in the other substantive terms? Brainstorm about this with your lawyer before you head into your settlement conference or mediation session.

2. What obstacles are common to you both in the negotiation of your divorce settlement? Do you share any common goals related to the children? Do you both have fears about going to court? Do you both want to control the outcome? How can you use these common concerns as a way to foster greater cooperation in settlement talks?

3. What are the weaknesses in your case? What concessions can you make in settlement to hedge against the risks of a less-than-ideal outcome at trial?

4. What are your dealbreakers that you will not give up without a court battle? How will you handle it when those dealbreaker items are challenged during the negotiation? Do you have a plan of how you will adjust your settlement proposals as the negotiation unfolds?

5. What is peace worth to you? How badly do you want to settle your case, and what are you willing to give up in order to reach a peaceful, amicable resolution of the issues? If you're becoming battle weary, start thinking about how you might buy your peace, either by giving him something you both want or by letting go of something you'd really hoped to get in the final resolution.

Resources

Never Split the Difference: Negotiating as If Your Life Depended on It—Chris Voss

Tactical Empathy movie (2022)

Getting to Yes: Negotiating Agreement Without Giving In—Roger Fisher and William Ury

Chapter Soundtrack

"You Can't Always Get What You Want"—The Rolling Stones

"We Just Disagree"—Dave Mason

"Goin' Through the Big D"—Mark Chesnutt

12

Tackling Trial

The Lord is my light and my salvation—whom shall I fear? The Lord is the stronghold of my life—of whom shall I be afraid? When the wicked advance against me to devour me, it is my enemies and my foes who will stumble and fall. Though an army besiege me, my heart will not fear; though war break out against me, even then I will be confident.

—Psalm 27:1-3

If all settlement efforts fail, you could soon find yourself preparing for a full-blown trial. It may scare you to death, but you will survive.

Go back and read the "Crush the First Hearing" chapter. A trial is like an initial hearing on steroids. Where I practice, a full divorce trial can be days long and involve many more witnesses than the initial hearing. The volume of evidence is overwhelming, as well, with sometimes hundreds of documents, lengthy videos and audio recordings and other exhibits coming into evidence for the judge or jury to consider. It's expensive, arduous, tedious and unpredictable. Even with the best preparation, witnesses can surprise you with what they say. It's a think-on-your-feet, shoot-from-the-hip siege. It's a heart-piercing retelling (and a reliving) of a couple's most painful, embarrassing moments. Only lawyers enjoy trials.

To be ready for trial, you must have reached a place of unwavering conviction in the truth of your story. If you don't have conviction in your voice as you answer the questions, if only the slightest hint of uncertainty comes across in your testimony, you'll make it much easier for your husband to get what he wants in the end. Your evidence must be locked and loaded, your thoughts must be organized well before you testify, and you must tell your story convincingly with some objective proof of each point at issue. A coherent presentation of your arguments will make all the difference.

Use the insight you gleaned at mediation to anticipate his arguments. Talk to your lawyer about how you can prepare for each of those arguments, and what documents, witnesses or other evidence is needed to refute each one. The key is good preparation. As the old Spartan proverb says, "He who sweats more in training will bleed less in war."

Bitterness is rarely rewarded. If you're struggling with bitterness and anger toward your ex, do not let it show at trial. Your attitude should be one of humility and fairmindedness.

Provide a complete list of your witnesses to your lawyer so subpoenas can be prepared well in advance. When you give your lawyer this list, include each witness's name, address, email address and phone number, along with the facts you will use each witness to establish. What has each witness seen? What can they testify to that will help you get the result you want in your case? I always appreciate having a list like this from my client because it's a most useful, one-page cheat sheet for trial and cuts my preparation time considerably.

A timeline of key events of the marriage is also a helpful thing for your lawyer to have. The timeline should be a succinct overview of places you've lived, moves, children's births, job changes, school changes, major illnesses, deaths in the family that impacted your marriage, incidents of domestic violence, revelations of adultery or other bad conduct which you perceive as major turning points (or even breaking points) in the marriage. Keep it high level for easier digestibility and quick reference at trial.

You may also need to provide your lawyer with updated evidence, financials, and responses due in discovery to perfect the record for trial. Check with your lawyer to make sure you meet all the court's expectations in this regard.

Pray the Armor of God (Ephesians 6) over yourself before you go into trial each day. If you have praying friends, get them to lift you up in prayer. You cannot be prayed up enough for this battle. It's the fight of your life, and—make no mistake—there is a spiritual component.

He already knows the outcome. You just have to walk through the fire and get it done now. May the Lord go before you into battle, Dear Sister. Know you are loved and that I'm here, praying for you and wishing you strength, wisdom and courage, wherever you are. Do the best you can to present your case, <u>do what your lawyer says</u>, and leave with peace of mind that you did all you could do. You can't control the outcome, and there's peace and comfort in that, too.

Questions for Reflection

1. Consider the words of Charles Spurgeon: "Your emptiness is but the preparation for your being filled, and your casting down is but the making ready for your lifting up." Apply this to your life. Are you ready for God to lift you up? Do you believe He can, and that He will? This emptiness is not the end of your story, friend. You are on the brink of something great!

2. Joshua 1:9 reminds us: "Have I not commanded you? Be strong and courageous. Do not be afraid; do not be discouraged, for the Lord your God will be with you wherever you go." Your divorce is not a surprise to the Lord. Find your strength in Him, and do not lose hope. There is a plan!

3. Do you feel overwhelmed by your ex and his flying monkeys? 2 Chronicles 20:15 tells us to "be not afraid nor dismayed by reason of this great multitude; for the battle is not yours, but God's." There's something bigger than you and your ex going on here. Trust the Lord to work it all out for your good and His glory. Ask Him to use your battle to encourage someone else, for whatever good purpose He has for it. Do you believe God can use your struggle to help someone else in a mighty way? When you look at it that way, you'll start counting your struggles as blessings.

Resources

The Art of War—Sun Tzu

Preparing Witnesses: A Practical Guide for Lawyers and Their Clients—Daniel Small

Win Your Case: How to Present, Persuade, and Prevail— Every Place, Every Time—Gerry Spence

Chapter Soundtrack

"Independence Day"– Martina McBride
"You Already Know"—JJ Heller
"The Lion and the Lamb"—Big Daddy Weave

13

Go Find Your Happy

Delight yourself in the LORD,
and he will give you the desires of your heart.
—Psalm 37:4

Blessed is she who has believed that the Lord would
fulfill his promises to her.
—Luke 1:45

It was a blazing hot August day in South Georgia. The tiny white frame Baptist church at the farm where I grew up, where all my mother's family is buried, with its gorgeous stained glass, giant live oak, wooden cross behind the pulpit and five rows of pews, was brimming with close friends and family. I wore a strapless, lace-overlay dress I'd bought for $200.00 online. It was a little long, but I couldn't care less. On my left hand was the engagement ring Jefferson asked his Alabama jeweler friend from college to design just for me, to make sure it was "exactly what you want," he'd said.

My longtime friend and photographer took our photos on the dirt road in front of the church, the same spot where I played as a child with my cousins every summer, the large trees framing Coon Pond in the background. In my right hand was a giant bouquet of the brightest blue hydrangeas I'd ever seen, arranged by Jefferson's mama's best friend. My favorite color.

I wore my late grandmother's sparkling diamond watch, fetched once again almost exactly twenty years since my last wedding, from the same safe deposit box, just for this day. Hanging from my neck was "something borrowed," my Aunt Lisa's pendant in the shape of a flower. In my ears were diamond studs, a gift from Jefferson after we'd decided the old ones had to go.

It was nothing fancy. No bridesmaids. No best man. No frills. No gift registries. No formalities. No stuffiness. No pressure. No pretense. No show. Just beautiful simplicity and the purest joy. Surrounded by so much love. Everything a wedding—and a marriage, for that matter—should be.

There I stood outside the church with my sweet Daddy looking so dashing in his seersucker suit that matched his blue eyes. Jefferson is the real deal, and there were no reservations about giving me away … not this time. My eyes puddled like they had twenty years ago at my first wedding, but these tears were different. They came from a wiser perspective, from the overwhelm of God's goodness and faithfulness to me, for bringing me through the storm and causing beauty to rise from my pile of ashes.

Nadia, a dear friend who had graciously agreed at the last minute to direct my wedding, told us it was time to walk in, and butterflies filled my stomach. I entered the church and saw the smiling faces of my little girls, the friends who had seen me through, the family who's always been there, and the amazing, supportive, loving family I'm about to join. And then, just ahead, is my genuine, kind-hearted, generous, selfless, always-boot-wearing Jefferson, in his navy suit and baby blue tie, flashing that perfect smile that could light up any room.

Beside him, his daddy also waited, Bible open on his palm, ready to marry us. I had to deliberately slow my steps down that short aisle. My heart wanted to run.

The ceremony itself took ten minutes, if that. After a few selfies, hugs from friends and wedding cake in the fellowship hall, we climbed into Jefferson's shiny black F-150. Plastic cups bearing our combined monogram waited in the cupholders for Farmer's Daughter Knockout, our favorite pinot noir. We rolled the windows down and waved as we rode away, rose petals still stuck in my hair and dirt-road dust flying up in our wake.

It was the most exuberant moment of my life.

How Breezy Got Her Groove Back

When I'd filed for divorce the previous year, I joked to everyone that I would never remarry unless I could marry John Mayer. I truly had no interest in any kind of romance as I was maneuvering my contentious divorce. The contentment of being by myself, taking care of my clients and my children, serving at church, spending my time with friends and enjoying my now-peaceful, quiet time home was all I wanted. Starting my life anew and doing things my own way for the first time in my adult life was empowering and liberating, but also terrifying. It was nice not to have to get someone else's approval for anything I wanted to do, but the unknown was ominous.

By the time the final papers were signed in early December, I had gotten back to my true self, by the grace of God. The energized optimism of my college years came rushing back over me, and I couldn't wait for each new day. Work was interesting and stimulating. After all the counseling, soul-searching, self-care and reflection, I was in a really, really good mental, spiritual and emotional place. My household was orderly and running well, and the children seemed okay with their timesharing arrangement at each parent's house. I had fully grieved the losses. After years of pain and the six months of gut-wrenching litigation it took to dissolve my marriage, I was healed, healthy and whole again. Single and secure. Right by myself.

Soon after my divorce, a friend told me about a guy she knew from work. "No pressure, but when you're ready, I know someone I think you would really like. You will be good friends, even if it isn't a love connection." She was right. I met him, really liked him, then really loved him, then loved his family, and couldn't stop myself from marrying him eight months later. Jefferson has just felt like home from the start. He's the male version of me. Undeniably meant to be. The perfect complement to my personality and life. My other half. My True North.

I used to tell my clients not to make any major decisions within the year following their divorces. I don't say that anymore. God's timing is not ours. Man's rules cannot—and should not—regulate or restrict His blessings.

I also used to counsel people to stay married as long as they could—for the children, to avoid the emotional pain and practical drudgery of litigation, to allow time to be sure before pulling the cord, and other suggestions. Projecting my own fears onto them, I advised folks to take what I thought was the safer route, the path of staying married and not rocking the boat unless absolutely necessary.

I don't give this advice anymore, either.

Today, I encourage people to run away as fast as they can from abusive, unhealthy home lives. Life can be so much better, and I now shout it from the rooftops! You do have the power to change your life like I did, if only you can find the courage.

I could write a hundred stories about the clients I've seen go on after divorce to meet their true soul mates. And I could probably write two hundred stories of women who—by finding themselves, their peace, and their unique purpose—impact the world in amazing ways after leaving abusive or toxic marriages, *without a new man.*

Over the years, I've observed that the happiest divorced people are those who know the importance of connecting with other people in a meaningful way. God put us on earth to love one another, to serve one another, to take care of one another's needs. What I've seen is when people look for ways to help and connect with other people, their souls are content. God gave you special, you-specific gifts to be used in the world for His glory. Use them. Connect. Love people. Hug them. Tell them you love them. Show your children how to love.

Show your warmth. Give compliments freely. Look for ways to brighten days. Throw away the fear. Embrace the future. Believe good things are possible. Reconnect with your unjaded twenty-year-old self. Be open to new experiences. Use your gifts and volunteer your time. Use your pain to help those with the same struggles. Bear their burdens and let them help you bear yours. Show your children how to live in community. It's what life is really all about.

You have great value. Go contribute something meaningful! When you give of yourself, it's amazing how much life enrichment you get back. And when you find fulfillment as a single person, that's usually when you meet some other single someone—maybe a really cute single someone—doing the same things. All in God's timing.

God cares about the small details of our lives. He knows the longings of our hearts. He is faithful and He is with you. He wants to bless you—with new relationships, experiences, fun times, greater confidence, a renewed sense of purpose.

When your divorce is over, I want you to be proud of yourself for pushing through and not allowing it to break you. You've done a very hard thing! My prayer is that your heart be fully healed, that you will feel God's love for you in the depth of your spirit, and that you will lean into His goodness and plan for you, knowing that nothing is impossible with God.

Get excited, girl! There is so much adventure and fun to be had! Life is far from over for you, friend. Believe it. Live it. Love it! I'll be right here rooting for you. xo, BSH

Questions for Reflection

1. What do you want your life to look like in one year? Two years? Five years?
2. What can you do to invest in the hearts and lives of others?
3. What gifts do you have to share with the world around you?
4. What do you want people to say about you after you're gone? What legacy do you want to leave behind?
5. What is the deepest desire of your heart? Find your delight in the Lord and pray that these desires will be fulfilled. I'll be praying with you. 🩶

Chapter Soundtrack

"Bless the Broken Road"—Rascal Flatts
"Cowboy Take Me Away"—The Chicks
"Perfect"—Ed Sheeran
"Slide"—Goo Goo Dolls
"High On You"—Survivor
"She's In Love"—Mark Wills
"Power of Two"—Indigo Girls

"I See It Now"—Tracy Lawrence

"Love Will Come to You"—Indigo Girls

"Safe in the Arms of Love"—Martina McBride

"Everything Has Changed"—Ed Sheeran & Taylor Swift

"Coming Around Again"—Carly Simon

"Taking You Home"—Don Henley

"Last Train Home"—John Mayer

"Hanging By a Moment"—Lifehouse

"Goodness of God"—The Worship Initiative, Bethany Barnard

Acknowledgements

This two-year labor of love was inspired by my children and my sweet Jefferson. I live each day to make all of you proud, and I love you more than words can say.

The idea for the book came to me around a dinner table with new friends at Cape Santa Maria, a sacred place so dear to Jefferson and me, an isolated utopia of warmth, kindness, love and peace, precious stray cats, conch fritters and pineapple rum drinks, which came to be the place I've written some of my favorite chapters—both of my life and of this book. I first fell in love with Jefferson there, and I fall more in love with him each time we go. If ever you visit the Cape, you're guaranteed to go back.

I would not have been able to pull off this work without the love and support of my family and friends. Mom and Daddy, you have always made me know how loved I was, and it's been that foundation that gave me the courage to step out and share my thoughts so vulnerably. You are the best parents any kid ever had.

To my family at the farm on Dias Road and from spots throughout the Great State of Baker, I wouldn't be me without all of you. Farm love, Riverview bus rides, long talks on hay bales, late-night manicures, Chase from Lolly, pickup truck sing-alongs, chip dip from a yellow Tupperware, and 24-hour coffee forever!

To Aunt Sheila and Aunt Donna, it was so great being the only girl in the sea of boy cousins. Thank you for always being so kind and nurturing to me, and for supporting my dad while also remaining friendly with my mother after their divorce. You showed me this kind of grace is possible. Pop and Mama Chris raised y'all right.

To my step-people from Bainbridge, thank you for never treating me like a "step-anything." I loved Linda so much, and I love you all.

To Sutton Howell Fyfe, your positivity and kindness in all things inspire me. I always wanted a sister, and you are the perfect one. God gave me a tremendous gift when He gave you, your parents, and Will to me.

Special thanks to Nicole, Leigh Ann and Claley for putting up with me at the office every day. You are the backbone of my practice, and you bless our clients. There's no way I could do this job without you!

To the Smart Girls Travel Club who taught me to embrace adventure and to step out of my comfort zone, time with each of you is life-giving. Now that the book is done, let's plan our next trip!

To Susan, Julie, Cindy, Kristin, Caroline, Cheryl, Allison, Kelly, Deb, Nadia, Janna, Jaci, Tricia, Leah, Laura, Jennifer, April, Ursula, Janet, Sherri, Sophie, Cheryl, Leigh, my church family and praise team, Diane Allen and Tracy Bane, who got me through my divorce and showed me life could be good again. You don't even know how much you've blessed my heart with your kind words, reassurance, and encouragement to keep going.

To Christine Lamb, Rebecca McKemie, Jennifer D., Jennifer B., and the ladies of Ally B Boutique, Nailsville and Thomasville Zoom Tan, all of whom who helped me gussy up and get my groove back. You made it a little less stressful to go on my first date in 20 years. 😜

I also thank fellow authors Amy Smith Hobbs, Nadia Watts and Felicia Dilbert, book coaches Michelle Melton Cox and Suzette Mullen, and copyright/trademark attorney Angie Avard Turner for all your helpful insight. You are all phenomenal, fierce women I want to be more like.

To UGA Professor Dr. Charles Bullock, Mercer Law School Professor Jack Sammons, and my first employer, Tommy James, thank you for believing in me and encouraging me as a thinker, as a writer and as a lawyer. You set my career on its course and taught me so much.

There would have been no book without the influence of all the fine judges and brilliant colleagues who've taught me so much over the years. Our life's work is to fight with one another for our clients, but our respect for the law and for one another makes the practice of law such a high calling. Thank you for the on-the-job training!

I especially thank you, my clients, for I would have no wisdom to share if you hadn't invited me to join you on your legal and personal journeys. I was thinking of you—and speaking to you—with every page of this work.

Above all, I praise and thank my Jesus for loving me, being ever so near in all of the low places of my life, for touching my heart, for giving me hope, for closing some doors while he was opening others, and for providing the tools to get my thoughts on paper. I pray these pages bring him glory.

About the Author

Bree Sullivan-Howell, J.D., with her impeccable record of academic achievements and commitment to justice, has distinguished herself as a top divorce lawyer over her twenty-year career. After graduating with a perfect GPA from the University of Georgia, and then from Mercer University School of Law with honors, Bree quickly established herself as a force in family law. Beyond the courtroom, Bree is an unwavering advocate for domestic abuse survivors and children. Bree's combination of vast legal expertise and profound personal experiences make her debut book, *Crush Your Divorce & Keep Your Faith* an essential guide of encouragement and empowerment for Christian women walking through the harsh reality of divorce. A devoted wife to her beloved Jefferson, and loving mother of three, Bree is living proof that life goes on after divorce, and that God's plans for us are always good, even when we can't see it yet. Her passion is to help men and women crush the hold divorce has over their lives with grace, integrity and grit, and to give them hope for the brighter day to come.

Let's connect!

Instagram: @lawyerbree || @crushyourdivorce
Facebook: Sullivan Law Firm
Linked In: Bree Sullivan-Howell, J.D.
www.sullivan-firm.com || www.crushyourdivorce.com
#crushyourdivorce® || Crush Your Divorce®

Printed in the USA
CPSIA information can be obtained
at www.ICGtesting.com
LVHW012017260624
784057LV00001B/26